**Ivy Global**

# ISEE
## PRACTICE
### 1ST EDITION

IVY GLOBAL, NEW YORK

This publication was written and edited by the team at Ivy Global.

Editors: Corwin Henville and Laurel Perkins
Layout Editor: Sacha Azor
Contributors: Sarah Atkins, Ali Candib, Tamara Jordan, Nathan Létourneau, Sarah Pike, and Julia Romanski
Producers: Lloyd Min and Junho Suh

**About Ivy Global**
Ivy Global is a pioneering education company that provides a wide range of educational services.

E-mail: info@ivyglobal.com
Website: http://www.ivyglobal.com

# CONTENTS

# INTRODUCTION

## CHAPTER 1

# HOW TO USE THIS BOOK

Welcome, students and parents! This book is intended for students practicing for the Lower, Middle, or Upper Level Independent School Entrance Exam (ISEE). For students applying to many top private and independent schools in North America, the ISEE is a crucial and sometimes daunting step in the admissions process. By exposing you to the format of the ISEE, Ivy Global will help you build your confidence and maximize your score on this important exam.

This book is right for you if:

- you are applying to a private or independent school that requires the ISEE for admission
- you will be in Grades 4-5 (Lower Level), 6-7 (Middle Level), or 8-11 (Upper Level) when you take the ISEE
- you would like to practice for the ISEE exam using full-length practice tests under simulated testing conditions
- you are a parent, family member, or tutor looking for new ways to help your Lower, Middle, or Upper Level ISEE student

Ivy Global's *ISEE Practice* provides six full-length exams to help students practice for the ISEE under simulated testing conditions. This book includes:

- an up-to-date introduction to the ISEE's administration, format, and scoring practices
- instructions for taking a full-length practice test for the ISEE under simulated testing conditions
- 2 full-length practice tests for the ISEE Lower Level
- 2 full-length practice tests for the ISEE Middle Level
- 2 full-length practice tests for the ISEE Upper Level
- detailed scoring instructions for each exam

To make the best use of this book, work through the exams that are appropriate to your level. After you have finished an exam, take time to assess your strengths and weaknesses. Then, spend some time reviewing the concepts you found challenging before you test yourself again.

To get started, continue reading for an overview of the ISEE. Good luck in this exciting new step for your education!

**Ivy Global**

# ABOUT THE ISEE

The **ISEE (Independent School Entrance Exam)** is a standardized test administered to students in grades 1-11 to help determine placement into certain private and independent schools. Many secondary schools worldwide use the ISEE as an integral part of their admissions process. The ISEE is owned and published by the Educational Records Bureau.

You will register for one of four ISEE tests, depending on your grade level:

- The **Primary Level** exam is for students currently in grades 1-3.
- The **Lower Level** exam is for students currently in grades 4-5.
- The **Middle Level** exam is for students currently in grades 6-7.
- The **Upper Level** exam is for students currently in grades 8-11.

The Primary Level exam is administered only with the use of a computer, and includes auditory content. All other levels may be taken on a computer or in a paper-and-pencil format. Among levels, the exams differ in difficulty, length, and the types of questions which may appear. The Lower Level exam is shorter than the Middle or Upper level exams.

## WHEN IS THE TEST ADMINISTERED?

Administration dates for the ISEE vary between test locations. ISEE test sites and administration dates can be found online, at ERBlearn.org. In addition to taking the test at a school that administers large group tests, students applying to grades 5-12 can register to take the ISEE at a Prometric Testing Center, which administers computer-based exams.

## HOW MANY TIMES CAN I TAKE THE TEST?

Students may only take the ISEE once per admission season. The version of the test doesn't matter: a student who has taken a paper-and-pencil test may not take another test on a computer, and a student who has taken a computer-based test may not take another test in a paper-and-pencil format.

## HOW DO I REGISTER?

The easiest and fastest way to register is to complete the **online application**. Visit www.ERBlearn.org to register for an exam in your area. It is also possible to register over the phone by calling (800) 446-0320 or (919) 956-8524, or to register by mail. To register by mail, you must complete and submit the application form available only in the printed ISEE student guide. Visit www.ERBlearn.org to order a printed copy of the ISEE student guide.

## WHAT IS THE FORMAT OF THE ISEE?

The Lower, Middle, and Upper Level ISEE exams consist of four scored sections (**Verbal Reasoning**, **Quantitative Reasoning**, **Reading Comprehension**, and **Mathematics Achievement**), plus an **Essay** that is used as a writing sample. The format of the test differs based on the level of the exam:

| LOWER LEVEL | | | |
|---|---|---|---|
| **Section** | **Questions** | **Length** | **Topics Covered** |
| Verbal Reasoning | 34 | 20 min | Synonyms, Sentence Completion |
| Quantitative Reasoning | 38 | 35 min | Logical Reasoning, Pattern Recognition (Word Problems) |
| Reading Comprehension | 25 | 25 min | Short Passages |
| Math Achievement | 30 | 30 min | Arithmetic, Algebra, Geometry, Data Analysis |
| Essay | 1 | 30 min | One age-appropriate essay prompt |
| Total testing time: 2 hours 20 minutes | | | |

Ivy Global

| MIDDLE AND UPPER LEVEL | | | |
|---|---|---|---|
| **Section** | **Questions** | **Length** | **Topics Covered** |
| Verbal Reasoning | 40 | 20 min | Synonyms, Sentence Completion |
| Quantitative Reasoning | 37 | 35 min | Logical Reasoning, Pattern Recognition (Word Problems and Quantitative Comparison) |
| Reading Comprehension | 36 | 35 min | Short Passages |
| Math Achievement | 47 | 40 min | Arithmetic, Algebra, Geometry, Data Analysis |
| Essay | 1 | 30 min | One age-appropriate essay prompt |
| *Total testing time: 2 hours 40 minutes* | | | |

Except for the Essay, all questions are **multiple-choice** (A) to (D). You are not normally allowed to use calculators, rulers, dictionaries, or other aids during the exam. However, students with documented learning disabilities or physical challenges may apply to take the test with extra time, aids, or other necessary accommodations that they receive in school. For more information about taking the ISEE with a documented disability, visit the ISEE Website at ERBlearn.org.

## HOW IS THE ISEE SCORED?

All of the multiple-choice questions on the ISEE are equal in value, and your **raw score** for these sections is the total number of questions answered correctly. There is no penalty for incorrect answers.

Within each section, there are also 5-6 **experimental questions** that do not count towards your raw score for the section. The ISEE uses these questions to measure exam accuracy and to test material for upcoming exams. You won't be told which questions are the experimental questions, however, so you have to do your best on the entire section.

Your raw score for each section is then converted into a **scaled score** that represents how well you did in comparison to other students who have taken the same exam. Scaled scores range from about 760-950 for each section, with total scaled scores ranging from about 2280-2850.

The **Essay** is not scored, but is sent to the schools you are applying to as a sample of your writing skills. Admissions officers may use your essay to evaluate your writing ability when they are making admissions decisions.

Scores are released to families, and to the schools that families have designated as recipients, within 7-10 business days after the test date. Scores will be mailed to the address you provided when registering for the ISEE, and to up to six schools and/or counselors. You may request expedited score reports, or send score reports to additional schools or counselors, for an additional fee.

## WHAT ARE THE ISEE PERCENTILES AND STANINES?

The ISEE score report also provides **ISEE percentile** rankings for each category, comparing your performance to that of other students in the same grade who have taken the test in the past three years. If you score in the 60th percentile, this means you are scoring higher than 60% of other students in your grade taking the exam.

These percentile rankings provide a more accurate way of evaluating student performance at each grade level. However, the ISEE percentiles are a comparison against only other students who have taken the ISEE, and these tend to be very high-achieving students. Students should not be discouraged if their percentile rankings appear low.

The following chart shows the median (50th percentile) ISEE scores for students applying to grades 5-12.

Ivy Global

| MEDIAN SCORES (ISEE 50TH PERCENTILE) FOR 2012 | | | | | |
|---|---|---|---|---|---|
| Level | Grade Applying To | Verbal Reasoning | Quantitative Reasoning | Reading Comprehension | Mathematics Achievement |
| Lower Level | 5 | 840 | 843 | 834 | 848 |
| | 6 | 856 | 856 | 848 | 863 |
| Middle Level | 7 | 863 | 865 | 866 | 871 |
| | 8 | 869 | 871 | 871 | 876 |
| Upper Level | 9 | 879 | 878 | 880 | 882 |
| | 10 | 883 | 882 | 886 | 886 |
| | 11 | 886 | 885 | 889 | 890 |
| | 12 | 881 | 884 | 880 | 889 |

The ISEE score report also includes **stanine** rankings. A stanine is a number from 1-9 obtained by dividing the entire range of students' scores into 9 segments, as shown in the table below:

| percentile rank | stanine |
|---|---|
| 1 – 3 | 1 |
| 4 – 10 | 2 |
| 11 – 22 | 3 |
| 23 – 39 | 4 |
| 40 – 59 | 5 |
| 60 – 76 | 6 |
| 77 – 88 | 7 |

| 89 – 95 | 8 |
|---------|---|
| 96 – 99 | 9 |

Stanine scores are provided because small differences in percentile rankings may not represent a significant difference in ability. Stanines represent a range of percentile rankings, and are intended to provide a better representation of student ability.

## HOW DO SCHOOLS USE THE ISEE?

Schools use the ISEE as one way to assess potential applicants, but it is by no means the only tool that they are using. Schools also pay very close attention to the rest of a student's application—academic record, teacher recommendations, extracurricular activities, writing samples, and interviews—in order to determine which students might be the best fit for their program. The personal components of a student's application sometimes give schools a lot more information about the student's personality and potential contributions to the school's overall community. Different schools place a different amount of importance on ISEE and other test scores within this process, and admissions offices are good places to find out how much your schools of interest will weight the ISEE.

**Ivy Global**

# TEST-TAKING STRATEGIES

## CHAPTER 2

# APPROACHING THE ISEE

Before you review the content covered on the ISEE, you need to focus on *how* you take the ISEE. If you approach the ISEE *thoughtfully* and *strategically*, you will avoid common traps and tricks planted in the ISEE by the test makers. Think of the ISEE as a timed maze—you need to make every turn cleverly and quickly so that you avoid getting stuck at a dead end with no time to spare.

In this section, you will learn about the ISEE's format and structure; this awareness will help you avoid any surprises or shocks on test day. The ISEE is a very predictable exam and will seem less challenging once you understand what it looks like and how it works. By learning and practicing the best test-taking strategies and techniques, you will discover how to work as quickly and efficiently as possible. Once you know what to expect, you can refine your knowledge of the actual material tested on the ISEE, such as the verbal and math skills that are based on your grade level in school.

This section on ISEE strategies will answer the following **major questions**:

1. How does the ISEE differ from a test you take in school?
2. What preparation strategies can you learn before you take the ISEE?
3. What strategies can you learn to use during the ISEE?
4. How can you manage stress before and during the ISEE?

In the process of answering your big questions, this section will also highlight key facts about smart test-taking:

- Your answer choice matters—your process does not. Enter your answer choices correctly and carefully to earn points. You have a set amount of time per section, so spend it wisely.

- The ISEE's format and directions do not change, so learn them now.

- All questions have the same value.

- Each level of the ISEE corresponds to a range of grades, and score expectations differ based on your grade level.

- Identify your areas of strength and weakness, and review any content that feels unfamiliar.

- Apply universal strategies—prediction-making, Process of Elimination, back-solving, and educated guessing—to the multiple-choice sections.
- Stay calm and be confident in your abilities as you prepare for and take the ISEE.

**Ivy Global**

# HOW DOES THE ISEE DIFFER FROM A TEST YOU TAKE IN SCHOOL?

The ISEE differs from tests you take in school in four major ways:

1. It is not concerned with the process behind your answers. Your answer is either right or wrong: there is no partial credit.
2. You have a set amount of time per section (and for the exam as a whole).
3. It is divided into four levels that correspond to four grade ranges of students.
4. It is extremely predictable given that its format, structure, and directions never vary.

## NO PARTIAL CREDIT

At this point in your school career, you have probably heard your teacher remark, "Be sure to show your work on the test!" You are most likely familiar with almost every teacher's policy of "No work, no credit." However, the ISEE completely ignores this guideline. The machine that grades your exam does not care that you penciled brilliant logic in the margins of the test booklet—the machine only looks at your answer choice. Your answer choice is either right or wrong: **there is no partial credit**.

## SET AMOUNT OF TIME

You have a **set amount of time per section**, so spend it wisely. The ISEE test proctors will never award you extra time after a test section has ended because you spent half of one section struggling valiantly on a single problem. Instead, you must learn to work within each section's time constraints.

You also must view the questions as equal because **each question is worth the same number of points** (one). Even though some questions are more challenging than others, they all carry the same weight. Rather than dwell on a problem, you should skip it, work through the rest of the section, and come back to it if you have time.

## FOUR LEVELS

There are four levels of the ISEE—Primary, Lower, Middle, and Upper—each of which is administered to a specific range of students. The Primary Level is given to students applying to grades 2, 3, and 4; the Lower Level is given to students applying to grades 5 and 6; the Middle Level is given to students applying to grades 7 and 8; and the Upper Level is given to students applying to grades 9, 10, 11, and 12. While you might be used to taking tests in school that are completely tailored to your grade, the ISEE is different: each test level covers content for a specific range of grade levels.

**Score expectations differ** based on your grade level. You are not expected to answer every question correctly on an Upper Level exam if you are only in eighth grade. Conversely, if you are in eleventh grade, you are expected to answer the most questions correctly on the Upper Level exam because you are one of the oldest students taking that exam.

## STANDARD FORMAT

The ISEE is, by definition, a **standardized test**, which means that its format and directions are standard and predictable. While your teachers might change formats and directions for every assessment they administer, you can expect to see the same format and directions on every ISEE.

Ivy Global

# WHAT PREPARATION STRATEGIES CAN YOU LEARN BEFORE YOU TAKE THE ISEE?

Now that you are familiar with how the ISEE differs from the tests you take in school, you are ready to learn some test tips. You can prepare for the ISEE by following these three steps:

1. Learn the format and directions of the test.
2. Identify your areas of strength and weakness.
3. Create a study schedule to review and practice test content.

## LEARN THE FORMAT AND DIRECTIONS

The structure of the ISEE is entirely predictable, so learn this now. Rather than wasting precious time reading the directions and understanding the format on test day, take the time now to familiarize yourself with the test's format and directions.

Refer to the tables on pages 6 and 7 for an overview of the ISEE's format. Continue reading for specific directions for the Verbal Reasoning, Reading Comprehension, and Essay sections. Specific directions for the Quantitative Reasoning and Mathematics Achievement sections can be found in Ivy Global's *ISEE Math*.

## IDENTIFY YOUR STRENGTHS AND WEAKNESSES

To determine your areas of strength and weakness and to get an idea of which concepts you need to review, take a full-length, accurate practice exam to serve as a diagnostic test. Practice exams for the ISEE can be found in this book.

Make sure you simulate test day conditions by timing yourself. Then, check your answers against the correct answers. Write down how many questions you missed in each section, and note the topics or types of questions you found most challenging. What was hard about the test? What did you feel good about? Did you leave a lot of questions blank because of timing issues, or did you leave questions blank because you did not know how to solve them? Reflecting on these questions, in addition to looking at your score breakdown, will help you determine your strengths, weaknesses, and areas for improvement.

## CREATE A STUDY SCHEDULE

After determining your areas of strength and weakness, create a study plan and schedule for your ISEE preparation to review content. Work backward from your test date until you arrive at your starting point for studying. The number of weeks you have until your exam will determine how much time you can (and should) devote to your preparation. Remember, practice is the most important!

To begin, try using this sample study plan as a model for your own personalized study schedule.

## SAMPLE STUDY PLAN

My test date is: _____.

I have _____ weeks to study. I will make an effort to study _____ minutes/hours each night, and I will set aside extra time on _____ to take timed sections.

I plan to take _____ full-length tests between now and my test date. I will study for _____ weeks and then take a practice test. My goal for this test is to improve my score in the following sections:

_____

_____

_____

_____

_____

_____

_____

If I do not make this goal, then I will spend more time studying.

Ivy Global

## STUDY SCHEDULE

| Date | Plan of Study | Time Allotted | Time Spent | Goal Reached? |
|------|---------------|---------------|------------|---------------|
| 1/1 | Learn 5 words and review perimeter of polygons | 1 hour | 44 minutes | Yes, I know 5 new words and can calculate perimeter! |
| 1/3 | Learn 5 words and review area of triangles | 1 hour | 1 hour | I know 5 new words, but I'm still confused about the area of triangles. I'll review this again next time and ask a teacher, tutor, or parent for help. |
| | | | | |
| | | | | |
| | | | | |
| | | | | |
| | | | | |
| | | | | |
| | | | | |
| | | | | |

**Ivy Global**

# WHAT STRATEGIES CAN YOU LEARN TO USE DURING THE TEST?

Once you have grown accustomed to the ISEE through practice, you are ready to learn strategies to use during the ISEE. The following points will prepare you to take the test as cleverly and efficiently as possible:

1.  Enter your answer choices correctly and carefully.
2.  Pace yourself to manage your time effectively.
3.  Learn a strategic approach for multiple-choice questions.

## ENTERING ANSWER CHOICES

Whether you are taking a pencil-and-paper or a computer-based exam, you must follow the directions carefully to enter your answers. In school you probably take tests that, for the most part, do not ask you to enter your answers in a specific format. However, the ISEE streamlines the grading process by only reviewing the answers you have entered on your answer sheet or into the computer program. This means that any notes or work you have written on your scratch paper will not be reviewed, and you will only receive credit for entering your answers correctly.

On a computer-based exam, you will click an answer on the computer screen in order to enter your response. Follow the directions carefully to make sure your answer has been recorded. Within each section, you will be able to go back to questions earlier in the section and change your answers. You will also be able to skip questions and come back to them later. However, you will not be able to review questions from sections that come earlier or later in the exam; you will only be able to review your answers for the questions in the section you are currently working on. Make sure all of your answers have been entered correctly before your time is up for the section.

On a pencil-and-paper exam, you will enter your answers on a separate answer sheet. You must grid in your multiple-choice answers onto this sheet using an HB pencil to fill in the circle that corresponds to your answer. This sheet is scanned and scored by a highly sensitive computer. You will also write your Essay on separate lined pages of this answer sheet.

Since you have to take an additional step to record your answers, it is important that you avoid making gridding mistakes. Sadly, many students get confused and mismark their answer sheets. Remember, even if you arrive at the right answer, it is only correct and counted in your favor if you grid correctly on your answer sheet.

To grid correctly and carefully to maximize your points, consider the following tips:

**Keep your answer sheet neat.** Since your answer sheet is graded by a machine, your score is calculated based on what your marks look like. The machine cannot know what you really meant if you picked the wrong bubble. Stray marks can harm your score, especially if you darken the correct answer but accidentally make a mark that confuses the machine! Avoid this and other errors by consulting the following image, which shows the difference between answers that are properly shaded and those that are not.

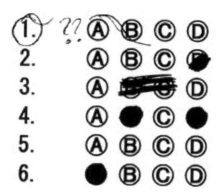

Answer 1 is *wrong* because no answer is selected and there are stray marks.
Answer 2 is *wrong* because choice (D) has not been darkened completely.
Answer 3 is *wrong* because two answers have been selected.
Answer 4 is *wrong* because two answers have been selected.
Answer 5 is *neither right nor wrong* because it was left blank.
Answer 6 is *right* because choice (A) has been darkened properly.

Train yourself to **circle your answer choice in your test booklet**. If you have time to go back and check your answers, you can easily check your circled answers against your gridded ones.

You should also **create a system for marking questions that you skipped** or that you found confusing (see the next section for more information about skipping quesions). Try circling those question numbers only in your test booklet so that you can find them later if you want to solve them or check your work. Be aware of these questions when gridding answers on your answer sheet.

Finally, **grid your answers in batches of four, five, or six answer choices.** That way, you do not have to go back and forth between your test booklet and your answer sheet every minute. If you choose to use this strategy, keep an eye on the clock—you do not want to get to the end of the section and find you have not gridded any answers. Depending on how much time you have left to check your work (if you happen to finish early), you can either review every problem or spot-check a series of questions on your answer sheet against your test booklet.

# TIME MANAGEMENT (PACING)

Manage your time effectively to boost your score. The ISEE has an element of time pressure, so it is important to keep moving on the exam rather than spending too much time on any single question.

**You can come back to questions** within each section of the ISEE. Each question is only worth one point, regardless of its difficulty. If you are stuck on a problem, you should make your best guess and move on to try to answer another problem. It makes more sense to answer as many questions as possible (and get as many points as possible) rather than spending all your time on one question. If you come across a question you want to come back to, circle it in your question booklet or mark it on your scratch paper. Remember not to make any stray marks on your answer sheet.

By moving quickly through each question of the section, you will ensure that: 1) you see every question in the section; 2) you gain points on questions that are easy for you; 3) you return to more challenging problems and figure out as many as you can with your remaining time. It is also important to note that you might not be able to answer several questions in each section if you are on the younger end of the testing group for your particular test level. In that case, you should make your best guess based on the information you do know, but shouldn't worry if the content is unfamiliar.

Even if you are unsure about a question and want to come back to it later, you should **always make a guess.** The ISEE doesn't take off any points for answering questions incorrectly, so you should never leave a question blank! Even if you guess a completely random answer, you have a small chance of gaining a point. If you can rule out one or two choices that you know are wrong, you have even better odds of guessing the right answer. Therefore, always make a guess on every question, even if you are planning to come back to it later. When your time is up, you want to make sure that you have entered an answer for every question!

Follow this step-by-step process for moving through a section:

1. Look through the section and answer the questions that are easy for you. If a question seems difficult or is taking too long, make a guess and circle it to come back to later.
2. After answering all the easier questions, go back to the questions you have circled and spend some time working on ones that you think you might be able to solve. If you figure out that the answer you originally guessed was incorrect, change that answer on your answer sheet.
3. If you have no idea how to solve a question, leave your best guess as your answer.
4. If you have any time remaining, check your work for the questions you solved.

**Ivy Global**

# STRATEGIES FOR MULTIPLE-CHOICE QUESTIONS

**Apply universal strategies**—prediction-making, Process of Elimination, back-solving, and educated guessing—to the multiple-choice sections. To illustrate the value of these strategies, read through the following example of a synonym question from the Verbal Reasoning section:

HAPPY:

(A) delighted
(B) unhappy
(C) crazy
(D) nice

*Answer: (A). "Delighted" is the correct answer because it is the word that most nearly means "happy."*

Regardless of whether the answer choices are easy, difficult, or somewhere in between, you can use certain tricks and tips to your advantage. To approach ISEE questions effectively, you need to step into the test makers' minds and learn to avoid their traps.

**Make predictions.** When you see a question, try to come up with an answer on your own before looking at the answer choices. You can literally cover the answer choices with your hand so that you must rely on your own intelligence to predict an answer instead of being swayed by answer choices that you see. If you look at the answer choices first, you might be tempted to pick an answer without thinking about the other options and what the question is asking you. Instead, make a prediction so that you understand the question fully and get a clear sense of what to look for in the answers. In the synonym example above, you could predict that a possible synonym for "happy" would be something like "glad."

**Use the Process of Elimination**. For each multiple-choice question, you must realize that the answer is right in front of you. To narrow down your answer choices, think about the potential incorrect answers and actively identify those to eliminate them. Even if you can eliminate just one answer, you will set yourself up for better odds if you decide to guess. For the synonym example above, test your prediction of "glad" against the answer choices and immediately eliminate "unhappy" since it is opposite in meaning. You can also probably eliminate "crazy" and "nice" since those words do not match your prediction. This leaves you with "delighted," which is the correct answer.

**Try back-solving.** This strategy is most useful on the math sections, especially when you are given a complicated, multi-step word problem. Instead of writing an equation, try plugging in the answer choices to the word problem. Take a look at the following question:

Catherine has a basket of candy. On Monday, she eats ½ of all the candy. On Tuesday, she eats 2 pieces. On Wednesday, she eats twice the amount of candy that she consumed on Tuesday. If she only has 4 pieces left on Thursday, how many pieces did she initially have?

(A) 12

(B) 14

(C) 16

(D) 20

To use back-solving, start with answer choice (C) and plug it into the word problem. If (C) is the correct answer, you are done. If not, you will then know whether you should test (B) or (D). When we start with 16 pieces of candy, we subtract 8 on Monday, then 2 more for Tuesday, and then 4 more for Wednesday. By Thursday, Catherine only has two pieces of candy left, which is less than the amount we wanted. Therefore, we know our answer has to be bigger, so we eliminate choices (A), (B), and (C) and try (D), which works.

(*Fun Fact:* If you think about it, you will have to plug in three answer choices at most to determine the right answer.)

Armed with these strategies, you might feel that the ISEE is starting to look more manageable because you now have shortcuts that will help you navigate the maze of questions quickly and cleverly.

Take a look at this example to practice using the strategies you just read about.

Because Kaitlin was -------- from her soccer game, she went to bed early.

(A) thrilled

(B) exhausted

(C) competitive

(D) inspired

1. Assess the question and recognize what it is testing. In this case, the question tests whether you can pick a word to complete the sentence.

2. Make a prediction. What about Kaitlin's soccer game would cause her to go to bed early? Maybe it wore her out, so we could look for something like "tired" to go in the blank.

3. Look for inaccurate answer choices and eliminate them. If Kaitlin were "thrilled," "competitive," or "inspired" as a result of her soccer game, this wouldn't explain why she had to go to bed early. Therefore, you can eliminate answers (A), (C), and (D).

4.  Make an educated guess, or choose the answer you feel most confident about. Since you made a fantastic prediction and used Process of Elimination, you only have one choice left: (B). "Exhausted" is the correct answer—you just earned yourself a point!

# HOW CAN YOU MANAGE YOUR STRESS?

If you have ever taken a big test before, or had an important sports match, play, or presentation, then you know what anxiety feels like. Even if you are excited for an approaching event, you might feel nervous. You might begin to doubt yourself, and you might feel as if your mind is racing while butterflies flutter in your stomach!

When it comes to preparing for the ISEE, the good news is that a little anxiety (or adrenaline) goes a long way. Anxiety is a natural, motivating force that will help you study hard in the days leading up to your test. That anxiety will also help you stay alert and work efficiently during the test.

Sometimes, however, anxiety might become larger than life and start to get the best of you. To prevent anxiety and nerves from clouding your ability to work effectively and believe in yourself, you should try some of the suggestions below. Many of these suggestions are good ideas to use in everyday life, but they become especially important in the final week before your test and on test day itself.

- **Relax and slow down.** To center yourself and ease your anxiety, take a big, deep breath. Slowly inhale for a few seconds and then slowly exhale for a few seconds. Shut your eyes and relax. Stretch your arms, roll your neck gently, crack your knuckles—get in the zone of Zen! Continue to breathe deeply and slowly until you can literally feel your body calm down.
- **Picture your goals.** Close your eyes or just pause to reflect on what you want to achieve on test day. Visualize your success, whether that means simply answering all the math questions or getting a top score and gaining acceptance into the school of your dreams. Acknowledge your former successes and abilities, and believe in yourself.
- **Break it down.** Instead of trying to study a whole section at once, break up your studying into small and manageable chunks. Outline your study goals before you start. For example, instead of trying to master the entire Reading Comprehension section at once, you might want to work on one type of passage at a time.
- **Sleep.** Make sure you get plenty of rest and sleep, especially the two nights leading up to your exam!
- **Fuel up.** Eat healthy, filling meals that fuel your brain. Also, drink lots of water to stay hydrated.
- **Take a break.** Put down the books and go play outside, read, listen to music, exercise, or have a good conversation with friend or family member. A good break can be just as restful as a nap. However, watching television will provide minimal relaxation.

**Ivy Global**

**On the night before the exam**, study only lightly. Make a list of your three biggest fears and work on them, but don't try to learn anything new. Pick out what you are going to wear to the exam—try wearing layers in case the exam room is hotter or colder than you expect. Organize everything you need to bring. Know where the test center is located and how long it will take to get there. Have a nutritious meal and get plenty of sleep!

**On the morning of the exam**, let your adrenaline kick in naturally. Eat a good breakfast and stay hydrated; your body needs fuel to endure the test. Bring along several pencils and a good eraser. Listen carefully to the test proctor's instructions and let the proctor know if you are left-handed so you can sit at an appropriate desk. Take a deep breath and remember: you are smart and accomplished! Believe in yourself and you will do just fine.

# PRACTICE TESTS

## CHAPTER 3

# PRACTICE TEST 1

## LOWER LEVEL

# HOW TO TAKE THIS PRACTICE TEST

To simulate an accurate testing environment, sit at a desk in a quiet location free of distractions—no TV, computers, phones, music, or noise—and clear your desk of all materials except pencils and erasers. Remember that no calculators, rulers, protractors, dictionaries, or other aids are allowed on the ISEE.

Give yourself the following amounts of time for each section:

| SECTION | SUBJECT | TIME LIMIT |
|---------|---------|------------|
| 1 | Verbal Reasoning | 20 minutes |
| 2 | Quantitative Reasoning | 35 minutes |
| *5 minute break* | | |
| 3 | Reading Comprehension | 25 minutes |
| 4 | Mathematics Achievement | 30 minutes |
| *5 minute break* | | |
| 5 | Essay | 30 minutes |

Have an adult help you monitor your time, or use a watch and time yourself. Only give yourself the allotted time for each section; put your pencil down when your time is up.

Follow the instructions carefully. As you take your test, bubble your answers into the answer sheets provided. Use the test booklet as scratch paper for notes and calculations. Remember that you are not granted time at the end of a section to transfer your answers to the answer sheet, so you must do this as you go along.

When you are finished, check your answers against the answer keys provided. Then, score your exam using the directions at the end of the book.

Ivy Global

Note: students with diagnosed learning disabilities who apply for testing with accommodations may receive extra time, or may be allowed to use certain assistive devices during the ISEE. For more information, visit http://erblearn.org/parents/admission/isee/accommodations.

# Ivy Global

# ISEE
# LOWER LEVEL TEST 1

## MARKING INSTRUCTIONS

- Use a #2 or HB pencil only on pages 34 and 35.
- Use a ballpoint pen for your essay on pages 36 and 37.
- Make dark marks that completely fill the circle.
- Erase clearly any mark you wish to change.
- Make no stray marks on this form.
- Do not fold or crease this form.

Correct Mark    Incorrect Marks
●              ⊗ ◯ ✓ ● ⊖

## 1 VERBAL REASONING

1 Ⓐ Ⓑ Ⓒ Ⓓ    15 Ⓐ Ⓑ Ⓒ Ⓓ    29 Ⓐ Ⓑ Ⓒ Ⓓ
2 Ⓐ Ⓑ Ⓒ Ⓓ    16 Ⓐ Ⓑ Ⓒ Ⓓ    30 Ⓐ Ⓑ Ⓒ Ⓓ
3 Ⓐ Ⓑ Ⓒ Ⓓ    17 Ⓐ Ⓑ Ⓒ Ⓓ    31 Ⓐ Ⓑ Ⓒ Ⓓ
4 Ⓐ Ⓑ Ⓒ Ⓓ    18 Ⓐ Ⓑ Ⓒ Ⓓ    32 Ⓐ Ⓑ Ⓒ Ⓓ
5 Ⓐ Ⓑ Ⓒ Ⓓ    19 Ⓐ Ⓑ Ⓒ Ⓓ    33 Ⓐ Ⓑ Ⓒ Ⓓ
6 Ⓐ Ⓑ Ⓒ Ⓓ    20 Ⓐ Ⓑ Ⓒ Ⓓ    34 Ⓐ Ⓑ Ⓒ Ⓓ
                                    **Lower Level Ends**
7 Ⓐ Ⓑ Ⓒ Ⓓ    21 Ⓐ Ⓑ Ⓒ Ⓓ    35 Ⓐ Ⓑ Ⓒ Ⓓ
8 Ⓐ Ⓑ Ⓒ Ⓓ    22 Ⓐ Ⓑ Ⓒ Ⓓ    36 Ⓐ Ⓑ Ⓒ Ⓓ
9 Ⓐ Ⓑ Ⓒ Ⓓ    23 Ⓐ Ⓑ Ⓒ Ⓓ    37 Ⓐ Ⓑ Ⓒ Ⓓ
10 Ⓐ Ⓑ Ⓒ Ⓓ    24 Ⓐ Ⓑ Ⓒ Ⓓ    38 Ⓐ Ⓑ Ⓒ Ⓓ
11 Ⓐ Ⓑ Ⓒ Ⓓ    25 Ⓐ Ⓑ Ⓒ Ⓓ    39 Ⓐ Ⓑ Ⓒ Ⓓ
12 Ⓐ Ⓑ Ⓒ Ⓓ    26 Ⓐ Ⓑ Ⓒ Ⓓ    40 Ⓐ Ⓑ Ⓒ Ⓓ
                                    **Middle/Upper Level Ends**
13 Ⓐ Ⓑ Ⓒ Ⓓ    27 Ⓐ Ⓑ Ⓒ Ⓓ
14 Ⓐ Ⓑ Ⓒ Ⓓ    28 Ⓐ Ⓑ Ⓒ Ⓓ

## 2 QUANTITATIVE REASONING

| 1 | (A) (B) (C) (D) | 15 | (A) (B) (C) (D) | 29 | (A) (B) (C) (D) |
|---|---|---|---|---|---|
| 2 | (A) (B) (C) (D) | 16 | (A) (B) (C) (D) | 30 | (A) (B) (C) (D) |
| 3 | (A) (B) (C) (D) | 17 | (A) (B) (C) (D) | 31 | (A) (B) (C) (D) |
| 4 | (A) (B) (C) (D) | 18 | (A) (B) (C) (D) | 32 | (A) (B) (C) (D) |
| 5 | (A) (B) (C) (D) | 19 | (A) (B) (C) (D) | 33 | (A) (B) (C) (D) |
| 6 | (A) (B) (C) (D) | 20 | (A) (B) (C) (D) | 34 | (A) (B) (C) (D) |
| 7 | (A) (B) (C) (D) | 21 | (A) (B) (C) (D) | 35 | (A) (B) (C) (D) |
| 8 | (A) (B) (C) (D) | 22 | (A) (B) (C) (D) | 36 | (A) (B) (C) (D) |
| 9 | (A) (B) (C) (D) | 23 | (A) (B) (C) (D) | 37 | (A) (B) (C) (D) Middle/Upper Level Ends |
| 10 | (A) (B) (C) (D) | 24 | (A) (B) (C) (D) | 38 | (A) (B) (C) (D) Lower Level Ends |
| 11 | (A) (B) (C) (D) | 25 | (A) (B) (C) (D) | | |
| 12 | (A) (B) (C) (D) | 26 | (A) (B) (C) (D) | | |
| 13 | (A) (B) (C) (D) | 27 | (A) (B) (C) (D) | | |
| 14 | (A) (B) (C) (D) | 28 | (A) (B) (C) (D) | | |

## 4 MATHEMATICS ACHIEVEMENT

| 1 | (A) (B) (C) (D) | 18 | (A) (B) (C) (D) | 35 | (A) (B) (C) (D) |
|---|---|---|---|---|---|
| 2 | (A) (B) (C) (D) | 19 | (A) (B) (C) (D) | 36 | (A) (B) (C) (D) |
| 3 | (A) (B) (C) (D) | 20 | (A) (B) (C) (D) | 37 | (A) (B) (C) (D) |
| 4 | (A) (B) (C) (D) | 21 | (A) (B) (C) (D) | 38 | (A) (B) (C) (D) |
| 5 | (A) (B) (C) (D) | 22 | (A) (B) (C) (D) | 39 | (A) (B) (C) (D) |
| 6 | (A) (B) (C) (D) | 23 | (A) (B) (C) (D) | 40 | (A) (B) (C) (D) |
| 7 | (A) (B) (C) (D) | 24 | (A) (B) (C) (D) | 41 | (A) (B) (C) (D) |
| 8 | (A) (B) (C) (D) | 25 | (A) (B) (C) (D) | 42 | (A) (B) (C) (D) |
| 9 | (A) (B) (C) (D) | 26 | (A) (B) (C) (D) | 43 | (A) (B) (C) (D) |
| 10 | (A) (B) (C) (D) | 27 | (A) (B) (C) (D) | 44 | (A) (B) (C) (D) |
| 11 | (A) (B) (C) (D) | 28 | (A) (B) (C) (D) | 45 | (A) (B) (C) (D) |
| 12 | (A) (B) (C) (D) | 29 | (A) (B) (C) (D) | 46 | (A) (B) (C) (D) |
| 13 | (A) (B) (C) (D) | 30 | (A) (B) (C) (D) Lower Level Ends | 47 | (A) (B) (C) (D) Middle/Upper Level Ends |
| 14 | (A) (B) (C) (D) | 31 | (A) (B) (C) (D) | | |
| 15 | (A) (B) (C) (D) | 32 | (A) (B) (C) (D) | | |
| 16 | (A) (B) (C) (D) | 33 | (A) (B) (C) (D) | | |
| 17 | (A) (B) (C) (D) | 34 | (A) (B) (C) (D) | | |

## 3 READING COMPREHENSION

| 1 | (A) (B) (C) (D) | 15 | (A) (B) (C) (D) | 29 | (A) (B) (C) (D) |
|---|---|---|---|---|---|
| 2 | (A) (B) (C) (D) | 16 | (A) (B) (C) (D) | 30 | (A) (B) (C) (D) |
| 3 | (A) (B) (C) (D) | 17 | (A) (B) (C) (D) | 31 | (A) (B) (C) (D) |
| 4 | (A) (B) (C) (D) | 18 | (A) (B) (C) (D) | 32 | (A) (B) (C) (D) |
| 5 | (A) (B) (C) (D) | 19 | (A) (B) (C) (D) | 33 | (A) (B) (C) (D) |
| 6 | (A) (B) (C) (D) | 20 | (A) (B) (C) (D) | 34 | (A) (B) (C) (D) |
| 7 | (A) (B) (C) (D) | 21 | (A) (B) (C) (D) | 35 | (A) (B) (C) (D) |
| 8 | (A) (B) (C) (D) | 22 | (A) (B) (C) (D) | 36 | (A) (B) (C) (D) Middle/Upper Level Ends |
| 9 | (A) (B) (C) (D) | 23 | (A) (B) (C) (D) | | |
| 10 | (A) (B) (C) (D) | 24 | (A) (B) (C) (D) | | |
| 11 | (A) (B) (C) (D) | 25 | (A) (B) (C) (D) Lower Level Ends | | |
| 12 | (A) (B) (C) (D) | 26 | (A) (B) (C) (D) | | |
| 13 | (A) (B) (C) (D) | 27 | (A) (B) (C) (D) | | |
| 14 | (A) (B) (C) (D) | 28 | (A) (B) (C) (D) | | |

Ivy Global

STUDENT NAME _____ GRADE APPLYING FOR _____

Use a blue or black ballpoint pen to write the final draft of your essay on this sheet.

You must write your essay topic in this space.

_____

_____

_____

Use specific details and examples in your response.

_____

_____

_____

_____

_____

_____

_____

_____

_____

_____

_____

_____

_____

_____

_____

_____

_____

_____

_____

_____

_____

_____

_____

Ivy Global

# Section 1
# Verbal Reasoning

This section is divided into two parts that contain two different types of questions. As soon as you have completed Part One, answer the questions in Part Two. You may write in your test booklet. For each answer you select, fill in the corresponding circle on your answer document.

## PART ONE — SYNONYMS

Each question in Part One consists of a word in capital letters followed by four answer choices. Select the one word that is most nearly the same in meaning as the word in capital letters.

---

SAMPLE QUESTION:

CHARGE:

(A) release
(B) belittle
(C) accuse
(D) conspire

The correct answer is "accuse," so circle C is darkened.

Sample Answer

Ⓐ Ⓑ ● Ⓓ

---

*Go on to the next page* ➡

## PART TWO — SENTENCE COMPLETION

Each question in Part Two is made up of a sentence with one blank. Each blank indicates that a word or phrase is missing. The sentence is followed by four answer choices. Select the word or phrase that will best complete the meaning of the sentence as a whole.

---

SAMPLE QUESTIONS:

<u>Sample Answer</u>

It rained so much that the streets were -------.

● Ⓑ Ⓒ Ⓓ

(A) flooded

(B) arid

(C) paved

(D) crowded

The correct answer is "flooded," so circle A is darkened.

Ⓐ Ⓑ Ⓒ ●

The house was so dirty that it took -------.

(A) less than ten minutes to wash it.

(B) four months to demolish it.

(C) over a week to walk across it.

(D) two days to clean it.

The correct answer is "two days to clean it," so circle D is darkened.

---

STOP. Do not go on
until told to do so.

## PART ONE – SYNONYMS

**Directions:** Select the word that is most nearly the same in meaning as the word in capital letters.

1. DENIAL
   (A) flow
   (B) lie
   (C) rejection
   (D) encouragement

2. SIMPLE
   (A) boring
   (B) silent
   (C) plain
   (D) nice

3. QUAKE
   (A) stake
   (B) fall
   (C) slam
   (D) shake

4. SIGNAL
   (A) obscure
   (B) assail
   (C) indicate
   (D) assume

5. AUTHORIZE
   (A) approve
   (B) demand
   (C) replenish
   (D) attempt

6. YIELD
   (A) imply
   (B) avoid
   (C) announce
   (D) surrender

7. HERALD
   (A) dance
   (B) announce
   (C) protect
   (D) insult

8. TRUCE
   (A) pine
   (B) tractor
   (C) declaration
   (D) ceasefire

9. SEVERITY
   (A) harshness
   (B) drought
   (C) division
   (D) wound

10. SAGE
    (A) spicy
    (B) ancient
    (C) false
    (D) wise

*Go on to the next page* ➡

11. RESTRAINT

    (A) reserve

    (B) pressure

    (C) repetition

    (D) rescue

12. WARBLE

    (A) trip

    (B) worry

    (C) assail

    (D) sing

13. RECOIL

    (A) escape

    (B) braid

    (C) unbind

    (D) withdraw

14. ENVELOP

    (A) enclose

    (B) entrust

    (C) freeze

    (D) inside

15. CREED

    (A) belief

    (B) avarice

    (C) guilt

    (D) admiration

16. IMMUNITY

    (A) disrespect

    (B) resistance

    (C) ability

    (D) dirtiness

17. FORLORN

    (A) short

    (B) evil

    (C) lonely

    (D) hidden

*Go on to the next page* ➡

## PART TWO – SENTENCE COMPLETION

**Directions:** Select the word that best completes the sentence.

18. Seeing that the conditions were ---------- for surfing, Liya quickly grabbed her wetsuit.

    (A) insufficient

    (B) faulty

    (C) ideal

    (D) honest

19. Mazen left his cake in the oven too long, but he hoped he could ---------- it by covering it with icing.

    (A) salvage

    (B) secure

    (C) escape

    (D) measure

20. The nature guide always warns hikers not to touch any snakes that they ---------- on the trail, as many local species are poisonous.

    (A) elude

    (B) oppose

    (C) reject

    (D) encounter

21. The new book received ---------- reviews for its meticulous coverage, high-quality illustrations, and engaging discussion.

    (A) calm

    (B) negative

    (C) moveable

    (D) favorable

22. Joan travelled to Thailand, where she learned to prepare ---------- Pad Thai from traditional chefs.

    (A) artificial

    (B) authentic

    (C) distressing

    (D) useless

23. Scientists in Brazil were ------------ when they discovered a new species of river dolphin.

    (A) thrilled

    (B) eager

    (C) dejected

    (D) bored

24. When Maya learned that Tommy played piano, ran track and field, and volunteered with seniors, she was impressed by the ---------- of his interests.

    (A) increase

    (B) resemblance

    (C) variety

    (D) community

25. Charlie Chaplin was a British comic actor, filmmaker, and composer who rose to ---------- in the silent era.

    (A) prominence

    (B) elevation

    (C) dependence

    (D) creation

*Go on to the next page* ➡

26. Wujie was ---------- when his class was cancelled, because it gave him more time to complete important homework.

    (A) disappointed
    (B) relieved
    (C) confused
    (D) aggravated

27. Sainte-Enimie, in southern France, is the location of several monasteries and other interesting ---------- sites.

    (A) mundane
    (B) religious
    (C) offensive
    (D) theoretical

28. Sheep's wool is the most widely used animal fiber, and is usually ---------- by shearing.

    (A) planted
    (B) concluded
    (C) dispersed
    (D) harvested

29. John knew a healthy diet called for a variety of vegetables, but ----------.

    (A) he ate numerous kinds.
    (B) he enjoyed many kinds of fruit.
    (C) he only ate spinach.
    (D) he was adept at preparing desserts.

30. Although the author claimed her work was pure fiction, those who knew her well ----------.

    (A) recognized many real events from her life.
    (B) bought several copies.
    (C) did not understand it.
    (D) supported her career as a writer.

31. Since she was a skilled surgeon, Dr. Gavora ----------.

    (A) had a passion for skiing.
    (B) successfully performed the operation.
    (C) enjoyed watching foreign films.
    (D) had been interested in medicine from a young age.

32. Jolie had been looking forward to the recital, but she ----------.

    (A) bought new shoes for the occasion.
    (B) fell ill and was unable to perform.
    (C) was planning to perform her favorite song.
    (D) knew how to play in a variety of musical styles.

33. In contrast to the realistic and conventional style of his early paintings, Pablo Picasso's later work in the Cubist style ----------.

    (A) was not well known by critics.
    (B) looked very life-like and natural.
    (C) was far more abstract and experimental.
    (D) was not popular, causing him to lose money.

34. Ceres was the first asteroid ever discovered, but ----------.

    (A) researchers initially thought it was a planet.
    (B) researchers study objects in space.
    (C) there are many different types of asteroids.
    (D) telescopes have become more powerful in recent years.

STOP. Do not go on until told to do so.

# Section 2
# Quantitative Reasoning

Each question is followed by four suggested answers. Read each question and then decide which one of the four suggested answers is best.

Find the row of spaces on your answer document that has the same number as the question. In this row, mark the space having the same letter as the answer you have chosen. You may write in your test booklet.

---

SAMPLE QUESTIONS:                                                        <u>Sample Answer</u>

What is the value of the expression $(4 + 6) \div 2$?                    Ⓐ Ⓑ ● Ⓓ

(A) 2

(B) 4

(C) 5

(D) 7

The correct answer is 5, so circle C is darkened.

A square has an area of 25cm². What is the length of one of its         Ⓐ ● Ⓒ Ⓓ

sides?

(A) 1 cm

(B) 5 cm

(C) 10 cm

(D) 25 cm

The correct answer is 5 so circle B is darkened.

---

STOP. Do not go on
until told to do so.

**Ivy Global**

1. The large square shown below has been divided into smaller squares.

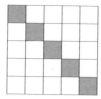

   What fraction of the large square is shaded?

   (A) $^5/_5$

   (B) $^1/_2$

   (C) $^1/_3$

   (D) $^1/_5$

2. Which expression is equivalent to the expression $(2 + 3) \div 4$?

   (A) $5 + 4$

   (B) $5 \times 4$

   (C) $\frac{2}{3} + 4$

   (D) $5 \times \frac{1}{4}$

3. Four students were asked to walk, jog, and sprint around a track. Every two minutes, their speeds were recorded in the table below.

| Times | Walking Student | Jogging Student | Sprinting Student |
|---|---|---|---|
| 2 min | 5.00 km/hr | 11.50 km/hr | 20.00 km/hr |
| 4 min | 5.00 km/hr | 11.00 km/hr | 16.00 km/hr |
| 6 min | 5.00 km/hr | 10.50 km/hr | 14.00 km/hr |
| 8 min | 5.00 km/hr | 10.00 km/hr | 13.00 km/hr |

According to the pattern in this table, what would be the predicted speed of the sprinting student at 10 minutes?

   (A) 14.00 km/hr

   (B) 12.50 km/hr

   (C) 10.00 km/hr

   (D) 8.50 km/hr

*Go on to the next page* ➡

4.  Which story best suits the equation $21 \div 7 = 3$?

    (A) Susie has 21 pieces of gum that she wants to share equally between her 7 friends. How many pieces of gum does she give each friend?

    (B) Susie had 21 pieces of gum and ate 7. How many pieces of gum did she have left?

    (C) Susie has 21 packs of gum, each with 7 pieces. How many pieces of gum does Susie have?

    (D) Susie has 21 pieces of gum and gives 3 packs of gum to her friend. How many packs of gum does Susie have left?

5.  Use the number line to answer the question.

    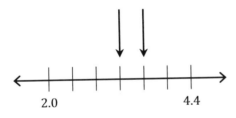

    What values are the arrows pointing to?

    (A) 2.3, 2.4

    (B) 2.8, 3.2

    (C) 3.2, 3.6

    (D) 4.0, 4.1

6.  Which is the smallest fraction?

    (A) $^2/_3$

    (B) $^{14}/_{30}$

    (C) $^4/_7$

    (D) $^5/_{10}$

7.  Which equation can be read as "4 less than half a number is equal to 2 more than the number?" Let $a$ represent the unknown number.

    (A) $(a - 4) \times \frac{1}{2} = 2 + a$

    (B) $a + \frac{1}{2} - 4 = a - 2$

    (C) $a \div 2 + 4 = 2 - a$

    (D) $\frac{a}{2} - 4 = a + 2$

8.  Use the pattern to help answer the question.

    X X O, X X X O, X X X X O, ...

    Which comes next?

    (A) X X X X X X O

    (B) O X X X X X O

    (C) O X X X X X

    (D) X X X X X O

9.  Andrea and Zach walk home together after school at a constant speed of 13 kilometers per hour. Zach's house is three times farther from school than Andrea's house. If it takes Zach 33 minutes to walk home, how long does it take Andrea to walk home?

    (A) 11 minutes

    (B) 13 minutes

    (C) 39 minutes

    (D) 66 minutes

10. Jeff is thinking of a prime number between 1 and 20. Jeff says that the number is greater than 11 and less than 17. What number is Jeff thinking of?

    (A) 11

    (B) 12

    (C) 13

    (D) 15

*Go on to the next page* ➡

11. A survey of 32 artists' favorite colors is displayed in the circle graph below.

**Artists' Favorite Colors**

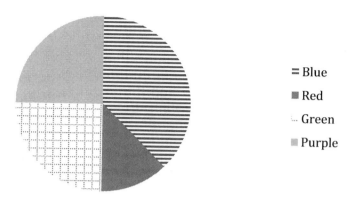

≡ Blue
▦ Red
⋯ Green
▨ Purple

Approximately what fraction of the artists chose blue as their favorite color?

(A) $^1/_8$

(B) $^1/_4$

(C) $^2/_7$

(D) $^3/_8$

12. The triangle below has an area of $A$ inches. If the formula for the area of a triangle is $area = \frac{1}{2} base \times height$, which equation would tell you the length of the triangle's base in inches?

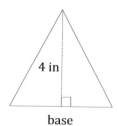

4 in

base

(A) base $= A \div 2$

(B) base $= A \times 2$

(C) base $= A \times 2 - 4$

(D) base $= A \div 4 + 4$

13. Use the equations to answer the question.

$$4a = 8$$
$$2 + b = 3$$

What is the sum of $a$ and $b$?

(A) 1

(B) 2

(C) 3

(D) 6

*Go on to the next page* ➡

**Ivy Global**

14. Use the diagram to answer the question.

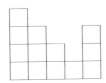

Which piece would complete the diagram to make a square?

(A)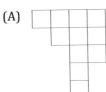

(B)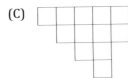

(C)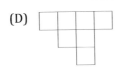

(D)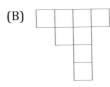

15. Use the following equation to answer the question.

$$p \times 15 = q$$

By which number can $q$ be divided without leaving a remainder?

(A) 2

(B) 3

(C) 4

(D) 10

16. Lucy has a bag full of marbles of various colors. The probability of choosing a red marble is 5 out of 12. Which combination of marbles is possible?

(A) 5 red marbles and 12 others

(B) 15 red marbles and 36 others

(C) 24 red marbles and 10 others

(D) 20 red marbles and 28 others

17. For which pair of symbols below do both symbols have the same number of lines of symmetry?

(A) ↗ ♈

(B) ⊘ ○

(C) ★ ✳

(D) △ ✗

18. Use the Venn diagram to answer the question.

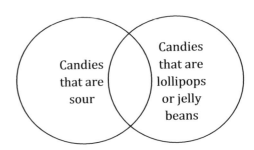

What candy could be found in the overlapping area of the Venn diagram?

(A) A sugary lollipop

(B) A sour jelly bean

(C) A sugary jelly bean

(D) A sour piece of gum

*Go on to the next page* ➡

19. The figure below shows Julie's juice box after she drank some of the juice.

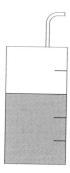

Julie has 150 mL of juice left. If the juice box was completely full before she started drinking, how much juice did Julie drink?

(A) 250 mL

(B) 200 mL

(C) 150 mL

(D) 100 mL

20. Use the table to determine the rule.

| Input | Output |
|-------|--------|
| ● | ✧ |
| 1 | 0 |
| 2 | 3 |
| 4 | 9 |
| 10 | 27 |
| 26 | 75 |

What is the rule for the function?

(A) ● + 3 − 3 = ✧

(B) 3● − 3 = ✧

(C) ● × 2 + 7 = ✧

(D) 4● − 1 = ✧

21. Rachel has four bags of candy. Two of the bags weigh $3\frac{1}{2}$ lb, one bag weighs 4 lb, and one bag weighs 5 lb. What is the mean weight of all four bags?

(A) 4 lb

(B) $4\frac{1}{4}$ lb

(C) $4\frac{3}{8}$ lb

(D) $4\frac{1}{2}$ lb

22. The perimeter of a square is 16w. What is the length of one side?

(A) 4

(B) 8

(C) 4w

(D) 8w

23. The length of $AB$ is $x$, the length of $BC$ is $y$, and the length of $BD$ is $z$.

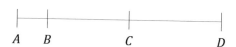

What is the length of $AD$?

(A) $x + y + z$

(B) $x − y + z$

(C) $yz$

(D) $x + z$

24. Use the two equations below to answer the question:

$$3 ● + 2 ☺ = 18$$
$$☺ = 3$$

What is the value of ●?

(A) 2

(B) 3

(C) 4

(D) 5

*Go on to the next page* ➡

25. Use the figure below to answer the question.

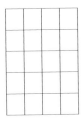

If the length and the width of the figure were both increased by two units, what would be the new perimeter of the figure?

(A) 22 units

(B) 26 units

(C) 28 units

(D) 42 units

26. What is the value of *b* in the expression below?

$$\frac{16 \times 48 \div 24}{8} = b$$

(A) 2

(B) 4

(C) 6

(D) 8

27. Leslie bought 416 erasers for $0.27 each. Which expression gives the best estimate of the total amount of money she spent?

(A) $42 \div 3$

(B) $41 \times 27$

(C) $400 \times 0.3$

(D) $300 \times 2.7$

28. 8 small boxes can fit into a larger rectangular box. One of the small boxes is shown inside the large rectangular box below.

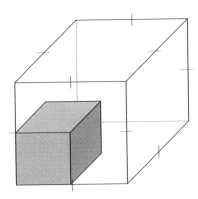

The volume of the large rectangular box is 16 units³. What is the volume of each small box?

(A) 1 units³

(B) 2 units³

(C) 4 units³

(D) 64 units³

29. Sam has a bag with 18 pieces of chocolate, gummies, and mints. There are three times as many chocolates as there are gummies, and twice as many gummies as there are mints. How many mints does Sam have?

(A) 6

(B) 4

(C) 2

(D) 1

*Go on to the next page* ➡

30. Rushen had three bottles of soda. Each bottle contained two liters of soda, and she divided the soda equally into 20 glasses for her friends. How much soda did she pour into each glass?

    (A) $\frac{1}{10}$ L

    (B) $\frac{3}{10}$ L

    (C) $\frac{1}{2}$ L

    (D) 6 L

31. Kim's house is 11 km from Joe's house. On a map, this distance is represented by 5.75 cm. How many centimeters would represent 66 km on the map?

    (A) 30 cm

    (B) 34.5 cm

    (C) 40.75 cm

    (D) 52 cm

32. Use the figure shown to answer the question.

    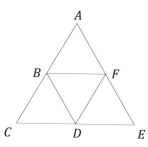

    Lucy wants to use the figure above to draw different quadrilaterals. She can only trace the straight lines connecting the points *A, B, C, D, E,* and *F*. How many quadrilaterals can she draw?

    (A) 0

    (B) 3

    (C) 4

    (D) 6

33. Alex did the problem shown with his calculator.

    $$\frac{27 \times 189}{59}$$

    What is a reasonable estimation for his answer?

    (A) between 50 and 150

    (B) between 150 and 250

    (C) between 500 and 1,500

    (D) between 1,500 and 2,500

34. How many small unit squares would you need to build a larger square where each side has a length of 3 unit squares?

    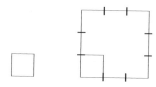

    unit square     larger square

    (A) 3

    (B) 8

    (C) 9

    (D) 12

35. Use the number line shown to answer the question.

    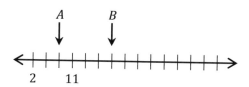

    The value of *B* is the difference between another number and *A*. What is the other number?

    (A) 28

    (B) 20

    (C) 8

    (D) 2

*Go on to the next page* ➡

36. Five students timed how long it takes them to walk to school and recorded the data in the graph shown below.

**Time Spent Walking to School**

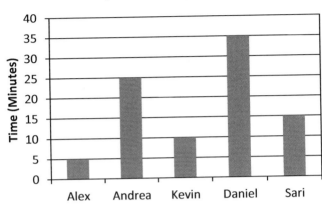

Which of the following statements is correct?

(A) The mean (average) walking time is between 25 and 35 minutes

(B) It takes Andrea twice as long to walk to school as it does Kevin.

(C) The range of the data is greater than the number of minutes it takes Andrea to walk to school.

(D) It takes Daniel longer to walk to school than all of the other students combined.

---

37. The perimeter of the shape below is 16.5 inches.

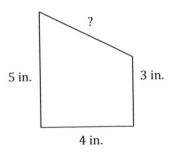

What is the length of the missing side?

(A) 6 in.

(B) 4.5 in.

(C) 3.5 in.

(D) 2 in.

38. Eloise flips a two-sided coin 100 times. The coin has an equal probability of landing on the "heads" side or landing on the "tails" side, and Eloise records which side it lands on after each flip. Which of the following most likely resembles Eloise's results?

(A) 94 heads, 6 tails

(B) 100 heads, 100 tails

(C) 47 heads, 53 tails

(D) 0 heads, 100 tails

**STOP. Do not go on until told to do so.**

# Section 3
# Reading Comprehension

This section contains five short reading passages. Each passage is followed by five questions based on its content. Answer the questions following each passage on the basis of what is <u>stated</u> or <u>implied</u> in that passage. You may write in your test booklet.

Questions 1–5

1      I remember from my childhood an
2 occasion on which my teacher enthusiastically
3 announced to the class that we would be going
4 on a field trip. While a field trip is always
5 welcome news, I wasn't thrilled about our
6 destination: we were going to visit some
7 ancient earthen mounds. Our teacher informed
8 us that the mounds pre-dated the pyramids of
9 Egypt. She told us that when European
10 explorers first encountered the mounds, the
11 people living in the region had no memory of
12 when they were built or who built them. She
13 read with us about the lost people who built
14 them and also built cities thousands of years
15 before the arrival of European settlers in North
16 America.
17      Just the month before, my brother's class
18 had gone to a zoo! As much as our teacher tried
19 to instill in us a sense of the historical
20 significance of the site we were going to visit,
21 observing large piles of old dirt still seemed

22 less exciting than spending a day gawking at
23 exotic animals and buying treats from carts. It
24 was difficult for me not to feel as though this
25 was going to be a second-rate field trip, and on
26 the long bus ride I thought mainly of how much
27 more fun a trip the zoo would have been.
28      But when we arrived, I couldn't help but
29 be affected by the mounds. As we walked
30 among them and our guide described the lives
31 of the people whose bodies were now interred
32 within them, I felt the weight of their history as
33 I had not when I had been only reading about
34 it. History transformed from a collection of
35 facts to real human experience: people had
36 been there, and they lived, grew up, grew old,
37 and died. Their cities dissolved, and they had
38 been almost completely forgotten, but their
39 works left a mark in history—and thousands of
40 years later, we were learning their stories. It
41 was a haunting and humbling experience. On
42 the ride home, I didn't think of the zoo at all.

*Go on to the next page* ➡

1.  The author's main purpose in this passage is to

    (A) describe an ancient civilization.
    (B) express an opinion about earthen mounds.
    (C) explain why she has never been to a zoo.
    (D) tell a story about a field trip.

2.  As it is used in the passage, the word "interred" (line 31) most nearly means

    (A) in-between.
    (B) buried.
    (C) entered.
    (D) studied.

3.  In the second paragraph (lines 17-27), the narrator's attitude as a child could best be described as

    (A) rational.
    (B) joyful.
    (C) enthusiastic.
    (D) pessimistic.

4.  With which of the following statements would the author most likely agree?

    (A) A field trip to the zoo would have been better than the field trip to the mounds.
    (B) Reading too much about your destination in advance can ruin the experience of a field trip.
    (C) Tour guides are usually better at teaching than classroom teachers are.
    (D) Some lessons are easier to learn through experience than by just reading about them.

5.  According to information in the passage, the earthen mounds were

    (A) even more ancient than the pyramids in Egypt.
    (B) built by European explorers, but later forgotten.
    (C) similar in construction to the pyramids in Egypt.
    (D) built in the first North American cities.

*Go on to the next page* ➡

# RC

1    Fireflies are common insects found
2    throughout temperate and tropical
3    environments. These insects are well-known
4    for a light that they produce using a chemical
5    reaction. Many of us have seen fireflies lighting
6    up the night-time air in parks and open fields,
7    or have even tried to catch them in order to
8    watch them glow up close.
9        These flying adult fireflies are most likely
10   using their glow in order to attract mates. In
11   many species, the male firefly creates flashes of
12   light while flying around an area, and then the
13   female responds to these aerial flashes with a
14   flash of her own. These mating behaviors vary
15   between species of firefly, however. In some
16   species, only the female adult flashes, and in
17   other species, only the males flash. In some
18   species, neither the male nor the female
19   flashes, and the fireflies instead use scent to
20   find mates.

21   Firefly larvae also glow, and for this
22   reason they are sometimes known as
23   glowworms. Larvae are the young form of
24   fireflies, and all firefly larvae glow, even in
25   species in which the adult fireflies do not glow.
26   This glowing is not intended to attract mates,
27   but is more likely intended to warn potential
28   predators against eating the young insects.
29   Most glowworms have a bad taste or may even
30   be poisonous to eat.
31       There are also some fireflies that use
32   their glow for another purpose altogether:
33   predation. In these species of firefly, the female
34   uses her flash to mimic the flash of a female of
35   another species. When males of the other
36   species are attracted by the flash, the predatory
37   females kill and eat them. This has earned
38   these fireflies the nickname "femme fatale."

*Go on to the next page* ➡

6. The primary purpose of this passage is to

   (A) disprove popular myths about fireflies.

   (B) describe several types of glowing insects.

   (C) provide information about various types of fireflies.

   (D) explain that certain fireflies use their glow to attract prey.

7. Based on information in the passage, we can infer that fireflies are probably

   (A) the only type of insect that uses a chemical reaction to glow.

   (B) larger and more complex than most flying insects.

   (C) found in many different places throughout the world.

   (D) more common in tropical environments than temperate ones.

8. Which question could be answered with information from the passage?

   (A) Are some fireflies predators?

   (B) Why don't all fireflies have the ability to glow as adults?

   (C) Which species of firefly is most common?

   (D) In what part of the world were fireflies first discovered?

9. According to the passage, glowworms are

   (A) a type of worm with similar traits to fireflies.

   (B) the only species of firefly that doesn't fly.

   (C) a predatory type of firefly.

   (D) the young form of any species of firefly.

10. In line 13, "aerial" most nearly means

   (A) in the air.

   (B) brighter than usual.

   (C) predatory.

   (D) warning.

*Go on to the next page* ➡

# RC

1     Chaji is a Japanese tea ceremony. The
2 guests arrive early and enter an interior
3 waiting room, where they leave their coats and
4 other possessions and put on fresh tabi—
5 special socks worn with traditional Japanese
6 sandals. The waiting room is decorated with a
7 hanging scroll which has artwork or writing on
8 it, and which usually has a seasonal theme.
9 When all the guests have arrived and finished
10 their preparations, they go to an outdoor
11 waiting bench in a simple garden outside the
12 teahouse, where they remain until summoned
13 by the host.
14     Following a silent bow between host and
15 guests, the guests take turns going to a stone
16 basin where they ritually purify themselves by
17 washing their hands and rinsing their mouths
18 with water. They remove their sandals and
19 enter the tea room, where they sit on mats.
20 Here, too, there is a hanging scroll.
21     In cool months, a fire is made at the
22 beginning of the chaji, before the meal.  In
23 warmer months, the fire is not made until after
24 the meal. The meal includes several courses
25 accompanied by rice wine and followed by a
26 small sweet. After the meal there is a break,
27 during which the guests return to the garden
28 while the host replaces the scroll with a flower
29 arrangement, opens the tea room's shutters,
30 and makes preparations for serving the tea.

*Go on to the next page* ➡

11. This passage is primarily about Japanese

    (A) manners.

    (B) food.

    (C) tea ceremonies.

    (D) gardens.

12. According to the passage, the guests at a Japanese tea ceremony remove their sandals

    (A) before entering the waiting room.

    (B) before entering the garden.

    (C) before entering the tea room.

    (D) before washing their hands.

13. The mood of a Japanese tea ceremony could best be described as

    (A) tense.

    (B) casual.

    (C) dark.

    (D) formal.

14. It can be inferred from the passage that during the meal

    (A) the host is not present.

    (B) the guests eat too much.

    (C) the host gets very tired.

    (D) the shutters of the tea room are shut.

15. As it is used in line 16, "purify" most nearly means

    (A) clean.

    (B) finish.

    (C) observe.

    (D) dabble.

*Go on to the next page* ➡

**Ivy Global**

Questions 16–20

1     It was a hot morning late in July when
2 the school opened. I trembled when I heard the
3 patter of little feet down the dusty road and
4 saw the growing row of dark solemn faces and
5 bright eager eyes facing me.
6     There they sat, nearly thirty of them, on
7 the rough benches, their faces shading from a
8 pale cream to a deep brown, the little feet bare
9 and swinging, the eyes full of expectation, with
10 here and there a twinkle of mischief, and the
11 hands grasping Webster's blue-back spelling-
12 book. I loved my school, and the fine faith the
13 children had in the wisdom of their teacher
14 was truly marvelous. We read and spelled
15 together, wrote a little, picked flowers, sang,
16 and listened to stories of the world beyond the
17 hill.

18     At times the school would dwindle away,
19 and I would start out. I would visit the Eddings,
20 who lived in two very dirty rooms, and ask why
21 little Lugene, whose flaming face seemed ever
22 ablaze with the dark-red hair uncombed, was
23 absent all last week, or why the unmistakable
24 rags of Mack and Ed were so often missing.
25 Then their father would tell me how the crops
26 needed the boys, and their mother would
27 assure me that Lugene must mind the baby.
28 "But we'll start them again next week." When
29 the Lawrences stopped, I knew that the doubts
30 of the old folks about book-learning had
31 conquered again, and so, toiling up the hill, I
32 put Cicero's "pro Archia Poeta" into the
33 simplest English, and usually convinced
34 them—for a week or so.

*Go on to the next page* ➡

16. How did the speaker feel about his job at the school?

    (A) He enjoyed having such easy and entertaining work.

    (B) He resented the fact that his students didn't appreciate his expertise.

    (C) He was bored by the simple activities he had to engage in with his students.

    (D) He was proud of his school and worked hard to maintain it.

17. According to the passage, when school attendance was low the speaker would

    (A) pay social calls to pass the time.

    (B) visit his students' families to find out why they were missing school.

    (C) bring homework assignments to his students in their homes.

    (D) entertain his students and their families with stories about history.

18. Based on the passage, we can infer that the narrator is most likely

    (A) the most dedicated and talented student in class.

    (B) a farmer in an isolated rural community.

    (C) the teacher in a small country school.

    (D) a traveler writing about his trip to a rural community.

19. What reasons do the Eddings give for their children's absence from school?

    (A) The children are being kept home as a punishment.

    (B) The children are needed at home to help with the farm and family.

    (C) The parents don't want their children to become more educated.

    (D) The children don't enjoy school and prefer to stay home.

20. It can be inferred from the passage that Cicero's "pro Archia Poeta" (line 32) is

    (A) a Latin treatise about farming.

    (B) a short story describing the benefits of studying geography.

    (C) a poem about the uneducated.

    (D) not written in simple English.

*Go on to the next page ➡*

# RC

Questions 21–25

1      During the "Golden Age" of Hollywood—
2 from the early 1920s through the early
3 1950s— Hollywood movies were produced
4 and distributed through what is known as the
5 studio system. The term "studio system" refers
6 to two important practices of large motion
7 picture studios at the time: they produced
8 movies primarily on their own filmmaking lots
9 with creative personnel under long-term
10 contracts; and they owned or effectively
11 controlled the movie theaters to which they
12 distributed their films. These two practices
13 helped the top studios maximize their profits
14 and maintain control of the industry.
15      Studios controlled almost completely
16 what jobs the actors under contract with them
17 could or could not do, which was
18 understandably frustrating for some
19 performers. In the late 1930s, Cary Grant
20 became the first Hollywood star to "go
21 independent" by not renewing his studio
22 contract. By leaving the studio system, Grant
23 gained control over every aspect of his career,

24 although he also ran the risk of that career
25 dwindling because no particular studio had a
26 long-term interest in promoting it. For Grant,
27 the risk paid off. Not only was he able to decide
28 which films he was going to appear in, he often
29 had personal choice of his directors and co-
30 stars. At times he even negotiated a share of
31 the gross revenue, something uncommon at the
32 time. Grant received more than $700,000 for
33 his 10% of the gross profits for *To Catch a*
34 *Thief,* while Alfred Hitchcock received less than
35 $50,000 for directing and producing it.
36      Later, the practices that the studio
37 system used to control movie theaters would
38 also come under attack. The studios were
39 investigated by the Federal Trade commission,
40 which determined that their practices were
41 against the law. At the end of a lawsuit in 1948,
42 they were forced to sell their movie theaters,
43 and give more control over what movies would
44 be purchased and shown to movie theater
45 operators.

*Go on to the next page* ➜

21. The main purpose of this passage is to

    (A) examine Cary Grant's surprising career choices.

    (B) describe the studio system and its decline.

    (C) demonstrate how larger studios were able to make higher profits.

    (D) argue that long-term contracts are unfair to creative staff.

22. According to the passage, which of the following practices defined the studio system as a method of film production?

    (A) forming long-term contracts with actors and other staff

    (B) paying independent stars like Cary Grant generously for their work

    (C) hiring talented directors like Alfred Hitchcock

    (D) fostering competition among theaters to buy new films

23. The passage suggests that Cary Grant decided to "go independent" (lines 20-21) mainly because

    (A) he wanted to own movie theaters and filmmaking lots.

    (B) he wanted more control over his career.

    (C) he wanted to work with Alfred Hitchcock.

    (D) he wanted to direct and produce his own films.

24. Which of the following questions is answered by information in the passage?

    (A) How much were Grant's co-stars paid for their roles in *To Catch a Thief*?

    (B) Who was responsible for starting the "Golden Age" of Hollywood?

    (C) Were any of the practices of the studio system against the law?

    (D) Who was Cary Grant's favorite director?

25. As it is used in line 31, the word "revenue" most nearly means

    (A) money spent.

    (B) money loaned.

    (C) money lost.

    (D) money earned.

# SECTION 4

# Mathematics Achievement

Each question is followed by four suggested answers. Read each question and then decide which one of the four suggested answers is best.

Find the row of spaces on your answer document that has the same number as the question. In this row, mark the space having the same letter as the answer you have chosen. You may write in your test booklet.

---

SAMPLE QUESTION:

<u>Sample Answer</u>

Which of the numbers below is NOT a factor of 364?

Ⓐ ● Ⓒ Ⓓ

(A) 13

(B) 20

(C) 26

(D) 91

The correct answer is 20, so circle B is darkened.

---

STOP. Do not go on
until told to do so.

*Ivy Global*

1. Which expression is equal to 98?

   (A) $2 \times (9 + 8 + 5)$

   (B) $8 \times (9 + 2) + 5$

   (C) $(8 + 9) + 2 \times 5$

   (D) $8 + 9 \times (2 \times 5)$

2. Jackie has 3 nickels, 4 dimes, and 1 quarter. Jackie puts 40 cents in her piggy bank. How much money does Jackie have left?

   (A) $0.20

   (B) $0.25

   (C) $0.40

   (D) $0.80

3. What is the mean of the following dataset?

   $$2, 3, 5, 6, 7, 7$$

   (A) 4

   (B) 5

   (C) 6

   (D) 7

4. The diagram below shows Terry's collection of black and white marbles.

   If one marble is picked out of Terry's collection at random, what is the probability that it will be a white marble?

   (A) 5 out of 5

   (B) 4 out of 11

   (C) 4 out of 7

   (D) 2 out of 3

5. Alex tracked the weight of a growing kitten, and made a graph. Use Alex's graph to complete the data table.

   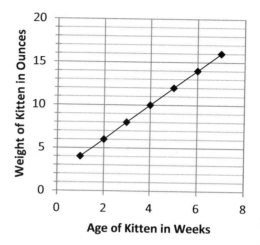

   | Age | Weight |
   |-----|--------|
   | 1 week | 4 oz. |
   | 2 weeks | 6 oz. |
   | 5 weeks | $a$ |
   | 6 weeks | 14 oz. |

   What is the value of $a$ in the data table?

   (A) 8 oz.

   (B) 10 oz.

   (C) 12 oz.

   (D) 13 oz.

6. Which expression correctly uses the distributive property to solve $15 \times (8 + 6)$?

   (A) $(15 + 8) + (15 + 6)$

   (B) $(15 \times 8) + 6$

   (C) $(15 \times 8) + (15 \times 6)$

   (D) $(15 \times 8) \times (15 \times 6)$

*Go on to the next page* ➡

7. How many vertices are there in the cube pictured below?

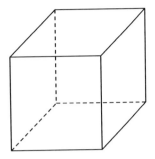

(A) 4

(B) 6

(C) 7

(D) 8

8. Shown below is a floor plan of Ana's bedroom.

10.5 ft

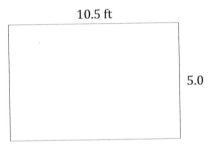

5.0

Ana is ordering new carpeting for her room so that the entire floor is covered. If her room is 10.5 feet wide and 5.0 feet long, how much carpet will Ana need?

(A) 15.5 ft²

(B) 22.5 ft²

(C) 52.5 ft²

(D) 105.5 ft²

9. Alyssa had a skipping rope that was 15.9 feet long. She cut the rope in half to create two smaller skipping ropes. How long are each of the shorter skipping ropes?

(A) $7\frac{7}{10}$ feet

(B) $7\frac{7}{8}$ feet

(C) $7\frac{19}{20}$ feet

(D) $8\frac{1}{10}$ feet

10. What is the name of the quadrilateral shown below?

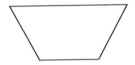

(A) Square

(B) Trapezoid

(C) Parallelogram

(D) Rhombus

11. Which number is equivalent to $\frac{3}{4}$?

(A) 0.34

(B) 0.66

(C) 0.75

(D) 3.33

12. A total of 34 students were split into three groups for track and field practice—running, jumping, and throwing. If 12 students were placed in the running group, and 9 students were placed in the jumping group, how many students were placed in the throwing group?

(A) 3

(B) 12

(C) 13

(D) 21

*Go on to the next page* ➡

13. What is the appropriate equation to determine the height of the triangle in the following diagram ($A = \frac{bh}{2}$ where $A$ = area, $b$ = base, $h$ = height)?

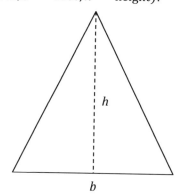

(A) $b = \frac{2A}{h}$

(B) $h = \frac{A}{2b}$

(C) $h = 2Ab$

(D) $h = \frac{2A}{b}$

14. What is the standard form for four hundred fifty thousand two hundred twenty-five?

(A) 425,055

(B) 450,025

(C) 450,225

(D) 452,025

15. Jason buys six bags of candy from the store weighing 47 grams, 112 grams, 695 grams, 619 grams, 98 grams, and 51 grams. What is the estimated total weight of Jason's candy?

(A) between 0 grams and 500 grams

(B) between 500 grams and 1,000 grams

(C) between 1,000 grams and 1,500 grams

(D) between 1,500 grams and 2,000 grams

16. Use the table to answer the question.

| STUDENT LUNCH CHOICES | | | | | |
|---|---|---|---|---|---|
| Lunch | Grade 3 | Grade 4 | Grade 5 | Grade 6 | Grade 7 |
| Turkey Sandwich | 56 | 45 | 40 | 38 | 36 |
| Tuna Sandwich | 10 | 11 | 19 | 17 | 15 |
| Salad | 7 | 6 | 9 | 13 | 19 |

What is the range of this set of data?

(A) 25

(B) 26

(C) 45

(D) 50

*Go on to the next page* ➡

17. Use the number sequence to answer the question.

$$1, 4, 10, 22, 46, \underline{\phantom{00}}$$

What is the next number in the sequence?

(A) 68

(B) 70

(C) 87

(D) 94

18. Use the coordinate grid to answer the question. Each grid square has a length of 1 unit.

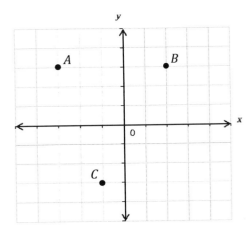

What are the coordinates of point $B$ in the figure?

(A) $(3, 2)$

(B) $(2, 3)$

(C) $(2, -3)$

(D) $(0, 2)$

19. Use the number line to answer the question.

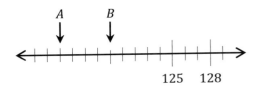

Points $A$ and $B$ represent what numbers?

(A) 107, 115

(B) 115, 119

(C) 116, 120

(D) 140, 135

20. If $\blacklozenge + 9(5 - 3) = 25$, what does $\blacklozenge$ equal?

(A) 47

(B) 43

(C) 41

(D) 7

21. Use the triangle to answer the question.

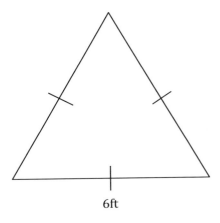

6ft

What is the perimeter of the triangle?
$(P = s + s + s)$

(A) 9 ft

(B) 12 ft

(C) 18 ft

(D) 26 ft

*Go on to the next page* ➡

22. What is the value of the expression 365 + 1,678?

    (A) 1,043

    (B) 1,044

    (C) 2,043

    (D) 2,044

23. Yonge Street is 1,900 kilometers long. Which street has a length closest to 3/4 that of Yonge Street?

    (A) Main Street, which is 1,450km long

    (B) Second Street, which is 1,100km long

    (C) Peter Street, which is 900km long

    (D) Mill Street, which is 425km long

24. The graph shows the number of pizzas given to each class for their pizza parties.

| PIZZA GIVEN TO FIVE CLASSES | |
|---|---|
| Ms. Fredrickson's Class | 🍕🍕🍕 |
| Mr. Johnson's Class | 🍕🍕🍕🍕🍕🍕🍕🍕 |
| Mrs. Smith's Class | 🍕🍕🍕🍕 |
| Mr. Nulman's Class | 🍕🍕🍕🍕🍕🍕 |
| Mr. Kim's Class | 🍕🍕 |

 = 8 slices of pizza

How many more slices of pizza did Mr. Nulman's class get than Ms. Fredrickson's class?

(A) 3

(B) 18

(C) 24

(D) 31

*Go on to the next page* ➡

25. Which fraction is between $\frac{5}{9}$ and $\frac{19}{27}$?

(A) $\frac{1}{10}$

(B) $\frac{1}{2}$

(C) $\frac{2}{3}$

(D) $\frac{7}{9}$

26. What is the value of the expression 35 × 42?

(A) 81

(B) 380

(C) 1,280

(D) 1,470

27. The number 11 is

(A) odd and even

(B) odd and prime

(C) even and composite

(D) even and prime

28. Which expression is equal to 75.6 × 90?

(A) 756 × 0.9

(B) 756 × 0.09

(C) 7.56 × 9

(D) 7.56 × 900

29. What is the sum of 3.3 + 1.5?

(A) $4\frac{4}{8}$

(B) $4\frac{7}{10}$

(C) $4\frac{3}{4}$

(D) $4\frac{4}{5}$

30. Four students were asked to walk, jog, and sprint around the track. Their speeds were collected at various times and recorded in the table below.

| Times | Walking Student | Jogging Student | Sprinting Student |
|---|---|---|---|
| 2 min | 5.00 km/hr | 11.50 km/hr | 20.00 km/hr |
| 4 min | 5.00 km/hr | 11.00 km/hr | 16.00 km/hr |
| 6 min | 5.00 km/hr | 10.50 km/hr | 14.00 km/hr |
| 8 min | 5.00 km/hr | 10.00 km/hr | 13.00 km/hr |

At the 6 minute mark, how much faster was the jogging student moving than the walking student?

(A) 9.00 km/hr

(B) 8.00 km/hr

(C) 5.50 km/hr

(D) 5.00 km/hr

STOP. Do not go on
until told to do so.

STOP

*Ivy Global*

# Essay Topic Sheet

The directions for the Essay portion of the ISEE are printed in the box below. Use the pre-lined pages on pages 36-37 for this part of the Practice Test.

You will have 30 minutes to plan and write an essay on the topic printed on the other side of this page. **Do not write on another topic. An essay on another topic is not acceptable.**

The essay is designed to give you an opportunity to show how well you can write. You should try to express your thoughts clearly. How well you write is much more important than how much you write, but you need to say enough for a reader to understand what you mean.

You will probably want to write more than a short paragraph. You should also be aware that a copy of your essay will be sent to each school that will be receiving your test results. You are to write only in the appropriate section of the answer sheet. Please write or print so that your writing may be read by someone who is not familiar with your handwriting.

You may make notes and plan your essay on the reverse side of the page. Allow enough time to copy the final form onto your answer sheet. You must copy the essay topic onto your answer sheet, on page 36, in the box provided.

Please remember to write only the final draft of the essay on pages 36-37 of your answer sheet and to write it in blue or black pen. Again, you may use cursive writing or you may print. Only pages 36-37 will be sent to the schools.

*Directions continue on the next page.*

**REMINDER:** Please write this essay topic on the first few lines of the first page of your essay sheet.

**Essay Topic**

Describe the perfect class field trip. Tell us where your class would go, and what you would do.

- Only write on this essay question
- Only pages 36 and 37 will be sent to the schools
- Only write in blue or black pen

# NOTES

_____

_____

_____

_____

_____

_____

_____

_____

_____

_____

_____

_____

_____

_____

_____

_____

_____

_____

_____

_____

Ivy Global

# PRACTICE TEST 2

## LOWER LEVEL

# HOW TO TAKE THIS PRACTICE TEST

To simulate an accurate testing environment, sit at a desk in a quiet location free of distractions—no TV, computers, phones, music, or noise—and clear your desk of all materials except pencils and erasers. Remember that no calculators, rulers, protractors, dictionaries, or other aids are allowed on the ISEE.

Give yourself the following amounts of time for each section:

| SECTION | SUBJECT | TIME LIMIT |
|---------|---------|------------|
| 1 | Verbal Reasoning | 20 minutes |
| 2 | Quantitative Reasoning | 35 minutes |
| 5 minute break | | |
| 3 | Reading Comprehension | 25 minutes |
| 4 | Mathematics Achievement | 30 minutes |
| 5 minute break | | |
| 5 | Essay | 30 minutes |

Have an adult help you monitor your time, or use a watch and time yourself. Only give yourself the allotted time for each section; put your pencil down when your time is up.

Follow the instructions carefully. As you take your test, bubble your answers into the answer sheets provided. Use the test booklet as scratch paper for notes and calculations. Remember that you are not granted time at the end of a section to transfer your answers to the answer sheet, so you must do this as you go along.

When you are finished, check your answers against the answer keys provided. Then, score your exam using the directions at the end of the book.

Ivy Global

Note: students with diagnosed learning disabilities who apply for testing with accommodations may receive extra time, or may be allowed to use certain assistive devices during the ISEE. For more information, visit http://erblearn.org/parents/admission/isee/accommodations.

# Ivy Global

# ISEE
## LOWER LEVEL TEST 2

| MARKING INSTRUCTIONS |
|---|
| • Use a #2 or HB pencil only on pages 76 and 77. |
| • Use a ballpoint pen for your essay on pages 78 and 79. |
| • Make dark marks that completely fill the circle. |
| • Erase clearly any mark you wish to change. |
| • Make no stray marks on this form. |
| • Do not fold or crease this form. |

Correct Mark        Incorrect Marks
●                    ⊗ ◯ ✓ ⊖ ☺

## 1 VERBAL REASONING

1  Ⓐ Ⓑ Ⓒ Ⓓ      15 Ⓐ Ⓑ Ⓒ Ⓓ      29 Ⓐ Ⓑ Ⓒ Ⓓ
2  Ⓐ Ⓑ Ⓒ Ⓓ      16 Ⓐ Ⓑ Ⓒ Ⓓ      30 Ⓐ Ⓑ Ⓒ Ⓓ
3  Ⓐ Ⓑ Ⓒ Ⓓ      17 Ⓐ Ⓑ Ⓒ Ⓓ      31 Ⓐ Ⓑ Ⓒ Ⓓ
4  Ⓐ Ⓑ Ⓒ Ⓓ      18 Ⓐ Ⓑ Ⓒ Ⓓ      32 Ⓐ Ⓑ Ⓒ Ⓓ
5  Ⓐ Ⓑ Ⓒ Ⓓ      19 Ⓐ Ⓑ Ⓒ Ⓓ      33 Ⓐ Ⓑ Ⓒ Ⓓ
6  Ⓐ Ⓑ Ⓒ Ⓓ      20 Ⓐ Ⓑ Ⓒ Ⓓ      34 Ⓐ Ⓑ Ⓒ Ⓓ
                                   **Lower Level Ends**
7  Ⓐ Ⓑ Ⓒ Ⓓ      21 Ⓐ Ⓑ Ⓒ Ⓓ      35 Ⓐ Ⓑ Ⓒ Ⓓ
8  Ⓐ Ⓑ Ⓒ Ⓓ      22 Ⓐ Ⓑ Ⓒ Ⓓ      36 Ⓐ Ⓑ Ⓒ Ⓓ
9  Ⓐ Ⓑ Ⓒ Ⓓ      23 Ⓐ Ⓑ Ⓒ Ⓓ      37 Ⓐ Ⓑ Ⓒ Ⓓ
10 Ⓐ Ⓑ Ⓒ Ⓓ      24 Ⓐ Ⓑ Ⓒ Ⓓ      38 Ⓐ Ⓑ Ⓒ Ⓓ
11 Ⓐ Ⓑ Ⓒ Ⓓ      25 Ⓐ Ⓑ Ⓒ Ⓓ      39 Ⓐ Ⓑ Ⓒ Ⓓ
12 Ⓐ Ⓑ Ⓒ Ⓓ      26 Ⓐ Ⓑ Ⓒ Ⓓ      40 Ⓐ Ⓑ Ⓒ Ⓓ
                                   **Middle/Upper**
13 Ⓐ Ⓑ Ⓒ Ⓓ      27 Ⓐ Ⓑ Ⓒ Ⓓ       **Level Ends**
14 Ⓐ Ⓑ Ⓒ Ⓓ      28 Ⓐ Ⓑ Ⓒ Ⓓ

## 2 QUANTITATIVE REASONING

| | | | |
|---|---|---|---|
| 1 Ⓐ Ⓑ Ⓒ Ⓓ | 15 Ⓐ Ⓑ Ⓒ Ⓓ | 29 Ⓐ Ⓑ Ⓒ Ⓓ |
| 2 Ⓐ Ⓑ Ⓒ Ⓓ | 16 Ⓐ Ⓑ Ⓒ Ⓓ | 30 Ⓐ Ⓑ Ⓒ Ⓓ |
| 3 Ⓐ Ⓑ Ⓒ Ⓓ | 17 Ⓐ Ⓑ Ⓒ Ⓓ | 31 Ⓐ Ⓑ Ⓒ Ⓓ |
| 4 Ⓐ Ⓑ Ⓒ Ⓓ | 18 Ⓐ Ⓑ Ⓒ Ⓓ | 32 Ⓐ Ⓑ Ⓒ Ⓓ |
| 5 Ⓐ Ⓑ Ⓒ Ⓓ | 19 Ⓐ Ⓑ Ⓒ Ⓓ | 33 Ⓐ Ⓑ Ⓒ Ⓓ |
| 6 Ⓐ Ⓑ Ⓒ Ⓓ | 20 Ⓐ Ⓑ Ⓒ Ⓓ | 34 Ⓐ Ⓑ Ⓒ Ⓓ |
| 7 Ⓐ Ⓑ Ⓒ Ⓓ | 21 Ⓐ Ⓑ Ⓒ Ⓓ | 35 Ⓐ Ⓑ Ⓒ Ⓓ |
| 8 Ⓐ Ⓑ Ⓒ Ⓓ | 22 Ⓐ Ⓑ Ⓒ Ⓓ | 36 Ⓐ Ⓑ Ⓒ Ⓓ |
| 9 Ⓐ Ⓑ Ⓒ Ⓓ | 23 Ⓐ Ⓑ Ⓒ Ⓓ | 37 Ⓐ Ⓑ Ⓒ Ⓓ |
| 10 Ⓐ Ⓑ Ⓒ Ⓓ | 24 Ⓐ Ⓑ Ⓒ Ⓓ | **Middle/Upper Level Ends** |
| 11 Ⓐ Ⓑ Ⓒ Ⓓ | 25 Ⓐ Ⓑ Ⓒ Ⓓ | 38 Ⓐ Ⓑ Ⓒ Ⓓ |
| 12 Ⓐ Ⓑ Ⓒ Ⓓ | 26 Ⓐ Ⓑ Ⓒ Ⓓ | **Lower Level Ends** |
| 13 Ⓐ Ⓑ Ⓒ Ⓓ | 27 Ⓐ Ⓑ Ⓒ Ⓓ | |
| 14 Ⓐ Ⓑ Ⓒ Ⓓ | 28 Ⓐ Ⓑ Ⓒ Ⓓ | |

## 4 MATHEMATICS ACHIEVEMENT

| | | |
|---|---|---|
| 1 Ⓐ Ⓑ Ⓒ Ⓓ | 18 Ⓐ Ⓑ Ⓒ Ⓓ | 35 Ⓐ Ⓑ Ⓒ Ⓓ |
| 2 Ⓐ Ⓑ Ⓒ Ⓓ | 19 Ⓐ Ⓑ Ⓒ Ⓓ | 36 Ⓐ Ⓑ Ⓒ Ⓓ |
| 3 Ⓐ Ⓑ Ⓒ Ⓓ | 20 Ⓐ Ⓑ Ⓒ Ⓓ | 37 Ⓐ Ⓑ Ⓒ Ⓓ |
| 4 Ⓐ Ⓑ Ⓒ Ⓓ | 21 Ⓐ Ⓑ Ⓒ Ⓓ | 38 Ⓐ Ⓑ Ⓒ Ⓓ |
| 5 Ⓐ Ⓑ Ⓒ Ⓓ | 22 Ⓐ Ⓑ Ⓒ Ⓓ | 39 Ⓐ Ⓑ Ⓒ Ⓓ |
| 6 Ⓐ Ⓑ Ⓒ Ⓓ | 23 Ⓐ Ⓑ Ⓒ Ⓓ | 40 Ⓐ Ⓑ Ⓒ Ⓓ |
| 7 Ⓐ Ⓑ Ⓒ Ⓓ | 24 Ⓐ Ⓑ Ⓒ Ⓓ | 41 Ⓐ Ⓑ Ⓒ Ⓓ |
| 8 Ⓐ Ⓑ Ⓒ Ⓓ | 25 Ⓐ Ⓑ Ⓒ Ⓓ | 42 Ⓐ Ⓑ Ⓒ Ⓓ |
| 9 Ⓐ Ⓑ Ⓒ Ⓓ | 26 Ⓐ Ⓑ Ⓒ Ⓓ | 43 Ⓐ Ⓑ Ⓒ Ⓓ |
| 10 Ⓐ Ⓑ Ⓒ Ⓓ | 27 Ⓐ Ⓑ Ⓒ Ⓓ | 44 Ⓐ Ⓑ Ⓒ Ⓓ |
| 11 Ⓐ Ⓑ Ⓒ Ⓓ | 28 Ⓐ Ⓑ Ⓒ Ⓓ | 45 Ⓐ Ⓑ Ⓒ Ⓓ |
| 12 Ⓐ Ⓑ Ⓒ Ⓓ | 29 Ⓐ Ⓑ Ⓒ Ⓓ | 46 Ⓐ Ⓑ Ⓒ Ⓓ |
| 13 Ⓐ Ⓑ Ⓒ Ⓓ | 30 Ⓐ Ⓑ Ⓒ Ⓓ | 47 Ⓐ Ⓑ Ⓒ Ⓓ |
| 14 Ⓐ Ⓑ Ⓒ Ⓓ | **Lower Level Ends** | **Middle/Upper Level Ends** |
| 15 Ⓐ Ⓑ Ⓒ Ⓓ | 31 Ⓐ Ⓑ Ⓒ Ⓓ | |
| 16 Ⓐ Ⓑ Ⓒ Ⓓ | 32 Ⓐ Ⓑ Ⓒ Ⓓ | |
| 17 Ⓐ Ⓑ Ⓒ Ⓓ | 33 Ⓐ Ⓑ Ⓒ Ⓓ | |
| | 34 Ⓐ Ⓑ Ⓒ Ⓓ | |

## 3 READING COMPREHENSION

| | | |
|---|---|---|
| 1 Ⓐ Ⓑ Ⓒ Ⓓ | 15 Ⓐ Ⓑ Ⓒ Ⓓ | 29 Ⓐ Ⓑ Ⓒ Ⓓ |
| 2 Ⓐ Ⓑ Ⓒ Ⓓ | 16 Ⓐ Ⓑ Ⓒ Ⓓ | 30 Ⓐ Ⓑ Ⓒ Ⓓ |
| 3 Ⓐ Ⓑ Ⓒ Ⓓ | 17 Ⓐ Ⓑ Ⓒ Ⓓ | 31 Ⓐ Ⓑ Ⓒ Ⓓ |
| 4 Ⓐ Ⓑ Ⓒ Ⓓ | 18 Ⓐ Ⓑ Ⓒ Ⓓ | 32 Ⓐ Ⓑ Ⓒ Ⓓ |
| 5 Ⓐ Ⓑ Ⓒ Ⓓ | 19 Ⓐ Ⓑ Ⓒ Ⓓ | 33 Ⓐ Ⓑ Ⓒ Ⓓ |
| 6 Ⓐ Ⓑ Ⓒ Ⓓ | 20 Ⓐ Ⓑ Ⓒ Ⓓ | 34 Ⓐ Ⓑ Ⓒ Ⓓ |
| 7 Ⓐ Ⓑ Ⓒ Ⓓ | 21 Ⓐ Ⓑ Ⓒ Ⓓ | 35 Ⓐ Ⓑ Ⓒ Ⓓ |
| 8 Ⓐ Ⓑ Ⓒ Ⓓ | 22 Ⓐ Ⓑ Ⓒ Ⓓ | 36 Ⓐ Ⓑ Ⓒ Ⓓ |
| 9 Ⓐ Ⓑ Ⓒ Ⓓ | 23 Ⓐ Ⓑ Ⓒ Ⓓ | **Middle/Upper Level Ends** |
| 10 Ⓐ Ⓑ Ⓒ Ⓓ | 24 Ⓐ Ⓑ Ⓒ Ⓓ | |
| 11 Ⓐ Ⓑ Ⓒ Ⓓ | 25 Ⓐ Ⓑ Ⓒ Ⓓ | |
| 12 Ⓐ Ⓑ Ⓒ Ⓓ | **Lower Level Ends** | |
| 13 Ⓐ Ⓑ Ⓒ Ⓓ | 26 Ⓐ Ⓑ Ⓒ Ⓓ | |
| 14 Ⓐ Ⓑ Ⓒ Ⓓ | 27 Ⓐ Ⓑ Ⓒ Ⓓ | |
| | 28 Ⓐ Ⓑ Ⓒ Ⓓ | |

**Ivy Global**

STUDENT NAME _____ GRADE APPLYING FOR _____

Use a blue or black ballpoint pen to write the final draft of your essay on this sheet.

You must write your essay topic in this space.

_____

_____

_____

Use specific details and examples in your response.

_____

_____

_____

_____

_____

_____

_____

_____

_____

_____

_____

_____

_____

_____

_____

_____

_____

_____

_____

_____

_____

_____

_____

Ivy Global

# Section 1
# Verbal Reasoning

| **34 Questions** | **Time: 20 minutes** |

This section is divided into two parts that contain two different types of questions. As soon as you have completed Part One, answer the questions in Part Two. You may write in your test booklet. For each answer you select, fill in the corresponding circle on your answer document.

## PART ONE — SYNONYMS

Each question in Part One consists of a word in capital letters followed by four answer choices. Select the one word that is most nearly the same in meaning as the word in capital letters.

---

SAMPLE QUESTION:

Sample Answer

Ⓐ Ⓑ ● Ⓓ

CHARGE:

(A) release
(B) belittle
(C) accuse
(D) conspire

The correct answer is "accuse," so circle C is darkened.

---

*Go on to the next page* ➜

# VR

## PART TWO — SENTENCE COMPLETION

Each question in Part Two is made up of a sentence with one blank. Each blank indicates that a word or phrase is missing. The sentence is followed by four answer choices. Select the word or phrase that will best complete the meaning of the sentence as a whole.

---

SAMPLE QUESTIONS:                                    <u>Sample Answer</u>

   It rained so much that the streets were -------.              ● Ⓑ Ⓒ Ⓓ

   (A) flooded

   (B) arid

   (C) paved

   (D) crowded

   The correct answer is "flooded," so circle A is darkened.        Ⓐ Ⓑ Ⓒ ●

   The house was so dirty that it took -------.

   (A) less than ten minutes to wash it.

   (B) four months to demolish it.

   (C) over a week to walk across it.

   (D) two days to clean it.

   The correct answer is "two days to clean it," so circle D is darkened.

---

STOP. Do not go on
until told to do so.              **STOP**

# VR

## PART ONE – SYNONYMS

**Directions:** Select the word that is most nearly the same in meaning as the word in capital letters.

1. VOLUNTEER
   (A) aid
   (B) offer
   (C) undergo
   (D) chatter

2. SYNCHRONIZE
   (A) wind
   (B) record
   (C) coordinate
   (D) measure

3. MOURN
   (A) imprison
   (B) lament
   (C) enjoy
   (D) discover

4. GLISTEN
   (A) shorten
   (B) collect
   (C) sparkle
   (D) exhale

5. RELENTLESS
   (A) insistent
   (B) impure
   (C) unfinished
   (D) soft

6. BRAND
   (A) oats
   (B) mark
   (C) business
   (D) bravery

7. RENDITION
   (A) refrain
   (B) article
   (C) song
   (D) version

8. COMMONPLACE
   (A) tasty
   (B) ordinary
   (C) liquid
   (D) invasive

9. HOIST
   (A) drop
   (B) plow
   (C) lift
   (D) strain

10. HEAP
    (A) compost
    (B) roll
    (C) rake
    (D) pile

*Go on to the next page* ➜

**Ivy Global**

11. SOW

    (A) pig

    (B) stitch

    (C) canal

    (D) sour

12. GLEE

    (A) gift

    (B) depression

    (C) joy

    (D) clarity

13. LINGER

    (A) revert

    (B) delay

    (C) hurry

    (D) remark

14. ADMIRE

    (A) impugn

    (B) sing

    (C) adore

    (D) count

15. PERSECUTE

    (A) invade

    (B) assume

    (C) oppress

    (D) govern

16. SKEPTICAL

    (A) captive

    (B) doubtful

    (C) tidy

    (D) uneasy

17. COUNSEL

    (A) letter

    (B) monitor

    (C) advice

    (D) carelessness

*Go on to the next page* ➡

**Ivy Global**

## PART TWO – SENTENCE COMPLETION

**Directions:** Select the word that best completes the sentence.

18. Harinder was ----------- to learn that his flight was cancelled, as it meant that he would miss his beloved grandfather's birthday party.

    (A) elated

    (B) dismayed

    (C) pleased

    (D) threatened

19. Although they are normally gentle creatures, pigs can become ----------- when forced to live in cramped pens.

    (A) playful

    (B) loving

    (C) aggressive

    (D) fatigued

20. Jake's rabbit was very -----------, and it would not come out of its cage when people were around.

    (A) nautical

    (B) annoying

    (C) political

    (D) timid

21. The beautiful vistas and abundant wildlife of the Galapagos Islands ----------- numerous visitors every year.

    (A) attract

    (B) paint

    (C) repel

    (D) reject

22. Ambreen was ----------- to make a suggestion during the school council meeting, as the school council president did not welcome input.

    (A) hesitant

    (B) excited

    (C) eager

    (D) confident

23. The museum guide told the students they must ----------- from touching any of the exhibits because they can be easily damaged.

    (A) admit

    (B) applaud

    (C) refrain

    (D) retain

24. Eli was the bakery's most ----------- customer; he continued to shop there even though the grocery store had lower prices.

    (A) fickle

    (B) knowledgeable

    (C) neutral

    (D) loyal

25. The story's villain was truly ----------- because he lied to the townsfolk and cheated during his duel with the hero.

    (A) despicable

    (B) relatable

    (C) charming

    (D) forgettable

*Go on to the next page* ➡

26. Feral cats are notoriously ----------- around people, while their housecat cousins are usually very comfortable with humans.

(A) bold

(B) tame

(C) impervious

(D) skittish

27. Because dark chocolate is her favorite food, Josie was ----------- to learn that it contains healthy antioxidants.

(A) ecstatic

(B) disappointed

(C) reluctant

(D) confused

28. Sally was proud of the ----------- in her neighborhood, which was home to people from a variety of countries, religions, and professions.

(A) repression

(B) anonymity

(C) altitude

(D) diversity

29. Unlike her brother, who never strays far from home, Rebecca -----------.

(A) does not travel far.

(B) is a world traveler.

(C) studies a variety of subjects.

(D) takes only a small suitcase on her trips.

30. Since Jodhi was a talented chef, -----------.

(A) she always prepared flavorful dishes.

(B) her father was an expert baker.

(C) she respected nature.

(D) poetry was her favorite thing to read.

31. Although Bret had spent many hours preparing for the test, -----------.

(A) he performed very well.

(B) his grade was not as high as he had hoped.

(C) it covered a wide range of material.

(D) the entire class had to take it.

32. Logan and his sister enjoyed watching basketball, but -----------.

(A) often watched games with friends.

(B) were not talented players themselves.

(C) followed a number of different teams.

(D) knew a lot about the sport.

33. I would love to volunteer at the harvest festival, but -----------.

(A) many students are available to help.

(B) the festival will involve a variety of activities.

(C) I believe that volunteering is important.

(D) I will sadly be out of town that weekend.

34. Although his books have sold millions of copies since his death, F. Scott Fitzgerald -----------.

(A) was well-known by critics of his era.

(B) often made money by selling short stories.

(C) had many financial difficulties during his career.

(D) made insightful observations about the 1920s in his writing.

STOP. Do not go on until told to do so.

# Section 2
# Quantitative Reasoning

Each question is followed by four suggested answers. Read each question and then decide which one of the four suggested answers is best.

Find the row of spaces on your answer document that has the same number as the question. In this row, mark the space having the same letter as the answer you have chosen. You may write in your test booklet.

---

SAMPLE QUESTIONS:

Sample Answer

What is the value of the expression $(4 + 6) \div 2$?

Ⓐ Ⓑ ● Ⓓ

(A) 2

(B) 4

(C) 5

(D) 7

The correct answer is 5, so circle C is darkened.

A square has an area of $25\text{cm}^2$. What is the length of one of its sides?

Ⓐ ● Ⓒ Ⓓ

(A) 1 cm

(B) 5 cm

(C) 10 cm

(D) 25 cm

The correct answer is 5, so circle B is darkened.

---

**STOP. Do not go on until told to do so.**

**STOP**

1.  Which story best fits the equation $24 \div 8 = 3$?

    (A) Jacqueline gives 8 of her headbands to her friend Lee. How many headbands does she have left?

    (B) Jacqueline has 8 times as many headbands as the number her friend Lee has. If Jacqueline has 24 headbands, how many headbands does Lee have?

    (C) Jacqueline has 8 headbands. If 24 headbands can fit in one bag, how many bags does she need to store her headbands?

    (D) Jacqueline has 24 friends, and each one has 8 headbands. How many headbands do her friends have in total?

2.  Use the figure below to answer the question.

    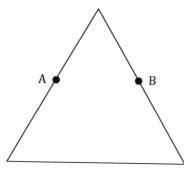

    If the triangle above were cut into two pieces along a straight line between points A and B, the resulting two pieces would be which shapes?

    (A) two rectangles

    (B) a triangle and a square

    (C) a triangle and a trapezoid

    (D) two triangles

3.  Use the diagram below to answer the question.

    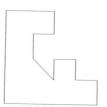

    Which shape completes the square?

    (A)

    (B)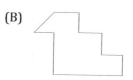

    (C)

    (D)

4.  Dividing a number $N$ by 6 leaves a remainder of 3. What is the remainder left when $2N$ is divided by 6?

    (A) 12

    (B) 6

    (C) 3

    (D) 0

*Go on to the next page* ➡

**Ivy Global**

5. Which of the following expressions is equivalent to $0.5 \times \text{♫} + \frac{\bigstar}{2}$?

   (A) $2(\text{♫} + \bigstar)$

   (B) $0.5(\text{♫} + \frac{\bigstar}{2})$

   (C) $\frac{\text{♫} + \bigstar}{0.5}$

   (D) $\frac{\text{♫} + \bigstar}{2}$

6. Use the Venn Diagram to answer the question.

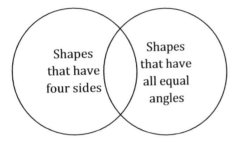

   Which shape could be found in the overlapping area of the Venn diagram?

   (A)

   (B)

   (C)

   (D)

7. A survey asked 100 students what their favorite season was. The results showed that 50 students prefer summer, 25 students prefer fall, 13 students prefer spring, and 12 students prefer winter. Which of the following circle graphs best represents the data from this survey?

   (A)

   (B)

   (C)

   (D)

*Go on to the next page* ➡

**Ivy Global**

8. Use the pattern to answer the question.

$$888 = 6 + 9 \times 98$$
$$8{,}888 = 5 + 9 \times 987$$
$$88{,}888 = 4 + 9 \times 9{,}876$$
$$888{,}888 = 3 + 9 \times 98{,}765$$
$$\dots$$
$$88{,}888{,}888 = 1 + 9 \times m$$

What is the value of $m$?

(A) 9,876

(B) 987,654

(C) 8,888,888

(D) 9,876,543

9. Susan's jar holds 2 cups of water when filled to the top. As shown below, she fills it only partially.

If Susan drinks $\frac{1}{3}$ of the water in the jar and then accidentally spills $\frac{1}{4}$ of the remaining water, how many cups of water are left in the jar?

(A) $\frac{3}{4}$

(B) 1

(C) $1\frac{1}{12}$

(D) $1\frac{1}{4}$

10. Selena is estimating $113.6 \div 11$. Which is the best way for her to estimate?

(A) $100 \div 10$

(B) $100 \div 15$

(C) $113 \div 20$

(D) $150 \div 10$

11. A large cube is built out of smaller cubes, as shown in the diagram below.

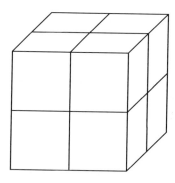

If the volume of the large cube is 32 cubic units, what is the volume of one of the smaller cubes?

(A) 1 cubic unit

(B) 4 cubic units

(C) 8 cubic units

(D) 16 cubic units

12. Which equation can be read as "three times two less than a number is equal to four more than the number"? Let $p$ represent the unknown number.

(A) $3 \times (p - 2) = p + 4$

(B) $3 \times (2 - p) = p + 4$

(C) $3 \times 2 \times p = p + 4$

(D) $2 \times (p - 3) = p + 4$

*Go on to the next page* ➡

13. The graph below shows the medals won by four different countries during the 1988 Summer Olympics.

**1988 Olympics Medal Count by Country and Medal Type**

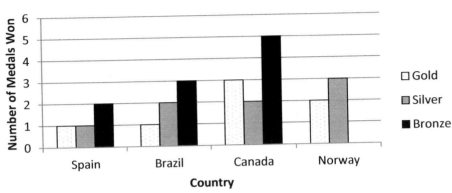

Based on the graph, which conclusion is true about the number of medals won by these four countries?

(A) The median number of silver medals won is greater than the range of bronze medals won.

(B) Brazil's total medal count is less than the number of bronze medals won by Canada.

(C) The median number of total medals won by each country is $5\frac{1}{2}$.

(D) The average (mean) number of gold medals won is greater than the average number of silver medals won.

---

14. It costs $9.95 to buy 1 pound of almonds. Sonja wants to know the price of a bag of almonds weighing 0.48 pounds. Which is the most reasonable estimation for the cost?

(A) $4.00

(B) $5.00

(C) $5.50

(D) $10.50

15. When Samson's two cats both stepped onto a scale, their measured weight was $X$ pounds. When one of the cats got off of the scale, the measured weight was $Y$ pounds. What was the weight of the cat that got off of the scale?

(A) $\frac{Y}{2}$

(B) $X + Y$

(C) $Y - X$

(D) $X - Y$

*Go on to the next page* ➡

Ivy Global

16. If $6 \times m = 42$, which of the number lines shown below shows the correct value of $m$?

(A)
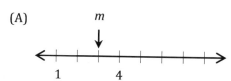
1    4

(B)
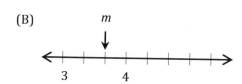
3    4

(C)
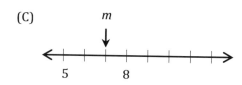
5    8

(D)
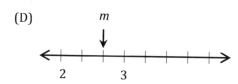
2    3

17. Jonathan had a square piece of paper. He cut a square with sides of 1 inch out of the paper, as shown by the dashed lines in the figure below.

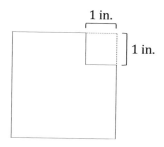

1 in.

1 in.

If the perimeter of the original piece of paper was $P$, what is the perimeter of the paper after it has been cut?

(A) $P$

(B) $P - 1$

(C) $P + 1$

(D) $\frac{1}{P}$

18. Jaron is plotting a square on a coordinate grid. So far, he has drawn three vertices at the coordinates $(0, 4)$ $(0, -4)$ $(-8, -4)$. To complete the square, what must be the coordinate of the fourth vertex?

(A) $(-8, 0)$

(B) $(-8, 4)$

(C) $(4, -8)$

(D) $(0, 8)$

19. Peter and Amrita both dove off a raft and began swimming in opposite directions. After five minutes, Amrita had swum two hundred meters. If Amrita swims twice as fast as Peter, how far apart were they after five minutes of swimming?

(A) 200 meters

(B) 300 meters

(C) 400 meters

(D) 600 meters

20. The largest square below is divided up into small squares.

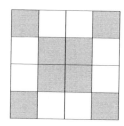

What is the ratio of the shaded region to the unshaded region?

(A) 8:1

(B) 2:1

(C) 1:2

(D) 1:1

*Go on to the next page* ➡

**Ivy Global**

21. What is the value of $R$ in the math equation $5 - 2R = 1$?

    (A) 2

    (B) 3

    (C) 4

    (D) 5

22. A group of friends is cutting a square card into pieces. The first friend cut it into four equal pieces, and passed it to the second friend. The second friend cut one of those pieces into four equal pieces, and passed it to the next friend, and so on. The figure below shows the card after it has been cut by three people.

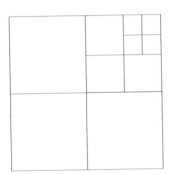

    If the card is cut by one more friend in the same fashion, how many square pieces will there be in total?

    (A) 4

    (B) 9

    (C) 10

    (D) 13

23. Which of the following numbers is greatest?

    (A) 0.309

    (B) $0.\overline{3}$

    (C) 0.334

    (D) 0.099

24. Ayumi has a small model of her bedroom built in her dollhouse. Everything in the dollhouse is built exactly to scale, and her 2-meter-long bed corresponds to a 5-centimeter-long doll bed. If Ayumi's bedroom desk is 1.5 meters wide, how wide is the doll's desk?

    (A) 2.5 centimeters

    (B) 3.75 centimeters

    (C) 4.25 centimeters

    (D) 5.0 centimeters

25. The figure below has three sides with a length of $x$ and three sides with a length of $y$.

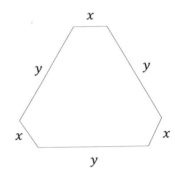

    If $x + y = 11$, what is the perimeter of the figure? (*Perimeter* $= s + s + s + s + s + s$)

    (A) 11

    (B) 14

    (C) 33

    (D) 40

26. Alastair is writing a list of prime numbers less than 50 in ascending order. If the first number on his list is 2, what is the fourth number on his list?

    (A) 5

    (B) 6

    (C) 7

    (D) 11

*Go on to the next page* ➡

27. Use the table to determine the rule.

| Input | Output |
|-------|--------|
| ✪ | ✧ |
| 1 | 1.5 |
| 3 | 4.5 |
| 8 | 12 |
| 10 | 15 |

(A) $✪ + \frac{1}{2}✪ = ✧$

(B) $✪ \times \frac{1}{2} = ✧$

(C) $✪ + \frac{3}{2} = ✧$

(D) $(✪ \times 2) - \frac{1}{2} = ✧$

28. Use the figure below to answer the question.

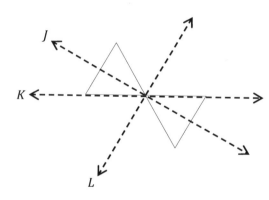

Which line(s) could NOT be a line of symmetry?

(A) $J$

(B) $K$

(C) $L$

(D) $J$ and $L$

29. Use the equations to answer the question.

$$c - 8 = 1$$
$$3 + d = 5$$

What is the value of $c - d$?

(A) 4

(B) 5

(C) 7

(D) 11

30. Jasmine and her mother have an average of 29.5 spools of thread between the two of them. If Jasmine has 12 spools of thread, how many spools does her mother have?

(A) 29.5

(B) 36

(C) 47

(D) 59

31. The net shown below can be folded into a six-sided cube. Each side has an equal chance of landing face-up when the cube is rolled.

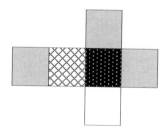

If someone rolls this cube, what is the probability that it will land with a grey side facing up?

(A) $\frac{1}{6}$

(B) $\frac{3}{7}$

(C) $\frac{1}{2}$

(D) $\frac{5}{6}$

*Go on to the next page* ➡

32. Use the table below to answer the question.

| POSTERS COMPLETED BY GROUP MEMBERS | |
|---|---|
| **Group Member** | **Number of Posters Completed** |
| Jessica | 2 |
| Augustus | $4\frac{1}{4}$ |
| Lupita | $3\frac{5}{8}$ |
| Hye Su | 4 |
| Ciaran | $6\frac{1}{8}$ |

What was the mean number of posters completed by a single group member?

(A) $3\frac{1}{4}$

(B) 4

(C) $4\frac{3}{8}$

(D) $5\frac{1}{4}$

33. Anton is thinking of a number that is greater than zero but less than six. He then says that it is a composite number. Which could be his number?

(A) 2

(B) 4

(C) 5

(D) 6

34. There are 14 animals in a pet shop which specializes in lizards, birds, and snakes. The total number of legs on these animals is 40, and there are three snakes. If each lizard has four legs and each bird has only two, how many birds are there?

(A) 2

(B) 4

(C) 9

(D) 11

*Go on to the next page* ➡

**Ivy Global**

35. Linus has twenty-two books that have either gray or black covers. He remembers that he left his bookmark in a book with a gray cover. If he has five books with black covers, what is the probability that his bookmark is in the first gray book he opens?

(A) $\frac{1}{22}$

(B) $\frac{1}{17}$

(C) $\frac{1}{10}$

(D) $\frac{1}{5}$

36. The height and base of a triangle are shown below.

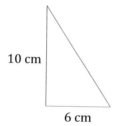

10 cm

6 cm

If the area of a triangle is $A = \frac{1}{2}$ base $\times$ height, what is the area of this triangle?

(A) 8 cm²

(B) 16 cm²

(C) 22 cm²

(D) 30 cm²

37. A pond contains goldfish, trout, koi fish, and frogs. If Vikram scoops a net through the pond and randomly catches one animal, he has a $\frac{1}{7}$ chance of catching a frog. Which of the following could be the composition of the pond's animals?

(A) 1 frog, 2 goldfish, 3 trout, 2 koi fish

(B) 1 frog, 8 goldfish, 1 trout, 3 koi fish

(C) 2 frogs, 3 goldfish, 7 trout, 2 koi fish

(D) 7 frogs, 7 goldfish, 7 trout, 7 koi fish

38. Alma has a piece of ribbon that is $x$ feet long. She cuts it into three equal pieces. She then decides that those pieces are too big, and cuts each of the three pieces into five equal pieces. How big is each piece, relative to the total length $x$?

(A) $\frac{x}{(3 \times 5)}$

(B) $\frac{x}{(3+5)}$

(C) $x \times 3 \times 5$

(D) $x - (\frac{1}{3} \times \frac{1}{5})$

STOP. Do not go on until told to do so.

**STOP**

# Section 3
# Reading Comprehension

| 25 Questions | Time: 25 minutes |
|---|---|

This section contains five short reading passages. Each passage is followed by five questions based on its content. Answer the questions following each passage on the basis of what is <u>stated</u> or <u>implied</u> in that passage. You may write in your test booklet.

STOP. Do not go on until told to do so. **STOP**

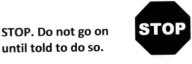

# RC

Questions 1–5

1      The sun shines with different degrees of
2  heating power at different parts of the world.
3  Where its effect is greatest, such as at the
4  tropics, the air is hottest. Now, imagine that at a
5  certain moment the air all around the globe is
6  at one temperature. Then suddenly the sun
7  shines and heats the air at one point until it is
8  much warmer than the surrounding air. The
9  heated air expands, rises, and spreads out
10  above the cold air. But because warm air has
11  less weight than an equal volume of cold air,
12  the cold air starts to rush towards another
13  point and squeeze the rest of the warm air out.
14  You can picture the atmosphere as made up of
15  a number of colder currents passing along the
16  surface of the earth to replace warm currents

17  rising and spreading over the upper surface of
18  the cold air.
19      Certain air currents interact repeatedly
20  in the same places. For example, temperature
21  differences between mountains and valleys
22  create special air currents called mountain and
23  valley breezes. During the day, air on mountain
24  slopes is heated more than air at the same
25  height over a nearby valley. This warm air rises
26  off the mountain and draws the cool air up
27  from the valley, creating a valley breeze. When
28  the sun goes down, the mountain slopes cool
29  more quickly than the valley air. This cool air
30  sinks, causing a mountain breeze to flow
31  downhill and cool the neighboring valley.

*Go on to the next page* ➜

1. At line 14, "picture" most nearly means

   (A) imagine.

   (B) paint.

   (C) sketch.

   (D) display.

2. The author's purpose in this passage is to

   (A) Confuse.

   (B) Entertain.

   (C) Educate.

   (D) Influence.

3. According to the passage, cold air currents

   (A) rise above hot air currents.

   (B) are created by snow.

   (C) cause storms.

   (D) sink beneath hot air currents.

4. What topic would the author most likely discuss next?

   (A) how air currents affect weather

   (B) qualities of the atmospheres on other planets

   (C) the importance of sunlight for plant growth

   (D) why hot air is less dense than cold air

5. The function of the last paragraph (lines 19–31) is to

   (A) summarize the main idea of the passage.

   (B) provide a specific example of the concept discussed in the first paragraph.

   (C) disprove the concept discussed in the first paragraph.

   (D) leave the reader with a question to consider.

*Go on to the next page* ➡

Questions 6–10

1    Migration is the regular seasonal
2    movement, often from north to south,
3    undertaken by many species of animals,
4    including birds. Most species migrate due to
5    low levels of food during certain seasons, or in
6    order to breed in a specific place.
7        Migration can be very risky. While on the
8    move, birds are more vulnerable to predators,
9    including human hunters, and can also be
10   harmed by flying into large human structures,
11   such as power lines. People further pose a
12   threat to migratory birds through habitat
13   destruction, which has affected "stopover" sites
14   that birds use for rest during long migratory
15   journeys.
16       While some of the challenges they face
17   may be new, birds have been migrating for
18   thousands of years. Ancient Greek authors

19   recorded the migration of species such as
20   storks, Turtle Doves, and swallows as much as
21   3,000 years ago. More recently, scientists have
22   used new technologies like satellite tracking to
23   observe the migration patterns of a wide range
24   of birds.
25       The distances birds fly to migrate can
26   vary drastically. Some birds that live in
27   mountain ranges, such as the Andes and
28   Himalayas, migrate by simply moving higher
29   up or lower down the mountain depending on
30   the season. By contrast, species such as the
31   Manx Shearwater migrate 14,000 km
32   (8,700 mi) between their northern breeding
33   grounds and the southern ocean. The long-
34   distance migration record for birds belongs to
35   the Arctic Tern, which travels between the
36   Arctic and Antarctic each year.

*Go on to the next page* ➡

6. This passage is primarily about
   (A) why animals migrate.
   (B) the Manx Shearwater.
   (C) how humans track bird migration.
   (D) bird migration.

7. Which statement about bird migration is supported by information in the passage?
   (A) Bird migration has been observed for at least 3,000 years.
   (B) Migration has become less dangerous for birds in recent years.
   (C) Migration only occurs in mountain ranges like the Andes and Himalayas.
   (D) Birds often become lost during migration.

8. It can be inferred from the passage that the distance flown by the Arctic Tern during migration is
   (A) exactly 14,000 km.
   (B) less than 14,000 km.
   (C) over 14,000 km.
   (D) impossible to calculate.

9. Which question could be answered by information given in the passage?
   (A) How does satellite tracking of birds work?
   (B) What is the best way to track migratory birds?
   (C) What are some reasons birds migrate?
   (D) What are some species of birds that do not migrate?

10. It can be inferred from the second paragraph (lines 7-15) that several of the different threats that birds face during migration are caused in some way by
    (A) habitat destruction.
    (B) new technologies like satellite tracking.
    (C) poor weather.
    (D) people.

*Go on to the next page* ➡

Questions 11–15

1     Holi is a spring festival also known as the
2 festival of colors. It is an ancient Hindu
3 religious festival that in recent years has
4 become popular with non-Hindus as well. Holi
5 is primarily observed in India and Nepal, and
6 other regions of the world with significant
7 Hindu, Indian, or Nepalese communities.
8 However, because of its growing popularity,
9 the festival has also spread to parts of Europe
10 and North America.
11     Holi is celebrated at the approach of the
12 spring equinox, on the last full moon day of the
13 month Phalguna, which is the twelfth month of
14 the Hindu calendar. The festival date thus
15 varies every year, but is typically sometime in
16 March or February.
17     The celebrations begin with a bonfire on
18 the night before Holi where people gather, sing
19 and dance. The next morning is a free-for-all
20 carnival of colors. People chase one another
21 with pigmented powder and tinted water,
22 trying to decorate one another with various
23 shades of the rainbow. Some participants get
24 creative with their approach to the festivities,
25 carrying water guns and balloons filled with
26 colored water. Anyone and everyone is fair
27 game: friend or stranger, rich or poor, child or
28 elder.
29     This giant water and color fight occurs in
30 the open streets, public parks, and outside
31 temples and buildings. Groups carry drums and
32 musical instruments, singing and dancing as
33 they move from place to place. People also visit
34 family, friends and even foes, first coloring one
35 another and then staying to laugh, chat, and
36 share Holi delicacies.

*Go on to the next page* ➡

**Ivy Global**

11. According to the passage, the date of Holi varies because

    (A) its date is based on the full moon and the hindu calendar.

    (B) people cannot decide when to hold the festival.

    (C) there needs to be good weather so everyone can be outside.

    (D) the festival is growing in popularity.

12. The function of the second paragraph (lines 11–16) is to

    (A) discuss the importance of holi.

    (B) describe the festivities that occur during holi.

    (C) explain when holi is celebrated.

    (D) argue that holi should be celebrated during a different month.

13. The mood of Holi celebrations could best be described as

    (A) solemn.

    (B) formal.

    (C) cheerful.

    (D) mournful.

14. Which question could be answered by information given in the passage?

    (A) When was the first Holi festival celebrated?

    (B) What are some favorite Holi delicacies?

    (C) In how many cities is Holi celebrated?

    (D) In what part of a city is Holi celebrated?

15. At line 24, "creative" most nearly means

    (A) productive.

    (B) inventive.

    (C) talented.

    (D) dull.

*Go on to the next page* ➡

**Ivy Global**

Questions 16–20

1  The Dust Bowl refers to an ecological
2  disaster during the 1930s, when severe dust
3  storms greatly damaged the ecology and
4  agriculture of the U.S. and Canadian prairies.
5  Severe drought and a failure to apply
6  appropriate farming methods to prevent the
7  loss of soil caused the phenomenon.
8       Extensive plowing of the natural
9  topsoil of the Great Plains during the previous
10  decade had displaced the native, deep-rooted
11  grasses that normally trapped soil and
12  moisture, even during periods of drought and
13  high winds. While the area had at one point
14  been considered unsuitable for growing crops,
15  new tools such as gasoline tractors and
16  combine harvesters led to a huge increase in
17  farming, despite the dry climate of the area.
18       These agricultural practices left the area
19  very vulnerable. Because there were no longer
20  grasses to keep the earth in place and retain
21  water, during the drought of the 1930s the
22  loose soil turned to dust. This dust was blown
23  by the strong local wind in large clouds that
24  blackened the sky. These dust storms could
25  become very dangerous, and were called "black
26  blizzards" or "black rollers." On April 14, 1935,
27  20 fierce "black blizzards" occurred all across
28  the Great Plains, from Canada down to Texas.
29  The storms caused extensive damage, and the
30  day became known as "Black Sunday."
31       The drought and erosion of the Dust
32  Bowl affected 100,000,000 acres that centered
33  on the panhandles of Texas and Oklahoma,
34  along with nearby sections of New Mexico,
35  Colorado, and Kansas. This forced tens of
36  thousands of families to abandon their farms.
37  Many of them migrated to California and other
38  states. However, because of the Great
39  Depression, the economic conditions and job
40  opportunities these families found were often
41  just as terrible as those they were trying to
42  escape in the prairies. The plight of such people
43  influenced many famous American artists, such
44  as folk singer Woody Guthrie and novelist John
45  Steinbeck.

*Go on to the next page* ➜

16. The passage implies that the extensive plowing in the Great Plains, which contributed to the Dust Bowl, took place during

    (A) the 1800s.
    (B) the 1920s.
    (C) the 1930s.
    (D) the 1960s.

17. In line 42 "plight" most nearly means

    (A) pledge.
    (B) predicament.
    (C) success.
    (D) achievement.

18. The primary purpose of the passage is to describe

    (A) the causes and outcomes of the dust bowl.
    (B) the best farming practices for prairie landscapes.
    (C) how people were affected by the great depression.
    (D) how the effects of the dust bowl were reversed.

19. Which word best describes the author's tone?

    (A) critical
    (B) neutral
    (C) admiring
    (D) humorous

20. The function of the last paragraph (lines 31–45) is to

    (A) list popular american artists of the era.
    (B) describe the climate of the american prairies.
    (C) summarize the causes of the dust bowl.
    (D) discuss how people were affected by the dust bowl.

*Go on to the next page* ➡

**Ivy Global**

Questions 21–25

1  From a young age, all I wanted to do was
2  write. Dancing was an acceptable pastime, and
3  singing was fine, but neither compared to the
4  thrill of creating stories. It was through writing
5  that I expressed and entertained myself. While
6  my classmates cut up colored paper or
7  experimented with watercolors, I was
8  constructing my next tale. After school, I would
9  routinely reject my neighbor's invitations to
10  play hide-and-seek, preferring to sit inside and
11  compose a new chapter. By writing, I could
12  easily transport myself to other lands, and
13  imagine myself as a fearless warrior or a regal
14  emperor. Best of all, by putting these fantasies
15  on paper, I could revisit them whenever I
16  wanted.
17  My writing process was as follows: first, I
18  would brainstorm a plot. A constant
19  daydreamer, I was rarely short on ideas. Next, I
20  would imagine who could handle the
21  adventures I had planned. My characters were
22  nearly always exaggerated versions of the real
23  people in my life, especially those I looked up
24  to. As soon as these basics were developed I
25  would start to write furiously. Once my pencil
26  touched the page I could not stop, scribbling
27  with the ferocity of a tiny tornado. Finally, I
28  would hand over my draft to my father, who
29  served as my ever-patient transcriber. He
30  would quickly type up my latest masterpiece,
31  handing me each page for my excited review.
32  At the tender age of 9, I undertook to
33  write my first novel. It was a thriller filled with
34  intrigue, mystery, and characters both noble
35  and despicable. Someone had stolen a priceless
36  ruby, and it was up to the story's heroes to
37  track it down. Their quest took them through
38  the capitals of Europe, where they ran up the
39  Eiffel Tower and chased thieves across St.
40  Peter's Square. Though it would be many years
41  before I ever visited these places myself, by
42  writing I felt as if I were already there.

*Go on to the next page* ➡

# RC

21. The passage supports which statement about the narrator?

    (A) Most of her early writing was fiction.

    (B) Her writing simply described the real events in her life.

    (C) She learned to write from her father.

    (D) She was discouraged from writing by those around her.

22. Which best expresses the main idea of the passage?

    (A) The narrator's first novel was published while she was only 9.

    (B) The narrator's constant daydreams seemed like a problem until she began to write.

    (C) The narrator was an enthusiastic writer, even as a child.

    (D) The narrator's first novel spanned the capitals of Europe, from the Eiffel tower to St. Peter's Square.

23. In line 27 "ferocity" most nearly means

    (A) accuracy.

    (B) frenzy.

    (C) fear.

    (D) calm.

24. The passage implies that the author visited Europe

    (A) numerous times as a young child.

    (B) while she was writing her first novel.

    (C) only in her imagination.

    (D) later in her life.

25. The author's attitude toward activities that are not writing is best described as one of

    (A) excitement.

    (B) curiosity.

    (C) sensitivity.

    (D) indifference.

**STOP. Do not go on until told to do so.** STOP

Ivy Global

# SECTION 4

# Mathematics Achievement

Each question is followed by four suggested answers. Read each question and then decide which one of the four suggested answers is best.

Find the row of spaces on your answer document that has the same number as the question. In this row, mark the space having the same letter as the answer you have chosen. You may write in your test booklet.

---

SAMPLE QUESTION:                                           <u>Sample Answer</u>

   Which of the numbers below is NOT a factor of 364?    (A) ● (C) (D)

(A) 13

(B) 20

(C) 26

(D) 91

The correct answer is 20, so circle B is darkened.

---

STOP. Do not go on
until told to do so.

**STOP**

1.  Use the figure below to answer the question.

    What is the name of the shape shown in the figure?

    (A) kite

    (B) rectangle

    (C) hexagon

    (D) pentagon

2.  Jeffrey baked a dozen sugar cookies with different designs on them, as shown in the diagram below.

    If his dog randomly eats one of the cookies, what is the chance that it will be a ♥ ?

    (A) 1 out of 12

    (B) 1 out of 8

    (C) 1 out of 6

    (D) 2 out of 3

3.  The chart below shows the growth of a tomato plant over the course of twelve days.

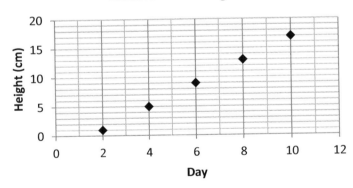

If the plant grew at a constant rate, what was the plant's height on the 7th day?

(A) 17 cm

(B) 11 cm

(C) 7 cm

(D) 6 cm

*Go on to the next page* ➔

4.  Use the triangle to answer the question.

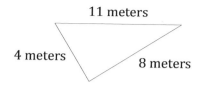

11 meters

4 meters

8 meters

What is the perimeter of the triangle?
($P = s + s + s$)

(A) 12 m

(B) 15 m

(C) 21 m

(D) 23 m

5.  Use the number line to answer the question.

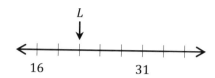

*L*

16    31

What number is represented by point *L* on the number line?

(A) 18

(B) 22

(C) 25

(D) 29

6.  The graph below shows the amount of snowfall in a town over five weeks.

| SNOWFALL | |
|---|---|
| Week 1 | ❄ ❄ |
| Week 2 | ❄ ❄ ❄ ❄ |
| Week 3 | ❄ |
| Week 4 | ❄ ❄ |
| Week 5 | ❄ ❄ ❄ ❄ ❄ |

❄ $= 1\frac{1}{2}$ inches of snow

How much snow fell from the beginning of Week 3 through the end of Week 5?

(A) 3 inches

(B) 8 inches

(C) 12 inches

(D) 14 inches

*Go on to the next page* ➡

**Ivy Global**

7. A total of 34 people were asked if they preferred cats or dogs. If 17 people said they preferred dogs and 11 people said they preferred cats, how many people did not have a preference at all?

   (A) 28

   (B) 13

   (C) 6

   (D) 0

8. Use the coordinate grid to answer the question.

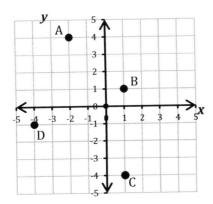

   Which of the four labeled points is closest to the coordinate point (-1, -4)?

   (A) A

   (B) B

   (C) C

   (D) D

9. Use the equations to answer the question

$$3 \times l = 12$$
$$6 + f = 4$$

   What is $\frac{l}{f}$?

   (A) 2

   (B) -2

   (C) 4

   (D) 3

10. A shape is drawn on a coordinate plane.

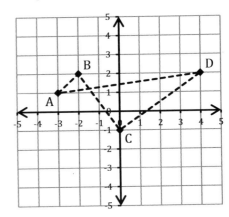

   What are the coordinates of point D?

   (A) (-3, 1)

   (B) (4, 2)

   (C) (-4, 2)

   (D) (-2, 2)

11. Lulu's candy shop charges $1.75 per pound of candy. Nate bought the following amounts of candy:

| Candy | Weight |
|---|---|
| Jellybeans | $\frac{1}{2}$ |
| Sour gummies | $\frac{3}{10}$ |
| Lollipops | $\frac{1}{5}$ |
| Butterscotch | ? |

   If Nate bought a total of 2 pounds of candy, how much did he spend on butterscotch?

   (A) $1.00

   (B) $1.75

   (C) $2.25

   (D) $3.50

*Go on to the next page* ➡

12. Which expression is equal to 16?

    (A) $\left(3 - \frac{1}{3}\right) \times 6$

    (B) $3 - \frac{1}{3} \times 6$

    (C) $\left(3 + \frac{1}{3}\right) \times 6$

    (D) $\frac{1}{3}(6 - 3)$

13. The diagram below shows a map of the distance from Solange's school to her house. Each grid on the map represents 2 km.

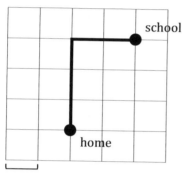

2 km

If Solange follows the path shown on the grid above, what is the distance that she will walk between school and home?

    (A) 5 km

    (B) 8 km

    (C) 10 km

    (D) 12 km

14. What is the standard form for three hundred fourteen thousand eight hundred twelve?

    (A) 300,412

    (B) 308,142

    (C) 314,812

    (D) 340,812

15. Which list is arranged from smallest to largest?

    (A) $\frac{3}{18}, \frac{3}{6}, \frac{16}{24}, \frac{10}{12}$

    (B) $\frac{3}{6}, \frac{3}{18}, \frac{16}{24}, \frac{10}{12}$

    (C) $\frac{16}{24}, \frac{10}{12}, \frac{3}{18}, \frac{3}{6}$

    (D) $\frac{10}{12}, \frac{16}{24}, \frac{3}{6}, \frac{3}{18}$

16. The transportation department asked a random sampling of people how many times they had taken public transportation in the past month. The results are shown in the stem-and-leaf plot below.

| 0 | 2 2 8 8 9 |
|---|---|
| 1 | 2 |
| 2 | 4 6 6 |
| 3 | 0 2 3 |
| 4 | 0 0 0 2 4 6 6 8 |
| 5 | 0 0 2 3 4 4 4 4 4 |

4 | 6 represents 46 trips using public transportation

How many people took public transportation 30 times or more in the past month?

    (A) 3

    (B) 9

    (C) 20

    (D) 56

*Go on to the next page* ➡

**4**

17. Use the set of numbers shown to answer the question.

$$\{0, 1, 3, 4, 6, ...\}$$

Which describes this set of numbers?

(A) odd numbers

(B) prime numbers

(C) integers

(D) negative numbers

18. Which expression is equal to 15?

(A) $(7 \times 2) + 5 - 4$

(B) $7 \times (2 + 5) - 4$

(C) $7 \times (2 + 5 - 4)$

(D) $7 \times 2 + (4 - 5)$

19. Pieces from an art collection were sold to different art collectors. Mr. Amati bought $\frac{1}{4}$ of the art pieces, Mrs. Brown bought $\frac{1}{3}$, Ms. Chen bought $\frac{1}{6}$, and Mr. Menounos bought the remainder. If Mr. Amati, Mrs. Brown, and Ms. Chen all donate their portions to a museum, what fraction of the total collection will the museum have?

(A) $\frac{3}{13}$

(B) $\frac{2}{3}$

(C) $\frac{3}{4}$

(D) $\frac{5}{6}$

20. What is the value of the expression 3,200 – 756?

(A) 1,444

(B) 2,444

(C) 2,454

(D) 2,544

21. Use the table to answer the question.

| PET OWNERSHIP | | | | | | | | |
|---|---|---|---|---|---|---|---|---|
| **Student** | Jason | Priya | Dominic | Nora | Liu | Floyd | Charu | Alex | Leah |
| **Number of Pets** | 4 | 0 | 1 | 2 | 2 | 1 | 3 | 6 | 1 |

What is the median of this set of data?

(A) 1

(B) 2

(C) 2.4

(D) 4

*Go on to the next page* ➡

**Ivy Global**

22. What number comes next in the sequence below?

$$1, 4, 16, 64, \_\_$$

(A) 60

(B) 68

(C) 256

(D) 264

23. Whitney ran 4 separate times in one week. She completed runs with lengths of 2.25 miles, 3.9 miles, 6.8 miles, and 4.9 miles. Which is the best estimation for the total number of miles that she ran during the week?

(A) between 17 and 19 miles

(B) between 19 and 21 miles

(C) between 21 and 23 miles

(D) between 23 and 25 miles

24. What is the missing number in the pattern below?

$$1, 1.5, 2, \_\_, 3, 3.5$$

(A) 25

(B) 2.5

(C) 2.75

(D) 4

25. Kim's school choir has a total of 83 singers. Which choir has a total number of singers closest to $\frac{1}{4}$ of Kim's choir?

(A) Nasim's choir, with 8 singers

(B) Johan's choir, with 14 singers

(C) Matt's choir, with 17 singers

(D) Husain's choir, with 21 singers

26. If $(3 + \Delta) \times 2 = 14$, what number does $\Delta$ stand for?

(A) 2

(B) 4

(C) 7

(D) 9

27. What is the sum of $\frac{1}{3} + \frac{1}{6}$?

(A) 0.11

(B) 0.3

(C) 0.5

(D) 0.6

28. If a rectangle has a length of 3, and an unknown width of $w$, which equation can be used to determine the rectangle's perimeter? ($P = 2 \times l + 2 \times w$, where $P$ = perimeter, $l$ = length, and $w$ = width.)

(A) $3 \times w$

(B) $3 + w + w + w$

(C) $6 + w$

(D) $6 + 2w$

29. In Marco's science class there are fifteen boy students and twelve girl students. If a student is randomly chosen to go up to the board, what is the chance that the student is a girl?

(A) 1 out of 27

(B) 1 out of 3

(C) 4 out of 9

(D) 5 out of 9

30. The sum of twice a number and five is equal to seventeen. What is the number?

(A) 6

(B) 7

(C) 10

(D) 12

**STOP. Do not go on until told to do so.**

STOP

# Essay Topic Sheet

The directions for the Essay portion of the ISEE are printed in the box below. Use the pre-lined pages on pages 78-79 for this part of the Practice Test.

You will have 30 minutes to plan and write an essay on the topic printed on the other side of this page. **Do not write on another topic. An essay on another topic is not acceptable.**

The essay is designed to give you an opportunity to show how well you can write. You should try to express your thoughts clearly. How well you write is much more important than how much you write, but you need to say enough for a reader to understand what you mean.

You will probably want to write more than a short paragraph. You should also be aware that a copy of your essay will be sent to each school that will be receiving your test results. You are to write only in the appropriate section of the answer sheet. Please write or print so that your writing may be read by someone who is not familiar with your handwriting.

You may make notes and plan your essay on the reverse side of the page. Allow enough time to copy the final form onto your answer sheet. You must copy the essay topic onto your answer sheet, on page 78, in the box provided.

Please remember to write only the final draft of the essay on pages 78-79 of your answer sheet and to write it in blue or black pen. Again, you may use cursive writing or you may print. Only pages 78-79 will be sent to the schools.

*Directions continue on the next page.*

Ivy Global

**REMINDER:** Please write this essay topic on the first few lines of the first page of your essay sheet.

### Essay Topic

**What do you think is the best kind of animal to keep as a pet? Explain why.**

- Only write on this essay question
- Only pages 78 and 79 will be sent to the schools
- Only write in blue or black pen

## NOTES

# PRACTICE TEST 3

## MIDDLE LEVEL

# HOW TO TAKE THIS PRACTICE TEST

To simulate an accurate testing environment, sit at a desk in a quiet location free of distractions—no TV, computers, phones, music, or noise—and clear your desk of all materials except pencils and erasers. Remember that no calculators, rulers, protractors, dictionaries, or other aids are allowed on the ISEE.

Give yourself the following amounts of time for each section:

| SECTION | SUBJECT | TIME LIMIT |
|---------|---------|------------|
| 1 | Verbal Reasoning | 20 minutes |
| 2 | Quantitative Reasoning | 35 minutes |
| 5 minute break | | |
| 3 | Reading Comprehension | 35 minutes |
| 4 | Mathematics Achievement | 40 minutes |
| 5 minute break | | |
| 5 | Essay | 30 minutes |

Have an adult help you monitor your time, or use a watch and time yourself. Only give yourself the allotted time for each section; put your pencil down when your time is up.

Follow the instructions carefully. As you take your test, bubble your answers into the answer sheets provided. Use the test booklet as scratch paper for notes and calculations. Remember that you are not granted time at the end of a section to transfer your answers to the answer sheet, so you must do this as you go along.

When you are finished, check your answers against the answer keys provided. Then, score your exam using the directions at the end of the book.

Ivy Global

Note: students with diagnosed learning disabilities who apply for testing with accommodations may receive extra time, or may be allowed to use certain assistive devices during the ISEE. For more information, visit http://erblearn.org/parents/admission/isee/accommodations.

# Ivy Global

# ISEE
# MIDDLE LEVEL TEST 1

## 1 VERBAL REASONING

1 Ⓐ Ⓑ Ⓒ Ⓓ    15 Ⓐ Ⓑ Ⓒ Ⓓ    29 Ⓐ Ⓑ Ⓒ Ⓓ

2 Ⓐ Ⓑ Ⓒ Ⓓ    16 Ⓐ Ⓑ Ⓒ Ⓓ    30 Ⓐ Ⓑ Ⓒ Ⓓ

3 Ⓐ Ⓑ Ⓒ Ⓓ    17 Ⓐ Ⓑ Ⓒ Ⓓ    31 Ⓐ Ⓑ Ⓒ Ⓓ

4 Ⓐ Ⓑ Ⓒ Ⓓ    18 Ⓐ Ⓑ Ⓒ Ⓓ    32 Ⓐ Ⓑ Ⓒ Ⓓ

5 Ⓐ Ⓑ Ⓒ Ⓓ    19 Ⓐ Ⓑ Ⓒ Ⓓ    33 Ⓐ Ⓑ Ⓒ Ⓓ

6 Ⓐ Ⓑ Ⓒ Ⓓ    20 Ⓐ Ⓑ Ⓒ Ⓓ    34 Ⓐ Ⓑ Ⓒ Ⓓ
                                  **Lower Level Ends**

7 Ⓐ Ⓑ Ⓒ Ⓓ    21 Ⓐ Ⓑ Ⓒ Ⓓ    35 Ⓐ Ⓑ Ⓒ Ⓓ

8 Ⓐ Ⓑ Ⓒ Ⓓ    22 Ⓐ Ⓑ Ⓒ Ⓓ    36 Ⓐ Ⓑ Ⓒ Ⓓ

9 Ⓐ Ⓑ Ⓒ Ⓓ    23 Ⓐ Ⓑ Ⓒ Ⓓ    37 Ⓐ Ⓑ Ⓒ Ⓓ

10 Ⓐ Ⓑ Ⓒ Ⓓ    24 Ⓐ Ⓑ Ⓒ Ⓓ    38 Ⓐ Ⓑ Ⓒ Ⓓ

11 Ⓐ Ⓑ Ⓒ Ⓓ    25 Ⓐ Ⓑ Ⓒ Ⓓ    39 Ⓐ Ⓑ Ⓒ Ⓓ

12 Ⓐ Ⓑ Ⓒ Ⓓ    26 Ⓐ Ⓑ Ⓒ Ⓓ    40 Ⓐ Ⓑ Ⓒ Ⓓ
                                  **Middle/Upper Level Ends**

13 Ⓐ Ⓑ Ⓒ Ⓓ    27 Ⓐ Ⓑ Ⓒ Ⓓ

14 Ⓐ Ⓑ Ⓒ Ⓓ    28 Ⓐ Ⓑ Ⓒ Ⓓ

## 2 QUANTITATIVE REASONING

| 1 Ⓐ Ⓑ Ⓒ Ⓓ | 15 Ⓐ Ⓑ Ⓒ Ⓓ | 29 Ⓐ Ⓑ Ⓒ Ⓓ |
|---|---|---|
| 2 Ⓐ Ⓑ Ⓒ Ⓓ | 16 Ⓐ Ⓑ Ⓒ Ⓓ | 30 Ⓐ Ⓑ Ⓒ Ⓓ |
| 3 Ⓐ Ⓑ Ⓒ Ⓓ | 17 Ⓐ Ⓑ Ⓒ Ⓓ | 31 Ⓐ Ⓑ Ⓒ Ⓓ |
| 4 Ⓐ Ⓑ Ⓒ Ⓓ | 18 Ⓐ Ⓑ Ⓒ Ⓓ | 32 Ⓐ Ⓑ Ⓒ Ⓓ |
| 5 Ⓐ Ⓑ Ⓒ Ⓓ | 19 Ⓐ Ⓑ Ⓒ Ⓓ | 33 Ⓐ Ⓑ Ⓒ Ⓓ |
| 6 Ⓐ Ⓑ Ⓒ Ⓓ | 20 Ⓐ Ⓑ Ⓒ Ⓓ | 34 Ⓐ Ⓑ Ⓒ Ⓓ |
| 7 Ⓐ Ⓑ Ⓒ Ⓓ | 21 Ⓐ Ⓑ Ⓒ Ⓓ | 35 Ⓐ Ⓑ Ⓒ Ⓓ |
| 8 Ⓐ Ⓑ Ⓒ Ⓓ | 22 Ⓐ Ⓑ Ⓒ Ⓓ | 36 Ⓐ Ⓑ Ⓒ Ⓓ |
| 9 Ⓐ Ⓑ Ⓒ Ⓓ | 23 Ⓐ Ⓑ Ⓒ Ⓓ | 37 Ⓐ Ⓑ Ⓒ Ⓓ  Middle/Upper Level Ends |
| 10 Ⓐ Ⓑ Ⓒ Ⓓ | 24 Ⓐ Ⓑ Ⓒ Ⓓ | 38 Ⓐ Ⓑ Ⓒ Ⓓ  Lower Level Ends |
| 11 Ⓐ Ⓑ Ⓒ Ⓓ | 25 Ⓐ Ⓑ Ⓒ Ⓓ | |
| 12 Ⓐ Ⓑ Ⓒ Ⓓ | 26 Ⓐ Ⓑ Ⓒ Ⓓ | |
| 13 Ⓐ Ⓑ Ⓒ Ⓓ | 27 Ⓐ Ⓑ Ⓒ Ⓓ | |
| 14 Ⓐ Ⓑ Ⓒ Ⓓ | 28 Ⓐ Ⓑ Ⓒ Ⓓ | |

## 4 MATHEMATICS ACHIEVEMENT

| 1 Ⓐ Ⓑ Ⓒ Ⓓ | 18 Ⓐ Ⓑ Ⓒ Ⓓ | 35 Ⓐ Ⓑ Ⓒ Ⓓ |
|---|---|---|
| 2 Ⓐ Ⓑ Ⓒ Ⓓ | 19 Ⓐ Ⓑ Ⓒ Ⓓ | 36 Ⓐ Ⓑ Ⓒ Ⓓ |
| 3 Ⓐ Ⓑ Ⓒ Ⓓ | 20 Ⓐ Ⓑ Ⓒ Ⓓ | 37 Ⓐ Ⓑ Ⓒ Ⓓ |
| 4 Ⓐ Ⓑ Ⓒ Ⓓ | 21 Ⓐ Ⓑ Ⓒ Ⓓ | 38 Ⓐ Ⓑ Ⓒ Ⓓ |
| 5 Ⓐ Ⓑ Ⓒ Ⓓ | 22 Ⓐ Ⓑ Ⓒ Ⓓ | 39 Ⓐ Ⓑ Ⓒ Ⓓ |
| 6 Ⓐ Ⓑ Ⓒ Ⓓ | 23 Ⓐ Ⓑ Ⓒ Ⓓ | 40 Ⓐ Ⓑ Ⓒ Ⓓ |
| 7 Ⓐ Ⓑ Ⓒ Ⓓ | 24 Ⓐ Ⓑ Ⓒ Ⓓ | 41 Ⓐ Ⓑ Ⓒ Ⓓ |
| 8 Ⓐ Ⓑ Ⓒ Ⓓ | 25 Ⓐ Ⓑ Ⓒ Ⓓ | 42 Ⓐ Ⓑ Ⓒ Ⓓ |
| 9 Ⓐ Ⓑ Ⓒ Ⓓ | 26 Ⓐ Ⓑ Ⓒ Ⓓ | 43 Ⓐ Ⓑ Ⓒ Ⓓ |
| 10 Ⓐ Ⓑ Ⓒ Ⓓ | 27 Ⓐ Ⓑ Ⓒ Ⓓ | 44 Ⓐ Ⓑ Ⓒ Ⓓ |
| 11 Ⓐ Ⓑ Ⓒ Ⓓ | 28 Ⓐ Ⓑ Ⓒ Ⓓ | 45 Ⓐ Ⓑ Ⓒ Ⓓ |
| 12 Ⓐ Ⓑ Ⓒ Ⓓ | 29 Ⓐ Ⓑ Ⓒ Ⓓ | 46 Ⓐ Ⓑ Ⓒ Ⓓ |
| 13 Ⓐ Ⓑ Ⓒ Ⓓ | 30 Ⓐ Ⓑ Ⓒ Ⓓ  Lower Level Ends | 47 Ⓐ Ⓑ Ⓒ Ⓓ  Middle/Upper Level Ends |
| 14 Ⓐ Ⓑ Ⓒ Ⓓ | 31 Ⓐ Ⓑ Ⓒ Ⓓ | |
| 15 Ⓐ Ⓑ Ⓒ Ⓓ | 32 Ⓐ Ⓑ Ⓒ Ⓓ | |
| 16 Ⓐ Ⓑ Ⓒ Ⓓ | 33 Ⓐ Ⓑ Ⓒ Ⓓ | |
| 17 Ⓐ Ⓑ Ⓒ Ⓓ | 34 Ⓐ Ⓑ Ⓒ Ⓓ | |

## 3 READING COMPREHENSION

| 1 Ⓐ Ⓑ Ⓒ Ⓓ | 15 Ⓐ Ⓑ Ⓒ Ⓓ | 29 Ⓐ Ⓑ Ⓒ Ⓓ |
|---|---|---|
| 2 Ⓐ Ⓑ Ⓒ Ⓓ | 16 Ⓐ Ⓑ Ⓒ Ⓓ | 30 Ⓐ Ⓑ Ⓒ Ⓓ |
| 3 Ⓐ Ⓑ Ⓒ Ⓓ | 17 Ⓐ Ⓑ Ⓒ Ⓓ | 31 Ⓐ Ⓑ Ⓒ Ⓓ |
| 4 Ⓐ Ⓑ Ⓒ Ⓓ | 18 Ⓐ Ⓑ Ⓒ Ⓓ | 32 Ⓐ Ⓑ Ⓒ Ⓓ |
| 5 Ⓐ Ⓑ Ⓒ Ⓓ | 19 Ⓐ Ⓑ Ⓒ Ⓓ | 33 Ⓐ Ⓑ Ⓒ Ⓓ |
| 6 Ⓐ Ⓑ Ⓒ Ⓓ | 20 Ⓐ Ⓑ Ⓒ Ⓓ | 34 Ⓐ Ⓑ Ⓒ Ⓓ |
| 7 Ⓐ Ⓑ Ⓒ Ⓓ | 21 Ⓐ Ⓑ Ⓒ Ⓓ | 35 Ⓐ Ⓑ Ⓒ Ⓓ |
| 8 Ⓐ Ⓑ Ⓒ Ⓓ | 22 Ⓐ Ⓑ Ⓒ Ⓓ | 36 Ⓐ Ⓑ Ⓒ Ⓓ  Middle/Upper Level Ends |
| 9 Ⓐ Ⓑ Ⓒ Ⓓ | 23 Ⓐ Ⓑ Ⓒ Ⓓ | |
| 10 Ⓐ Ⓑ Ⓒ Ⓓ | 24 Ⓐ Ⓑ Ⓒ Ⓓ | |
| 11 Ⓐ Ⓑ Ⓒ Ⓓ | 25 Ⓐ Ⓑ Ⓒ Ⓓ  Lower Level Ends | |
| 12 Ⓐ Ⓑ Ⓒ Ⓓ | 26 Ⓐ Ⓑ Ⓒ Ⓓ | |
| 13 Ⓐ Ⓑ Ⓒ Ⓓ | 27 Ⓐ Ⓑ Ⓒ Ⓓ | |
| 14 Ⓐ Ⓑ Ⓒ Ⓓ | 28 Ⓐ Ⓑ Ⓒ Ⓓ | |

Ivy Global

STUDENT NAME _____  GRADE APPLYING FOR _____

Use a blue or black ballpoint pen to write the final draft of your essay on this sheet.

You must write your essay topic in this space.

_____

_____

_____

Use specific details and examples in your response.

**Ivy Global**

## Section 1
## Verbal Reasoning

This section is divided into two parts that contain two different types of questions. As soon as you have completed Part One, answer the questions in Part Two. You may write in your test booklet. For each answer you select, fill in the corresponding circle on your answer document.

## PART ONE — SYNONYMS

Each question in Part One consists of a word in capital letters followed by four answer choices. Select the one word that is most nearly the same in meaning as the word in capital letters.

---

SAMPLE QUESTION:

**Sample Answer**
Ⓐ Ⓑ ● Ⓓ

CHARGE:

(A) release

(B) belittle

(C) accuse

(D) conspire

The correct answer is "accuse," so circle C is darkened.

---

## PART TWO — SENTENCE COMPLETION

Each question in Part Two is made up of a sentence with one blank. Each blank indicates that a word is missing. The sentence is followed by four answer choices. Select the word that will best complete the meaning of the sentence as a whole.

---

SAMPLE QUESTIONS:

**Sample Answer**
● Ⓑ Ⓒ Ⓓ

It rained so much that the streets were -------.

(A) flooded

(B) arid

(C) paved

(D) crowded

The correct answer is "flooded," so circle A is darkened.

---

**STOP. Do not go on until told to do so.**

# VR

## PART ONE – SYNONYMS

**Directions:** Select the word that is most nearly the same in meaning as the word in capital letters.

1. RESOLVE
   (A) reject
   (B) unify
   (C) settle
   (D) consolidate

2. LAST
   (A) claim
   (B) endure
   (C) invoke
   (D) seek

3. HABITUAL
   (A) usual
   (B) peculiar
   (C) prominent
   (D) unsurpassed

4. ANOMALOUS
   (A) verified
   (B) average
   (C) irregular
   (D) stimulating

5. WORTHY
   (A) demanding
   (B) deserving
   (C) forgotten
   (D) vicious

6. DIVERSITY
   (A) totality
   (B) variety
   (C) community
   (D) quality

7. LOATHE
   (A) delay
   (B) consider
   (C) anticipate
   (D) detest

8. HYPOTHESIS
   (A) supposition
   (B) resolution
   (C) exhibition
   (D) epiphany

9. DISTRUST
   (A) mutation
   (B) suspicion
   (C) charge
   (D) stealth

10. DELIBERATE
    (A) intentional
    (B) chronic
    (C) proportionate
    (D) incidental

11. LETHAL
    (A) morbid
    (B) cordial
    (C) deadly
    (D) capable

12. DECREASE
    (A) lessen
    (B) intensify
    (C) retract
    (D) conclude

*Go on to the next page* ➡

## Ivy Global

13. PROLONG

   (A) project
   (B) complicate
   (C) extend
   (D) upset

14. COMMENDABLE

   (A) laudable
   (B) pitiful
   (C) criminal
   (D) trivial

15. REVERSE

   (A) duplicate
   (B) invert
   (C) equal
   (D) support

16. ALLOW

   (A) obstruct
   (B) permit
   (C) adore
   (D) imply

17. FUSE

   (A) abandon
   (B) lose
   (C) combine
   (D) drop

18. CONTROL

   (A) express
   (B) consider
   (C) regulate
   (D) draw

19. OBLIGATION

   (A) comparison
   (B) duty
   (C) exemption
   (D) preference

20. PROVOKE

   (A) subdue
   (B) incite
   (C) investigate
   (D) predict

21. SOOTHE

   (A) reclaim
   (B) source
   (C) endorse
   (D) relieve

*Go on to the next page* ➡

## PART TWO – SENTENCE COMPLETION

**Directions:** Select the word that best completes the sentence.

22. During his trip abroad, Yosef endured much ----------; his baggage was lost, and he became violently ill.

    (A) irony

    (B) misfortune

    (C) casualty

    (D) felicity

23. The critic's review ---------- the actor's performance, describing it as affecting, stimulating, and believable.

    (A) praised

    (B) qualified

    (C) accredited

    (D) denounced

24. The Pilgrims' Way is a route ---------- taken by pilgrims to the shrine of Saint Thomas, although there are doubts about its name and exact location.

    (A) knowingly

    (B) unavoidably

    (C) supposedly

    (D) hardly

25. Reshma was forced to ---------- the entire project after her boss suddenly provided her with new guidelines regarding its intended goals.

    (A) overhaul

    (B) protect

    (C) regulate

    (D) repudiate

26. María Josefa Mujía was a Bolivian poet who drew on the death of her father to write plaintive and ---------- verses.

    (A) reserved

    (B) pedantic

    (C) jubilant

    (D) sorrowful

27. If you do not know how to sew, you can ---------- ribbons to a hat with glue.

    (A) clench

    (B) apprehend

    (C) release

    (D) affix

28. Fareed avoided punishment by ---------- replacing his mother's vase before she noticed it had been broken.

    (A) longingly

    (B) obviously

    (C) secretly

    (D) recklessly

29. To avoid being ---------- by his teacher, Jeremiah pretended that he had completed his assignment.

    (A) defeated

    (B) neglected

    (C) reprimanded

    (D) lost

*Go on to the next page* ➜

30. Although the new student was ----------- during her first few days of class, after a week she became quite talkative.

    (A) rude
    (B) reticent
    (C) gregarious
    (D) certain

31. In an attempt to ----------- the problem of declining public health, the state government is creating free exercise programs and introducing subsidies to lower the cost of fresh produce.

    (A) negotiate
    (B) endorse
    (C) ameliorate
    (D) condemn

32. The storeowner attempted to ----------- shoppers to his boutique through a variety of advertisements and promotions.

    (A) lure
    (B) reinforce
    (C) rectify
    (D) presage

33. Paula Radcliffe felt ----------- when she completed the 2003 London Marathon, as she had set a new world record.

    (A) enticed
    (B) elated
    (C) dejected
    (D) captivated

34. Be sure not to ----------- any ingredients while baking, as the delicate chemistry in recipes requires precise ratios.

    (A) appropriate
    (B) omit
    (C) include
    (D) measure

35. Activists were dismayed that the politician did not ----------- the actions of the rebel group, but instead gave only non-committal comments when pressed by reporters.

    (A) undertake
    (B) deliver
    (C) denounce
    (D) retrieve

36. Finding his insatiable greed -----------, most viewers were unable to sympathize with the film's protagonist.

    (A) gregarious
    (B) contagious
    (C) detectable
    (D) reprehensible

37. The climbers felt ----------- when they finally stood on the summit, relieved of the exhaustion of their long trek to the top.

    (A) hilarious
    (B) remorseful
    (C) abandoned
    (D) rejuvenated

*Go on to the next page* ➡

38. With a wide range of cakes, pastries, chocolates, and fruits on display, the party guests knew dessert would be -----------.

(A) decadent

(B) acknowledged

(C) sparse

(D) deliberate

39. Although she was constantly compared to her famous father, Laila Ali became a successful boxer based on her own ----------- in the ring.

(A) proficiency

(B) detachment

(C) leniency

(D) heritage

40. The author's writing was ----------- by beautiful photographs that helped bring her story to life.

(A) defended

(B) accompanied

(C) confined

(D) inspected

**STOP. Do not go on until told to do so.**

# Section 2
# Quantitative Reasoning

This section is divided into two parts that contain two different types of questions. As soon as you have completed Part One, answer the questions in Part Two. You may write in your test booklet. For each answer you select, remember to fill in the corresponding circle on your answer document.

Any figures that accompany the questions in this section may be assumed to be drawn as accurately as possible EXCEPT when it is stated that a particular figure is not drawn to scale. Letters such as $x$, $y$, and $n$ stand for real numbers.

## PART ONE — WORD PROBLEMS

Each question in Part One consists of a word problem followed by four answer choices. You may write in your test booklet; however, you may be able to solve many of these problems in your head. Next, look at the four answer choices given and select the best answer.

---

SAMPLE QUESTION:

What is the value of the expression $3 + 7 \times (6 - 4)^2 - 8 \div 2$?

(A) 14

(B) 16

(C) 27

(D) 32

The correct answer is 27, so circle C is darkened.

Sample Answer

Ⓐ Ⓑ ● Ⓓ

---

*Go on to the next page* ➡

Ivy Global

# QR

## PART TWO — QUANTITATIVE COMPARISONS

All questions in Part Two are quantitative comparisons between the quantities shown in Column A and Column B. Using the information given in each question, compare the quantity in Column A to the quantity in Column B, and choose one of these four answer choices:

(A) The quantity in Column A is greater.

(B) The quantity in Column B is greater.

(C) The two quantities are equal.

(D) The relationship cannot be determined from the information given.

---

SAMPLE QUESTIONS:

| Column A | Column B | Sample Answer |
|----------|----------|---------------|
| 5 | $\sqrt{25}$ | Ⓐ Ⓑ ● Ⓓ |

The quantity in <u>Column A</u> (5) is the same as the quantity in <u>Column B</u> (5), so circle C is darkened.

---

$$x = 6^2 - 3 \times 4$$

| Column A | Column B | Sample Answer |
|----------|----------|---------------|
| $x$ | 22 | ● Ⓑ Ⓒ Ⓓ |

The quantity in <u>Column A</u> (24) is greater than the quantity in <u>Column B</u> (22), so circle A is darkened.

---

**STOP. Do not go on until told to do so.**

**STOP**

## PART ONE – WORD PROBLEMS

**Directions:** Choose the best answer from the four choices given.

1. In the city of Townville, there are $C$ cars, $T$ tricycles, $B$ bicycles, and one high-speed train called the Arrow that runs on sixteen wheels. Which of the following expressions gives the total number of all wheels in Townville?

   (A) $2C + 3T + 2B + 16$

   (B) $4C + 3B + 2T + A$

   (C) $2C + 3T + 2B + A$

   (D) $4C + 3T + 2B + 16$

2. Dan is creating a list of songs in the following pattern: one classical song, one rock song, one country song, one jazz song, one blues song. If this pattern continues, the 48th song in his list will be

   (A) classical

   (B) rock

   (C) country

   (D) jazz

3. If $N$ is a negative number, which of the following expressions has the greatest value?

   (A) $-\frac{N}{2}$

   (B) $N - 2$

   (C) $N - 3$

   (D) $N$

4. If $Q$ is a positive number, which of the following expressions has the smallest value?

   (A) $-4 - Q$

   (B) $Q - 2$

   (C) $(-Q)^2$

   (D) $-Q$

5. Use the following equations to answer the question.

   $$n = \blacksquare x$$
   $$x = \bigcirc b$$

   What is the value of $n$ if $b = \blacksquare$?

   (A) $\bigcirc$

   (B) $\bigcirc\blacksquare$

   (C) $\blacksquare^2$

   (D) $\bigcirc\blacksquare^2$

6. In the figure below, four line segments are drawn from the midpoints of a large square to make a smaller shaded square. If the area of the large square is $4z$, then what is the area of the shaded square?

   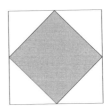

   (A) $\frac{1}{4}z$

   (B) $\frac{1}{3}z$

   (C) $z$

   (D) $2z$

7. 3 people can pack $x$ boxes in 15 minutes. If they work at the same rate, how many boxes can 6 people pack in 30 minutes?

   (A) $x/2$

   (B) $2x$

   (C) $(2x)^2$

   (D) $4x$

*Go on to the next page* ➡

8. Ashley has a number of boxes that measure $6 \times 5 \times 10$ inches. She wants to fill the boxes with books that are 5 inches wide, 9 inches tall, and 1.5 inches thick. What is the greatest number of books that Ashley can put in each box?

   (A) 2

   (B) 3

   (C) 4

   (D) 5

9. For all real numbers, $\boxed{a} = a^2 + 3^2$.

   For example, $\boxed{3} = 3^2 + 3^2 = 9 + 9 = 18$.

   What is the value of $\boxed{6}$?

   (A) 9

   (B) 36

   (C) 45

   (D) 72

10. Dave and Ryan spent $x$ dollars on a whole pizza. When they ate $3/4$ of the pizza, they had 4 slices left over. What was the average cost per slice of pizza?

    (A) $\frac{x}{16}$ dollars

    (B) $\frac{x}{4}$ dollars

    (C) $x$ dollars

    (D) $\frac{3x}{16}$ dollars

11. Kathy has replaced all of her incandescent light bulbs with fluorescent light bulbs that last 8 times longer. Compared with how frequently Kathy had to change her incandescent light bulbs previously, how frequently will she now have to change her new light bulbs?

    (A) 8% as frequently

    (B) 12.5% as frequently

    (C) 15% as frequently

    (D) 80% as frequently

12. In Figure 3, a cube has a side length of $n$. How much volume remains if we cut the cube in half diagonally?

    Figure 3

    (A) $\frac{n^2}{2}$

    (B) $\frac{n^3}{2}$

    (C) $n^2$

    (D) $n^3$

13. If $M = \frac{\boxed{\triangle}}{2}$ and $N = 4M$, which expression below is correct?

    (A) $N = \boxed{\triangle}$

    (B) $N = 2 \times \boxed{\triangle}$

    (C) $N = 4 \times \boxed{\triangle}$

    (D) $N = M$

14. There are 10 bathtubs each filled to $\frac{1}{3}$ of their capacity with water. Another bathtub is filled to $\frac{2}{3}$ of its capacity with water. If all bathtubs are the same shape and size, how much, on average, are each of the 11 bathtubs filled?

    (A) $\frac{1}{3}$ capacity

    (B) $\frac{4}{11}$ capacity

    (C) $\frac{2}{3}$ capacity

    (D) $\frac{11}{15}$ capacity

*Go on to the next page* ➡

**Ivy Global**

15. A school teacher needs to buy 8 erasers at $1.10 each. There is a fee of $5.00 for shipping and an additional tax of 5% calculated after the shipping cost has been added. What is the total cost for the teacher's order?

    (A) $7.91

    (B) $8.80

    (C) $13.80

    (D) $14.49

16. If the cube below is cut all the way through along the dashed lines, how many triangular sections are created?

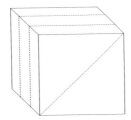

    (A) 1

    (B) 2

    (C) 3

    (D) 6

17. Two bedrooms of identical size and dimensions together form the shape of a rectangle. If their total length is $l$ and their total width is $w$, what is the perimeter of one bedroom?

    (A) $\frac{w}{2} + \frac{l}{2}$

    (B) $w + l$

    (C) $2w + 2l$

    (D) $2w \times 2l$

18. A number cube has 6 sides numbered 1 through 6. Erol is rolling two number cubes. What is the probability that the sum of his roll will be at least 10?

    (A) $\frac{1}{18}$

    (B) $\frac{1}{12}$

    (C) $\frac{1}{6}$

    (D) $\frac{11}{12}$

19. Brynne is digging river-ways for an oncoming flood. Each river-way is 1,000 feet long and is connected to one dam. At each dam, the incoming river-way branches off into three new river-ways. If he begins with one river-way and wants to build a total of 13 river-ways, how many dams does he need?

    (A) 3

    (B) 4

    (C) 13

    (D) 39

20. If $a = \frac{b}{c}$ and $d = \left(\frac{c}{b}\right) \div \left(\frac{a}{b}\right)$, which equation is equal to $d$?

    (A) $\frac{1}{b}$

    (B) $\frac{c^2}{b}$

    (C) 1

    (D) $\frac{b}{c}$

Go on to the next page ➡

21. The number of trains leaving Dumbleport Monday through Friday is shown in the chart below.

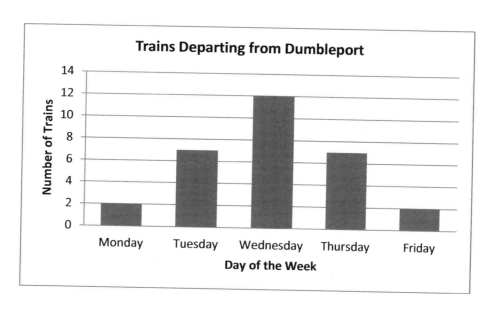

How many fewer trains left from Dumbleport on Friday when compared to the week's average number of daily train departures?

(A) 2

(B) 3

(C) 4

(D) 6

*Go on to the next page* ➡

# PART TWO – QUANTITATIVE COMPARISONS

**Directions:** Using the information given in each question, compare the quantity in column A to the quantity in Column B. All questions in Part Two have these answer choices:

(A) The quantity in Column A is greater.

(B) The quantity in Column B is greater.

(C) The two quantities are equal.

(D) The relationship cannot be determined from the information given.

$$y = -3x + 4$$

| Column A | Column B |
|---|---|
| 22. The value of $x$ when $y = -8$ | 3 |

| Column A | Column B |
|---|---|
| 23. $2^3 - 3^2$ | $3^2 - 2^3$ |

A vase costs $200.00.

| Column A | Column B |
|---|---|
| 24. A sales tax at 5% of the vase's cost | $15.00 |

Each person at a party eats four slices of pie. Every pie comes with enough slices to feed exactly three people.

| Column A | Column B |
|---|---|
| 25. The number of people needed to eat twenty slices of pie | The number of pies needed to feed fifteen people |

| Column A | Column B |
|---|---|
| 26. The slope between (1,2) and (0,3) | The slope of $0.5y = -x + 2$ |

Paper Route A

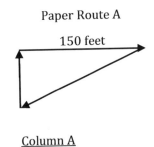

150 feet

Paper Route B

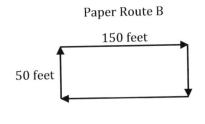

150 feet

50 feet

| Column A | Column B |
|---|---|
| 27. The distance of Paper Route A | The distance of Paper Route B |

*Go on to the next page* ➡

**Ivy Global**

# QR

---

**ANSWER CHOICES FOR ALL QUESTIONS ON THIS PAGE:**

(A) The quantity in Column A is greater.

(B) The quantity in Column B is greater.

(C) The two quantities are equal.

(D) The relationship cannot be determined from the information given.

---

A sample is randomly selected from two separate populations. This sample is asked whether they prefer water or milk. The percent of each sample to their respective population and the results of the survey are show in the table below.

| City | A | B |
|---|---|---|
| **Percent of City Surveyed** | 20% | 40% |
| **People Who Prefer Water** | 20 | 30 |
| **People Who Prefer Milk** | 15 | 30 |

| Column A | Column B |
|---|---|
| 28. The predicted number of people who prefer milk in City A | The predicted number of people who prefer milk in City B |

---

Laurel has to get to Chicago from New York. She stops at Allentown, Cleveland, and Toledo along the way to buy sandwiches.

| HIGHWAY DISTANCE BETWEEN CITIES | |
|---|---|
| New York to Allentown | 91 miles |
| Allentown to Cleveland | 380 miles |
| Cleveland to Toledo | 116 miles |
| Toledo to Chicago | 246 miles |
| New York to Allentown | 91 miles |

| Column A | Column B |
|---|---|
| 29. The distance remaining on Laurel's trip if she is leaving Cleveland | The distance that Laurel has already traveled if she is leaving Cleveland |

*Go on to the next page* ➡

**Ivy Global**

## ANSWER CHOICES FOR ALL QUESTIONS ON THIS PAGE:

(A) The quantity in Column A is greater.

(B) The quantity in Column B is greater.

(C) The two quantities are equal.

(D) The relationship cannot be determined from the information given.

A number cube has six sides numbered 1-6. A deck of cards has 52 cards in total, four of which are king cards.

| Column A | Column B |
|---|---|
| 30. The probability of rolling a 2 twice in a row with a number cube | The probability of picking one king from a deck of cards |

| | Column A | Column B |
|---|---|---|
| 31. | $\dfrac{\sqrt{25-9}}{\sqrt{36-25}}$ | $\dfrac{(5-3)}{(6-5)}$ |

A triangle is placed within a square as shown in the diagram below.

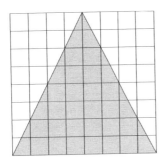

| | Column A | Column B |
|---|---|---|
| 32. | The area of the shaded triangle | The non-shaded area |

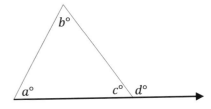

| | Column A | Column B |
|---|---|---|
| 33. | $a+b+c$ | $c+d$ |

$$M = \frac{1}{N} \qquad N = \frac{1}{L}$$

| | Column A | Column B |
|---|---|---|
| 34. | The value of $N$ if $L = \frac{1}{5}$ | The value of $M$ if $L = 6$ |

Eight pool balls are labeled 1-8 and placed in a bag.

| | Column A | Column B |
|---|---|---|
| 35. | The probability of picking a ball labeled with an even number | The probability of picking a ball labeled 6 or greater |

*Go on to the next page* ➡

**ANSWER CHOICES FOR ALL QUESTIONS ON THIS PAGE:**

(A) The quantity in Column A is greater.

(B) The quantity in Column B is greater.

(C) The two quantities are equal.

(D) The relationship cannot be determined from the information given.

| <u>Column A</u> | <u>Column B</u> |
|---|---|
| 36. The perimeter of a right angle triangle with one side that measures 5 cm | The perimeter of a right angle triangle with two sides that measure 3 cm and 4 cm |

Roland has one pair each of yellow, orange, and blue socks. He also has one pair each of yellow and black pants. Roland randomly selects one pair of socks and one pair of pants.

| <u>Column A</u> | <u>Column B</u> |
|---|---|
| 37. The probability that Roland will select a pair of yellow or blue socks with black pants | $\dfrac{1}{3}$ |

STOP. Do not go on until told to do so.

## Section 3
## Reading Comprehension

This section contains six short reading passages. Each passage is followed by six questions based on its content. Answer the questions following each passage on the basis of what is <u>stated</u> or <u>implied</u> in that passage. You may write in your test booklet.

**STOP. Do not go on
until told to do so.**

**STOP**

Questions 1–6

1  A green leaf is green because of the
2  presence of a pigment known as chlorophyll,
3  but chlorophyll is not the only pigment in a
4  leaf. Leaves also contain yellow and orange
5  pigments that are present in the leaf
6  throughout its life, and red and purple
7  pigments that develop under certain conditions
8  in the late summer. However, as long as the leaf
9  has plenty of chlorophyll, green will be the
10  dominant color.
11      Chlorophyll has a vital function: it
12  captures solar rays and utilizes the resulting
13  energy to manufacture the plant's food through
14  a process called photosynthesis, which can also
15  be observed in algae. The simple sugars that
16  are produced during this process from water
17  and carbon dioxide gas are the sole source of
18  the carbohydrates the plant needs for growth
19  and development.
20      Throughout the spring and summer, the
21  plant continually replenishes the chlorophyll in
22  its leaves so that they can keep producing its
23  food. In late summer, as daylight hours shorten

24  and temperatures cool, the veins that carry
25  fluids into and out of the leaf are gradually
26  closed off as a layer of special cork cells forms
27  at the base of each leaf. As this cork layer
28  develops, the flow of chlorophyll into the leaf
29  decreases, slowly at first, and then rapidly.
30  Eventually, the flow of the replacement
31  chlorophyll cannot keep pace with the rate at
32  which the chlorophyll is used up, and the leaf
33  begins to change colors. Without the
34  chlorophyll there to mask them, the yellow,
35  orange, red, and purple colors of the other leaf
36  pigments begin to show through.
37      The colors revealed by the absence of
38  chlorophyll can be vibrant and beautiful,
39  though they only last for a few weeks in the fall.
40  Certain areas, like southern Canada and the
41  eastern United States, are even internationally
42  famous for the brilliance of their "fall foliage."
43  These areas and others often attract tourists
44  called "leaf peepers" who travel great distances
45  for a chance to see the changing leaves.

*Go on to the next page* ➡

1.  According to the passage, a leaf's supply of chlorophyll is replenished by

    (A) the formation of cork cells at the base of each leaf.

    (B) water condensation from the atmosphere.

    (C) veins that transport fluids into each leaf.

    (D) the production of carbohydrates.

2.  As it is used in line 11, "vital" most nearly means

    (A) critical.

    (B) energetic.

    (C) active.

    (D) refreshing.

3.  Red, yellow, and purple leaf pigments reveal themselves

    (A) during the process of photosynthesis.

    (B) when a leaf has less chlorophyll.

    (C) on cloudy days.

    (D) when a leaf has more chlorophyll.

4.  Which question could be answered by information given in the passage?

    (A) What causes the seasons to change?

    (B) Why are leaves green, and why do they change color?

    (C) Why are some trees always green?

    (D) Why do plant leaves contain yellow and orange pigments?

5.  The function of the second paragraph (lines 11–19) is to

    (A) explain why leaves are green.

    (B) provide evidence that contradicts the first paragraph.

    (C) describe the role of chlorophyll in plants.

    (D) summarize the main idea of the passage.

6.  It can be inferred from the passage that the more chlorophyll a leaf has

    (A) the greener it will be.

    (B) the less green it will be.

    (C) the less food it can produce.

    (D) the colder it will be.

*Go on to the next page* ➡

Questions 7–12

1       Nicknamed the "City of Angels," Los
2 Angeles is a global city, known for its strengths
3 in business, entertainment, media, technology,
4 and sports. The city is home to renowned
5 cultural institutions like the Hollywood Bowl
6 and Getty Center, and is one of the most
7 substantial economies within the United States.
8       But this paradise is not without its
9 problems: owing to its geography, and heavy
10 traffic, Los Angeles suffers from debilitating air
11 pollution in the form of smog. The Los Angeles
12 Basin is susceptible to atmospheric inversion,
13 meaning the air closest to the earth's surface is
14 colder than the air above. This phenomenon
15 traps the cooler air and the exhaust from road
16 vehicles, airplanes, and other sources close to
17 the ground. Further, unlike other large cities
18 that rely on rain to clear smog, Los Angeles gets
19 only 15 inches of rain each year, allowing
20 pollution to accumulate over many consecutive
21 days. These factors make smog a pressing issue
22 for the city, and the 2006 and 2007 annual
23 reports of the American Lung Association
24 ranked the city as the most polluted in the
25 country.
26       To tackle this issue, Los Angeles decided
27 to take a legal approach. In 2008 a law was
28 passed allowing the city to collect fees from
29 those using its port for shipping, with the funds

30 raised directed to local air quality projects. The
31 state of California also updated its emission
32 standards in 2012, making them the strictest in
33 the country. As a result, the number of severe
34 smog alerts in Los Angeles has declined from
35 over 100 per year in the 1970s to almost zero
36 in recent years. Smog is expected to continue to
37 drop in the coming years due to new
38 technologies like electric and hybrid cars.
39       Despite these improvements, much work
40 remains to be done. Indeed, in 2013 Los
41 Angeles was still ranked as having the nation's
42 worst smog. One opportunity that the city
43 should consider is working to improve its
44 public transit system. While Los Angeles
45 already has an extensive bus network, which is
46 the second busiest in the country, only about
47 10% of the city's residents make use of it. By
48 contrast, other large American cities
49 sometimes see a quarter or more of their
50 inhabitants opting for buses, subways, and
51 trains; in recent years over 50% of New York
52 City residents used such methods to travel to
53 work. Encouraging more citizens to utilize
54 public transportation rather than taking their
55 own cars could be the final piece of the
56 pollution puzzle that gives Los Angeles the
57 cleaner air it craves.

*Go on to the next page* ➡

7. The main purpose of this passage is to

   (A) describe the history of innovation in Los Angeles.

   (B) explain the concept of atmospheric inversion.

   (C) discuss the problem of smog in Los Angeles and some possible solutions.

   (D) argue for better public transit in Los Angeles.

8. Which best describes the way the passage is organized?

   (A) A series of contradictory solutions are presented.

   (B) A problem and early solutions are described, and a further proposal is discussed.

   (C) A popular view is presented and then challenged by scientific evidence.

   (D) A problem is introduced and then analyzed.

9. In line 21, "pressing" most nearly means

   (A) serious.

   (B) forceful.

   (C) chronic.

   (D) constricted.

10. The author is most likely to agree with which one of the following statements?

    (A) The measures Los Angeles has already taken to limit smog have been helpful but insufficient.

    (B) So far Los Angeles has done nothing to fight smog.

    (C) Even without further action, the current levels of smog in Los Angeles are acceptable.

    (D) Improving public transit is the only way to further reduce smog in Los Angeles.

11. According to the passage, besides geography, the largest cause of smog and pollution in Los Angeles is

    (A) industry.

    (B) entertainment.

    (C) climate.

    (D) transportation.

12. It can be inferred from the passage that electric and hybrid cars

    (A) produce more pollution than traditional cars.

    (B) cannot be used in the Los Angeles basin.

    (C) will encourage more citizens to utilize public transportation.

    (D) produce less pollution than traditional cars.

*Go on to the next page* ➡

Questions 13–18

1     To buy a horse was my greatest
2 ambition. My father died; and as misfortunes
3 seldom come singly, the horse on which my
4 family depended to till our scanty fields died
5 shortly after its owner. Whenever the spring
6 arrived, our one chance to plant a crop was to
7 hire a mule from our nearest neighbor, the
8 tanner. I was the eldest son, and my mother
9 had only my work to offer in payment. The
10 tanner always greeted this proposition coldly.
11 The mule was needed to haul up piles of bark
12 from the depths of the woods to the tanyard.
13 Then, too, he had his own crops to plant.
14 Although the mule was a multifarious animal
15 that ploughed and worked in the bark-mill, and
16 hauled bark from the woods, and took long
17 journeys with the wagon or under the saddle, it
18 was impossible for her to be in all the places in
19 which she was urgently needed at the same
20 time. Therefore, to hire her out hardly seemed
21 to benefit her master. Nevertheless, this
22 bargain was struck every spring. My poverty-
23 stricken mother always congratulated herself
24 upon it, and it never occurred to her that the

25 amount of work that I did in the tanyard was
26 more than enough payment for the few days
27 that the tanner's mule ploughed our little fields.
28     I, however, was beginning to see that a
29 boy to drive that mule around the bark-mill
30 was as essential as the mule himself. As
31 Providence had failed to furnish the tanner
32 with a son for this purpose—his family
33 consisting of several small daughters—I
34 supplied a long-felt want.
35     I appreciated that my mother was
36 overreached, yet I could not see that she could
37 do otherwise. I sighed for independence, for a
38 larger opportunity. As I drove the mule round
39 the limited circuit, my mind was far away. I
40 anxiously canvassed the future. I cherished
41 fiery, ambitious schemes—but always with a
42 sense of their futility. With my time thus
43 mortgaged, I thought that my help to my
44 mother was far less than it might be. But until I
45 could have a horse of my own, there was no
46 hope—no progress. And for this I planned, and
47 dreamed, and saved.

*Go on to the next page* ➡

**Ivy Global**

13. When did the family's horse die?

   (A) in the spring.

   (B) before the father died.

   (C) after the father died.

   (D) while it was plowing the field.

14. What deal was struck every spring?

   (A) The tanner gave the narrator's family some bark, and the narrator's mother lent him their horse.

   (B) The narrator drove the tanner's wagon, and the tanner helped the narrator's mother in the field.

   (C) The narrator gave the tanner his crops, and the tanner gave the narrator a horse.

   (D) The tanner lent the narrator's mother his mule, and the narrator did work for the tanner.

15. What is the most likely reason that the narrator's family always struck this deal in the spring?

   (A) The spring was the time of the year when they needed to till their fields to plant a crop.

   (B) Their old horse died in the spring.

   (C) The spring was the time of the year when the tanner didn't need to use the mule.

   (D) It was too cold to walk to the tanner's house during any other time of the year.

16. The passage answers all of the following questions EXCEPT which one?

   (A) Did the narrator have an older brother?

   (B) What did the narrator's family need the mule for?

   (C) What did the narrator want more than anything?

   (D) How many siblings did the narrator have?

17. In line 31, the word "furnish" most nearly means

   (A) provide.

   (B) appoint.

   (C) include.

   (D) trade.

18. Which phrase means most nearly the same as "this bargain was struck" (lines 21-22)?

   (A) this deal was made.

   (B) we hit upon an idea.

   (C) the bargain was rejected.

   (D) we were astonished at the bargain.

*Go on to the next page* ➡

Questions 19–24

1   Proudly raising four fingers—
2   representing the four stripes of the Catalan
3   flag—the enxaneta is greeted by uproarious
4   applause, which he or she can usually enjoy
5   only for a moment before scrambling down the
6   other side of the human tower known as a
7   castell.
8       "Castell" is the Catalan word for, as an
9   English-speaker might guess, "castle." Castells
10  are a Catalan tradition dating back to the 18th
11  century, when they were first built during local
12  festivals in the city of Valls. Today, castell
13  teams—or colles—build elaborate human
14  towers during festivals throughout Catalonia,
15  as well as in competition.
16      While castell teams were traditionally
17  all-male, today's colles are as diverse as the
18  communities they come from, uniting men and
19  women of all ages in a feat that is bigger than
20  themselves. Each level of the castell is formed
21  by two to five people standing on the shoulders
22  of those in the level below. The enxaneta is the
23  brave soul, almost always a child, who climbs
24  to the top of a castell to mark its completion.
25  Then begins the treacherous process of
26  dismantling the many levels (as many as ten) of
27  castellers who make up the tower. This is the
28  most treacherous stage of the activity, when
29  participants are most likely to fall. But the
30  danger is not quite as great as it might seem—
31  hundreds of supporters form a pinya, or base,
32  for the castell, cushioning the fall of the
33  castellers in case of collapse. In a
34  demonstration of the sportsmanship found
35  among castellers, when not competing, even
36  members of rival colles will assist in forming a
37  pinya for another team that is attempting to
38  build a particularly difficult structure.
39      The traditional outfit for castellers
40  usually consists of a pair of white trousers and
41  a colorful shirt, often bearing the crest or
42  emblem of the casteller's team. The castellers
43  generally do not wear protective equipment,
44  with the exception of a sash, which provides
45  support for the lower back. Indeed, castellers
46  typically do not even wear shoes, which could
47  injure the people on the lower levels of the
48  Castell, and can actually make it harder to
49  balance.

*Go on to the next page* ➡

19. Which of the following statements would the author most likely NOT agree with?

    (A) The completion of a castell is an exciting moment for the audience.

    (B) Today's castell teams are better than those of the 18th century.

    (C) Building a castell is an impressive achievement.

    (D) Castellers are actually safer than their audience might imagine.

20. Which best expresses the main point of the passage?

    (A) Building castells started in the 18th century all over Catalonia as an activity that brought men and women together.

    (B) Castells were first built by all-male teams in 18th century Valls; today, men, women, and children build them together all over Catalonia.

    (C) Castells were once popular throughout Catalonia but today are mainly built by the inhabitants of Valls.

    (D) Building castells is a new sport that was designed to heal social rifts by uniting diverse groups in pursuit of a common goal.

21. The attitude of the author towards castells is best described as

    (A) alarmed.

    (B) critical.

    (C) disbelieving.

    (D) admiring.

22. According to the passage, what is the role of the pinya (lines 29-33)?

    (A) The pinya is a crowd of fans that will cheer the castellers even if they fail.

    (B) If the castellers lose their balance and fall, the supporters in the pinya will help them back onto their feet.

    (C) If the castellers lose their balance and fall, they will fall safely onto the pinya instead of hitting the ground.

    (D) The pinya is the child who goes to the top of the castell to signal its completion.

23. Which best describes the organization of the passage?

    (A) A specific event is introduced, and then its history and process are described.

    (B) A hypothesis is presented and arguments to support it are provided.

    (C) A specific event is introduced and then criticized.

    (D) An opinion is presented, followed by facts to support that opinion.

24. In line 13, the word "elaborate" most nearly means

    (A) complex.

    (B) frilly.

    (C) modest.

    (D) compact.

*Go on to the next page* ➡

Questions 25-30

*The following is an excerpt from a speech by Lyndon B. Johnson, delivered in 1964.*

1　　A third place to build the Great Society is
2　in the classrooms of America. There your
3　children's lives will be shaped. Our society will
4　not be great until every young mind is set free
5　to scan the farthest reaches of thought and
6　imagination. We are still far from that goal.
7　Today, 8 million adult Americans, more than
8　the entire population of Michigan, have not
9　finished 5 years of school. Nearly 20 million
10　have not finished 8 years of school. Nearly 54
11　million -- more than one quarter of all America
12　-- have not even finished high school.
13　　Each year more than 100,000 high school
14　graduates, with proved ability, do not enter
15　college because they cannot afford it. And if we
16　cannot educate today's youth, what will we do
17　in 1970 when elementary school enrollment
18　will be 5 million greater than 1960?

19　　In many places, classrooms are
20　overcrowded and curricula are outdated. Most
21　of our qualified teachers are underpaid, and
22　many of our paid teachers are unqualified. So
23　we must give every child a place to sit and a
24　teacher to learn from. Poverty must not be a
25　bar to learning, and learning must offer an
26　escape from poverty.
27　　But more classrooms and more teachers
28　are not enough. We must seek an educational
29　system which grows in excellence as it grows in
30　size. This means better training for our
31　teachers. It means preparing youth to enjoy
32　their hours of leisure as well as their hours of
33　labor. It means exploring new techniques of
34　teaching, to find new ways to stimulate the love
35　of learning and the capacity for creation.

*Go on to the next page* ➡

25. The passage above mainly focuses on

  (A) arguing for improvements in the educational system.

  (B) outlining the problems with education.

  (C) encouraging more people to stay in school and further their education.

  (D) addressing the issues of poverty by subsidizing education.

26. Which word best describes the speaker's tone when describing steps that should be taken to improve the system of education?

  (A) ambivalent

  (B) petulant

  (C) discouraged

  (D) emphatic

27. The second paragraph (lines 13-18) suggests that the speaker believes that

  (A) the cost of college helps to limit demand to just those students who will benefit the most.

  (B) college education should be made more affordable to capable students.

  (C) every citizen should be given a free college education.

  (D) college is expensive mainly because there are too many capable students.

28. When the speaker says that "we must give every child a place to sit" (line 23), he is making reference to

  (A) the large number of adults who have not graduated from high school.

  (B) the problem of overcrowded classrooms.

  (C) the outdated curricula still being used in schools.

  (D) the lack of schools in rural areas.

29. The passage suggests that a high quality education will help some students

  (A) grow up to escape the poverty of their childhood.

  (B) afford the cost of college tuition.

  (C) spend more of their time on leisure.

  (D) spend more of their time at work.

30. What best describes the speaker's tone when discussing the current state of the education system?

  (A) supportive

  (B) disinterested

  (C) neutral

  (D) critical

*Go on to the next page* ➜

# RC

1     Carrots contain vitamin A. A lack of
2 vitamin A can cause poor vision, including poor
3 night vision. In cases where poor vision is the
4 result of a vitamin deficiency, vision can be
5 restored by adding the vitamin back into the
6 diet. One way to do this is by eating plenty of
7 carrots. Some people, however, believe that the
8 relationship between carrots and vision goes
9 even further, arguing that eating large
10 quantities of carrots will improve vision
11 beyond normal limits and allow one to see in
12 the dark.
13     This misconception developed in part
14 from stories of British gunners in World War II,
15 who were able to shoot down German planes in
16 the darkness of night. The British gunners
17 were able to shoot down German planes thanks
18 to advances in radar technology, which used
19 radio waves to detect metallic objects like the
20 German planes and accurately target them
21 even in the dark. But the British Government
22 circulated a rumor that it was a diet which
23 included unusually large amounts of carrots
24 that enabled their pilots to see German planes
25 in the dark. This propaganda helped to
26 conceal the recent advances in technology from
27 the Germans by providing a plausible
28 alternative explanation for the success of
29 British gunners. Since German folktales already
30 included such stories about carrots, the story
31 was quite believable to the Germans.
32     This propaganda also helped to achieve
33 another important goal for the British by
34 increasing British carrot consumption. During
35 the war, ships importing food to Brittan were
36 often sunk, and there were constant shortages
37 of essential foodstuffs – but there was actually
38 a surplus of carrots. By increasing demand for
39 the vegetable with creative stories about its
40 health benefits, the British government was
41 able to encourage the population to consume
42 more of it, thereby relieving strain on the rest
43 of the food supply. Propaganda about carrots
44 also played a role in the "Dig for Victory"
45 campaign, which was designed to encourage
46 Britons to plant gardens and grow their own
47 food locally. The campaign was widely
48 successful, and carrots became an important
49 part of British gardens.

*Go on to the next page* ➡

**Ivy Global**

31. It can be inferred from the passage that

(A) British propaganda was more effective against the British than the Germans.

(B) many Britons planted gardens during the war.

(C) carrots actually aren't a healthy food after all.

(D) animals that have good night vision eat a lot of carrots

32. According to the passage, what role did the British Air Force play in the belief that carrots can provide the ability to see in the dark?

(A) The British Air Force intentionally spread this rumor to misinform the Germans.

(B) The British Air Force tried to stop this rumor from reaching the Germans.

(C) The British Air Force told this rumor to their pilots in order to justify the carrots in their rations.

(D) When the British Air Force heard this rumor, they encouraged their pilots to eat carrots.

33. According to the passage, the British gunners were actually able to shoot down German planes at night because

(A) the British ate carrots to improve their night vision.

(B) the light emitted by the German planes made them easy to see.

(C) the British had naturally better eyesight than the Germans.

(D) the British used radar technology to find the planes.

34. The main purpose of this passage is to

(A) give evidence of how carrots can help you see in the dark.

(B) document German folk stories about carrots.

(C) discuss the historical importance of carrots in Britain during World War II.

(D) provide an explanation of World War II-era radar technology.

35. In line 13, the word "misconception" most nearly means

(A) belief.

(B) vicious rumor.

(C) propaganda.

(D) faulty idea.

36. The passage suggests that propaganda

(A) had no effect on World War II.

(B) played an important role in accomplishing certain goals for the British.

(C) deceived many people and promoted ill will.

(D) reduced the consumption of carrots in Great Britain.

**STOP. Do not go on until told to do so.**

STOP

**Ivy Global**

# SECTION 4

# Mathematics Achievement

47 Questions

Time: 40 minutes

Each question is followed by four suggested answers. Read each question and then decide which one of the four suggested answers is best.

Find the row of spaces on your answer document that has the same number as the question. In this row, mark the space having the same letter as the answer you have chosen. You may write in your test booklet.

---

SAMPLE QUESTION:

If $a = 3$, what is the value $a^2 + (3 \times 4) \div 6$?

(A) 3.5

(B) 11

(C) 14.5

(D) 20

The correct answer is 11, so circle B is darkened.

Sample Answer

Ⓐ ● Ⓒ Ⓓ

---

STOP. Do not go on
until told to do so.

1. If $Q<2$ and $Q>-1$, which of the following could be a value of Q?

   (A) $-1$

   (B) 0

   (C) 2

   (D) 2.5

2. If the ratio of $5:12$ is the same as $X:144$, then $X =$

   (A) 25

   (B) 50

   (C) 55

   (D) 60

3. Joe bought a bag of 42 candies. He first gave $1/3$ of the bag to his brother, and he then gave 10 pieces of candy to his sister. How many pieces of candy did Joe have remaining?

   (A) 4

   (B) 18

   (C) 10

   (D) 52

4. Figure $AB$ is made from pieces $A$ and $B$.

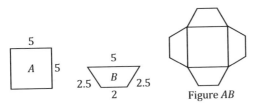

   If $A$ is a square and $B$ is a trapezoid, what is the perimeter of Figure $AB$?

   (A) 20

   (B) 26

   (C) 28

   (D) 32

5. If the area of a square is 1 cm², what is the perimeter of the square?

   (A) 1 cm

   (B) 2 cm

   (C) 3 cm

   (D) 4 cm

6. Mike's soccer team has won 4 games and lost 7 games. There are 11 more games left in the season. How many more games must Mike's team win in order to have an equal number of wins and losses for the whole season?

   (A) 4

   (B) 7

   (C) 9

   (D) 10

7. What is the value of the expression $\frac{5^2-1}{12}$?

   (A) $1/3$

   (B) $1/2$

   (C) 1

   (D) 2

8. Which of the following is closest to $0.32 \times 59$?

   (A) $1/6$ of 50

   (B) $1/3$ of 50

   (C) $1/2$ of 50

   (D) $1/3$ of 60

*Go on to the next page* ➡

9. The figure below shows two squares, one with a side length of 4 and one with a side length of 7.

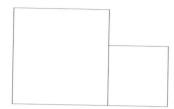

What is the perimeter of the entire figure?

(A) 16

(B) 20

(C) 33

(D) 36

10. A group of 3 knitters takes 3 hours to knit a total of 6 sweaters. Sally can knit 6 sweaters in 3 hours working by herself. If Sally joins the group of knitters, what will be the new average rate for each knitter?

(A) $1/2$ sweaters per hour

(B) $2/3$ sweaters per hour

(C) 1 sweater per hour

(D) $4/3$ sweaters per hour

11. There are 230 foxes in a forest. If the ratio of rabbits to foxes in the forest is 5:2, how many rabbits are in the forest?

(A) 460

(B) 575

(C) 720

(D) 1150

*Questions 12-13 refer to the chart below:*

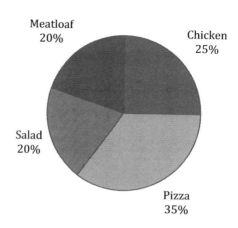

12. The chart above shows the breakdown of students' lunch orders at a cafeteria. If 120 lunches were ordered, how many students ordered pizza?

(A) 28

(B) 35

(C) 36

(D) 42

13. What fraction of students ordered meatloaf or salad?

(A) $1/5$

(B) $2/5$

(C) $1/4$

(D) $1/2$

*Go on to the next page* ➡

14. In the figure below, a square with a side length of 8 is adjacent to a triangle with a base of 8.

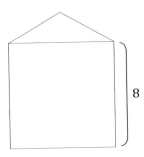

8

If the height of the entire figure is 10, what is its area?

(A) 56

(B) 64

(C) 72

(D) 80

15. A swimming pool is being filled with water at a rate of 120 cubic feet per hour. If the pool measures 10 feet long by 12 feet wide by 8 feet deep, how long will it take for the pool to be entirely full?

(A) 8 hrs

(B) 12 hrs

(C) 16 hrs

(D) 80 hrs

16. According to the chart below, Author A wrote approximately how many more books than Author E?

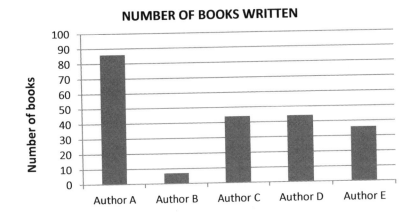

**NUMBER OF BOOKS WRITTEN**

(A) 40

(B) 50

(C) 60

(D) 70

*Go on to the next page* ➡

17. According to the chart below, what were the approximate average earnings of the three highest-grossing films during the weekend of July 13-15?

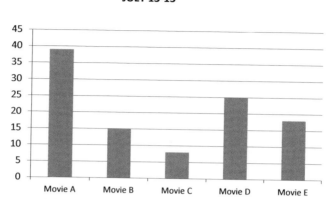

**WEEKEND BOX OFFICE EARNINGS,
JULY 13-15**

(A) $20 million

(B) $30 million

(C) $40 million

(D) $50 million

18. According to the graph below, pencils were produced at the greatest rate between which years?

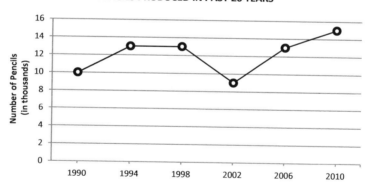

**PENCILS PRODUCED IN PAST 20 YEARS**

(A) 1994-1998

(B) 1998-2002

(C) 2002-2006

(D) 2006-2010

*Go on to the next page* ➡

**Ivy Global**

19. Which is equivalent to the following equation?

$$\frac{1}{x} \times \frac{1}{2} + \frac{1}{16} = y$$

(A) $x = \frac{1}{2y - \frac{1}{8}}$

(B) $x = y \times 2 - \frac{1}{16}$

(C) $x = y - \frac{1}{8}$

(D) $x = \left(y - \frac{1}{16}\right) \times 2$

20. If one fourth of the height of a giraffe is 5 ft, what is three fifths of the giraffe's height?

(A) 5 ft

(B) 8 ft

(C) 10 ft

(D) 12 ft

21. A T-shirt is on sale for 25% off of the regular price of $15.99. About how much less in dollars is the sale price?

(A) $3

(B) $4

(C) $8

(D) $12

22. If $\frac{2}{3} + M < \frac{1}{6}$, which of the following could be a value for $M$?

(A) $-\frac{2}{3}$

(B) $-\frac{1}{2}$

(C) $-\frac{1}{3}$

(D) $\frac{1}{3}$

23. The sum of three consecutive integers is 27. What is the smallest of the three integers?

(A) 8

(B) 9

(C) 10

(D) 11

24. If $\bigstar \times 5 = \blacklozenge \times 2$ and $\blacklozenge = 3$, what is the value of $\bigstar$?

(A) $\frac{2}{5}$

(B) $\frac{4}{5}$

(C) $\frac{6}{5}$

(D) 6

25. Gabrielle has packed 11 pieces of clothing for a vacation, including 5 scarves, 3 hats, and 3 pairs of gloves. If she wants to select an outfit that has one scarf, one hat, and one pair of gloves, how many choices does she have?

(A) 3

(B) 11

(C) 45

(D) 60

26. For two numbers $p$ and $s$, $p \times 2 = s + 2$. Which expression represents the value of $p \times 3$?

(A) $3 \times s$

(B) $\frac{3}{2} \times s + 3$

(C) $3 \times s + 3$

(D) $s + 6$

27. What is the closest value to $\sqrt{139}$?

(A) 11

(B) 12

(C) 13

(D) 20

*Go on to the next page* ➡

28. What is the difference between 5621–9586?

   (A) -4035

   (B) -3965

   (C) -3935

   (D) -3035

29. Ashley has 10 more pencils than Troy. If Troy has 5 pencils, what fraction of the total pencils does Troy have?

   (A) $\frac{1}{2}$

   (B) $\frac{1}{3}$

   (C) $\frac{1}{4}$

   (D) $\frac{1}{5}$

30. Sophia has written 8 novels during her 24-year career. If she continues to write the same average number of novels per year, how many total novels will she have written after another 10 years?

   (A) 8

   (B) 9

   (C) 10

   (D) 11

31. 20% of $a$ is equal to $b$. What is 35% of $b$, in terms of $a$?

   (A) $0.07a$

   (B) $0.14a$

   (C) $0.15a$

   (D) $0.35a$

32. If $x = \frac{2}{3}y$ and $z = \frac{1}{2}y$, $z$ is equal to

   (A) $\frac{x}{4}$

   (B) $\frac{3x}{4}$

   (C) $x$

   (D) $\frac{4x}{3}$

33. Jarred is rolling two six-sided number cubes, numbered 1-6. What is the probability that the sum of his rolls will equal 4?

   (A) $\frac{1}{36}$

   (B) $\frac{1}{18}$

   (C) $\frac{1}{12}$

   (D) $\frac{1}{9}$

34. Gerome's weekly wage in dollars ($W$) relates to the number of hours he works ($H$) according to the equation below:

$$W = H \times \$7 + \$40$$

What does this formula indicate?

   (A) For every 7 hours of work, Gerome makes $47.

   (B) When Gerome works 0 hours, his wage is $40.

   (C) Gerome pays $40 to begin his work.

   (D) Gerome works 47 hours per week.

35. The distance from Buxton to Elmswood is 15 miles. In order to get to Elmswood from Buxton, Sam has to pass through Milton. The distance from Buxton to Milton is 5 miles. What is the approximate distance from Milton to Elmswood, in kilometers? (Note: 1 mile ≈ 1.6 kilometers)

   (A) 10 kilometers

   (B) 16 kilometers

   (C) 24 kilometers

   (D) 5 kilometers

*Go on to the next page* ➡

36. What coordinate pair would complete a rhombus on the coordinate plane below?

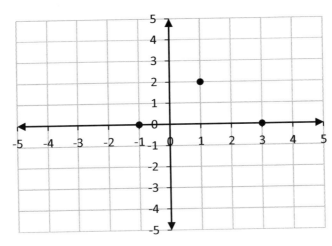

(A) $(-2,1)$

(B) $(1,-2)$

(C) $(0,0)$

(D) $(1,2)$

37. In the coordinate plane below, if $\triangle ABC$ were reflected along the y axis, what would be the new coordinates for point C?

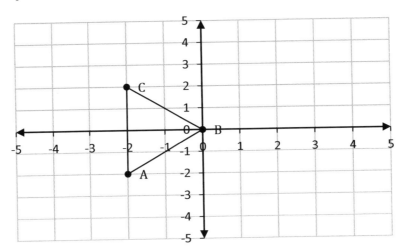

(A) $(-2,-2)$

(B) $(-2,2)$

(C) $(2,-2)$

(D) $(2,2)$

*Go on to the next page* ➡

**Ivy Global**

38. Two spinners are each equally divided into three parts with the colors red, green, and yellow. If Stacy spins both spinners, what is the probability that each spinner will land on red or green?

    (A) $\frac{2}{9}$

    (B) $\frac{4}{9}$

    (C) $\frac{4}{6}$

    (D) $\frac{5}{6}$

39. Which expression is equal to 144?

    (A) $3 + 1 \times 3 \times (4 \times 4 - 1)$
    (B) $(3 + 1) \times (3 \times 4) \times 4 - 1$
    (C) $3 + (1 \times 3) \times (4 \times 4) - 1$
    (D) $(3 + 1) \times 3 \times 4 \times (4 - 1)$

40. If $P = 2 \times (\pi \times r)$, what is $P$ when $r = 6.28$ inches?

    (A) $6.253\,\pi$ inches
    (B) $8\,\pi$ inches
    (C) $12.56\,\pi$ inches
    (D) $25.12\,\pi$ inches

41. What is the greatest common prime factor of 42 and 63?

    (A) 3
    (B) 7
    (C) 9
    (D) 11

42. Continue the pattern:

(A)

(B)

(C)

(D)

*Go on to the next page* ➡

43. What is the closest estimate of
$(63 \times 98) \div 5032$?

   (A) 0.1

   (B) 1.2

   (C) 1.5

   (D) 2.0

44. If $z = \frac{3}{4}y$ and $y = 1.2$, then which expression best represents the value of $2z$?

   (A) $\frac{21}{20}$

   (B) $\frac{3}{2}$

   (C) $\frac{24}{15}$

   (D) $\frac{9}{5}$

45. One candy bar costs $0.89, an orange costs $1.21, and a pair of tweezers costs $2.12. If Ho-jung has a $5.00 bill, how much change will he receive if he purchases a candy bar, an orange and one pair of tweezers?

   (A) $0.69

   (B) $0.78

   (C) $2.33

   (D) $3.20

46. If $\frac{3}{6x} = 21$, what is the value of $\frac{1}{3x}$?

   (A) 14

   (B) 18

   (C) 21

   (D) 36

47. The Opera Company of New York is planning its production run of the Magic Flute. The cost to pay its cast and crew is $2,401.51. The opera hall seats 200 people, tickets are $24.98 each, and the performance is sold out. What is the expected profit for the show after paying its cast and crew?

   (A) $2,534.49

   (B) $2,535.49

   (C) $2,594.49

   (D) $4,996.00

**STOP. Do not go on until told to do so.**  **STOP**

**Ivy Global**

# Essay Topic Sheet

The directions for the Essay portion of the ISEE are printed in the box below. Use the pre-lined pages on pages 122-123 for this part of the Practice Test.

---

You will have 30 minutes to plan and write an essay on the topic printed on the other side of this page. **Do not write on another topic. An essay on another topic is not acceptable.**

The essay is designed to give you an opportunity to show how well you can write. You should try to express your thoughts clearly. How well you write is much more important than how much you write, but you need to say enough for a reader to understand what you mean.

You will probably want to write more than a short paragraph. You should also be aware that a copy of your essay will be sent to each school that will be receiving your test results. You are to write only in the appropriate section of the answer sheet. Please write or print so that your writing may be read by someone who is not familiar with your handwriting.

You may make notes and plan your essay on the reverse side of the page. Allow enough time to copy the final form onto your answer sheet. You must copy the essay topic onto your answer sheet, on page 122, in the box provided.

Please remember to write only the final draft of the essay on pages 122-123 of your answer sheet and to write it in blue or black pen. Again, you may use cursive writing or you may print. Only pages 122-123 will be sent to the schools.

---

*Directions continue on the next page.*

## NOTES

_____

_____

_____

_____

_____

_____

_____

_____

_____

_____

_____

_____

_____

_____

_____

_____

_____

_____

_____

_____

Ivy Global

# PRACTICE TEST 4

## MIDDLE LEVEL

# HOW TO TAKE THIS PRACTICE TEST

To simulate an accurate testing environment, sit at a desk in a quiet location free of distractions—no TV, computers, phones, music, or noise—and clear your desk of all materials except pencils and erasers. Remember that no calculators, rulers, protractors, dictionaries, or other aids are allowed on the ISEE.

Give yourself the following amounts of time for each section:

| SECTION | SUBJECT | TIME LIMIT |
|---------|---------|------------|
| 1 | Verbal Reasoning | 20 minutes |
| 2 | Quantitative Reasoning | 35 minutes |
| 5 minute break | | |
| 3 | Reading Comprehension | 35 minutes |
| 4 | Mathematics Achievement | 40 minutes |
| 5 minute break | | |
| 5 | Essay | 30 minutes |

Have an adult help you monitor your time, or use a watch and time yourself. Only give yourself the allotted time for each section; put your pencil down when your time is up.

Follow the instructions carefully. As you take your test, bubble your answers into the answer sheets provided. Use the test booklet as scratch paper for notes and calculations. Remember that you are not granted time at the end of a section to transfer your answers to the answer sheet, so you must do this as you go along.

When you are finished, check your answers against the answer keys provided. Then, score your exam using the directions at the end of the book.

Ivy Global

Note: students with diagnosed learning disabilities who apply for testing with accommodations may receive extra time, or may be allowed to use certain assistive devices during the ISEE. For more information, visit http://erblearn.org/parents/admission/isee/accommodations.

# Ivy Global

# ISEE
# MIDDLE LEVEL TEST 2

## MARKING INSTRUCTIONS

- Use a #2 or HB pencil only on pages 168 and 169.
- Use a ballpoint pen for your essay on pages 170 and 171.
- Make dark marks that completely fill the circle.
- Erase clearly any mark you wish to change.
- Make no stray marks on this form.
- Do not fold or crease this form.

| Correct Mark | Incorrect Marks |
|:---:|:---:|
| ● | ⊗ ◌ ✓ ◉ ☺ |

## 1 VERBAL REASONING

| | | |
|---|---|---|
| 1 Ⓐ Ⓑ Ⓒ Ⓓ | 15 Ⓐ Ⓑ Ⓒ Ⓓ | 29 Ⓐ Ⓑ Ⓒ Ⓓ |
| 2 Ⓐ Ⓑ Ⓒ Ⓓ | 16 Ⓐ Ⓑ Ⓒ Ⓓ | 30 Ⓐ Ⓑ Ⓒ Ⓓ |
| 3 Ⓐ Ⓑ Ⓒ Ⓓ | 17 Ⓐ Ⓑ Ⓒ Ⓓ | 31 Ⓐ Ⓑ Ⓒ Ⓓ |
| 4 Ⓐ Ⓑ Ⓒ Ⓓ | 18 Ⓐ Ⓑ Ⓒ Ⓓ | 32 Ⓐ Ⓑ Ⓒ Ⓓ |
| 5 Ⓐ Ⓑ Ⓒ Ⓓ | 19 Ⓐ Ⓑ Ⓒ Ⓓ | 33 Ⓐ Ⓑ Ⓒ Ⓓ |
| 6 Ⓐ Ⓑ Ⓒ Ⓓ | 20 Ⓐ Ⓑ Ⓒ Ⓓ | 34 Ⓐ Ⓑ Ⓒ Ⓓ **Lower Level Ends** |
| 7 Ⓐ Ⓑ Ⓒ Ⓓ | 21 Ⓐ Ⓑ Ⓒ Ⓓ | 35 Ⓐ Ⓑ Ⓒ Ⓓ |
| 8 Ⓐ Ⓑ Ⓒ Ⓓ | 22 Ⓐ Ⓑ Ⓒ Ⓓ | 36 Ⓐ Ⓑ Ⓒ Ⓓ |
| 9 Ⓐ Ⓑ Ⓒ Ⓓ | 23 Ⓐ Ⓑ Ⓒ Ⓓ | 37 Ⓐ Ⓑ Ⓒ Ⓓ |
| 10 Ⓐ Ⓑ Ⓒ Ⓓ | 24 Ⓐ Ⓑ Ⓒ Ⓓ | 38 Ⓐ Ⓑ Ⓒ Ⓓ |
| 11 Ⓐ Ⓑ Ⓒ Ⓓ | 25 Ⓐ Ⓑ Ⓒ Ⓓ | 39 Ⓐ Ⓑ Ⓒ Ⓓ |
| 12 Ⓐ Ⓑ Ⓒ Ⓓ | 26 Ⓐ Ⓑ Ⓒ Ⓓ | 40 Ⓐ Ⓑ Ⓒ Ⓓ **Middle/Upper Level Ends** |
| 13 Ⓐ Ⓑ Ⓒ Ⓓ | 27 Ⓐ Ⓑ Ⓒ Ⓓ | |
| 14 Ⓐ Ⓑ Ⓒ Ⓓ | 28 Ⓐ Ⓑ Ⓒ Ⓓ | |

## 2 QUANTITATIVE REASONING

| | | | | | | |
|---|---|---|---|---|---|
| 1 Ⓐ Ⓑ Ⓒ Ⓓ | 15 Ⓐ Ⓑ Ⓒ Ⓓ | 29 Ⓐ Ⓑ Ⓒ Ⓓ |
| 2 Ⓐ Ⓑ Ⓒ Ⓓ | 16 Ⓐ Ⓑ Ⓒ Ⓓ | 30 Ⓐ Ⓑ Ⓒ Ⓓ |
| 3 Ⓐ Ⓑ Ⓒ Ⓓ | 17 Ⓐ Ⓑ Ⓒ Ⓓ | 31 Ⓐ Ⓑ Ⓒ Ⓓ |
| 4 Ⓐ Ⓑ Ⓒ Ⓓ | 18 Ⓐ Ⓑ Ⓒ Ⓓ | 32 Ⓐ Ⓑ Ⓒ Ⓓ |
| 5 Ⓐ Ⓑ Ⓒ Ⓓ | 19 Ⓐ Ⓑ Ⓒ Ⓓ | 33 Ⓐ Ⓑ Ⓒ Ⓓ |
| 6 Ⓐ Ⓑ Ⓒ Ⓓ | 20 Ⓐ Ⓑ Ⓒ Ⓓ | 34 Ⓐ Ⓑ Ⓒ Ⓓ |
| 7 Ⓐ Ⓑ Ⓒ Ⓓ | 21 Ⓐ Ⓑ Ⓒ Ⓓ | 35 Ⓐ Ⓑ Ⓒ Ⓓ |
| 8 Ⓐ Ⓑ Ⓒ Ⓓ | 22 Ⓐ Ⓑ Ⓒ Ⓓ | 36 Ⓐ Ⓑ Ⓒ Ⓓ |
| 9 Ⓐ Ⓑ Ⓒ Ⓓ | 23 Ⓐ Ⓑ Ⓒ Ⓓ | 37 Ⓐ Ⓑ Ⓒ Ⓓ **Middle/Upper Level Ends** |
| 10 Ⓐ Ⓑ Ⓒ Ⓓ | 24 Ⓐ Ⓑ Ⓒ Ⓓ | 38 Ⓐ Ⓑ Ⓒ Ⓓ **Lower Level Ends** |
| 11 Ⓐ Ⓑ Ⓒ Ⓓ | 25 Ⓐ Ⓑ Ⓒ Ⓓ | |
| 12 Ⓐ Ⓑ Ⓒ Ⓓ | 26 Ⓐ Ⓑ Ⓒ Ⓓ | |
| 13 Ⓐ Ⓑ Ⓒ Ⓓ | 27 Ⓐ Ⓑ Ⓒ Ⓓ | |
| 14 Ⓐ Ⓑ Ⓒ Ⓓ | 28 Ⓐ Ⓑ Ⓒ Ⓓ | |

## 4 MATHEMATICS ACHIEVEMENT

| | | |
|---|---|---|
| 1 Ⓐ Ⓑ Ⓒ Ⓓ | 18 Ⓐ Ⓑ Ⓒ Ⓓ | 35 Ⓐ Ⓑ Ⓒ Ⓓ |
| 2 Ⓐ Ⓑ Ⓒ Ⓓ | 19 Ⓐ Ⓑ Ⓒ Ⓓ | 36 Ⓐ Ⓑ Ⓒ Ⓓ |
| 3 Ⓐ Ⓑ Ⓒ Ⓓ | 20 Ⓐ Ⓑ Ⓒ Ⓓ | 37 Ⓐ Ⓑ Ⓒ Ⓓ |
| 4 Ⓐ Ⓑ Ⓒ Ⓓ | 21 Ⓐ Ⓑ Ⓒ Ⓓ | 38 Ⓐ Ⓑ Ⓒ Ⓓ |
| 5 Ⓐ Ⓑ Ⓒ Ⓓ | 22 Ⓐ Ⓑ Ⓒ Ⓓ | 39 Ⓐ Ⓑ Ⓒ Ⓓ |
| 6 Ⓐ Ⓑ Ⓒ Ⓓ | 23 Ⓐ Ⓑ Ⓒ Ⓓ | 40 Ⓐ Ⓑ Ⓒ Ⓓ |
| 7 Ⓐ Ⓑ Ⓒ Ⓓ | 24 Ⓐ Ⓑ Ⓒ Ⓓ | 41 Ⓐ Ⓑ Ⓒ Ⓓ |
| 8 Ⓐ Ⓑ Ⓒ Ⓓ | 25 Ⓐ Ⓑ Ⓒ Ⓓ | 42 Ⓐ Ⓑ Ⓒ Ⓓ |
| 9 Ⓐ Ⓑ Ⓒ Ⓓ | 26 Ⓐ Ⓑ Ⓒ Ⓓ | 43 Ⓐ Ⓑ Ⓒ Ⓓ |
| 10 Ⓐ Ⓑ Ⓒ Ⓓ | 27 Ⓐ Ⓑ Ⓒ Ⓓ | 44 Ⓐ Ⓑ Ⓒ Ⓓ |
| 11 Ⓐ Ⓑ Ⓒ Ⓓ | 28 Ⓐ Ⓑ Ⓒ Ⓓ | 45 Ⓐ Ⓑ Ⓒ Ⓓ |
| 12 Ⓐ Ⓑ Ⓒ Ⓓ | 29 Ⓐ Ⓑ Ⓒ Ⓓ | 46 Ⓐ Ⓑ Ⓒ Ⓓ |
| 13 Ⓐ Ⓑ Ⓒ Ⓓ | 30 Ⓐ Ⓑ Ⓒ Ⓓ **Lower Level Ends** | 47 Ⓐ Ⓑ Ⓒ Ⓓ **Middle/Upper Level Ends** |
| 14 Ⓐ Ⓑ Ⓒ Ⓓ | 31 Ⓐ Ⓑ Ⓒ Ⓓ | |
| 15 Ⓐ Ⓑ Ⓒ Ⓓ | 32 Ⓐ Ⓑ Ⓒ Ⓓ | |
| 16 Ⓐ Ⓑ Ⓒ Ⓓ | 33 Ⓐ Ⓑ Ⓒ Ⓓ | |
| 17 Ⓐ Ⓑ Ⓒ Ⓓ | 34 Ⓐ Ⓑ Ⓒ Ⓓ | |

## 3 READING COMPREHENSION

| | | |
|---|---|---|
| 1 Ⓐ Ⓑ Ⓒ Ⓓ | 15 Ⓐ Ⓑ Ⓒ Ⓓ | 29 Ⓐ Ⓑ Ⓒ Ⓓ |
| 2 Ⓐ Ⓑ Ⓒ Ⓓ | 16 Ⓐ Ⓑ Ⓒ Ⓓ | 30 Ⓐ Ⓑ Ⓒ Ⓓ |
| 3 Ⓐ Ⓑ Ⓒ Ⓓ | 17 Ⓐ Ⓑ Ⓒ Ⓓ | 31 Ⓐ Ⓑ Ⓒ Ⓓ |
| 4 Ⓐ Ⓑ Ⓒ Ⓓ | 18 Ⓐ Ⓑ Ⓒ Ⓓ | 32 Ⓐ Ⓑ Ⓒ Ⓓ |
| 5 Ⓐ Ⓑ Ⓒ Ⓓ | 19 Ⓐ Ⓑ Ⓒ Ⓓ | 33 Ⓐ Ⓑ Ⓒ Ⓓ |
| 6 Ⓐ Ⓑ Ⓒ Ⓓ | 20 Ⓐ Ⓑ Ⓒ Ⓓ | 34 Ⓐ Ⓑ Ⓒ Ⓓ |
| 7 Ⓐ Ⓑ Ⓒ Ⓓ | 21 Ⓐ Ⓑ Ⓒ Ⓓ | 35 Ⓐ Ⓑ Ⓒ Ⓓ |
| 8 Ⓐ Ⓑ Ⓒ Ⓓ | 22 Ⓐ Ⓑ Ⓒ Ⓓ | 36 Ⓐ Ⓑ Ⓒ Ⓓ **Middle/Upper Level Ends** |
| 9 Ⓐ Ⓑ Ⓒ Ⓓ | 23 Ⓐ Ⓑ Ⓒ Ⓓ | |
| 10 Ⓐ Ⓑ Ⓒ Ⓓ | 24 Ⓐ Ⓑ Ⓒ Ⓓ | |
| 11 Ⓐ Ⓑ Ⓒ Ⓓ | 25 Ⓐ Ⓑ Ⓒ Ⓓ **Lower Level Ends** | |
| 12 Ⓐ Ⓑ Ⓒ Ⓓ | 26 Ⓐ Ⓑ Ⓒ Ⓓ | |
| 13 Ⓐ Ⓑ Ⓒ Ⓓ | 27 Ⓐ Ⓑ Ⓒ Ⓓ | |
| 14 Ⓐ Ⓑ Ⓒ Ⓓ | 28 Ⓐ Ⓑ Ⓒ Ⓓ | |

Ivy Global

STUDENT NAME _____ GRADE APPLYING FOR _____

Use a blue or black ballpoint pen to write the final draft of your essay on this sheet.

You must write your essay topic in this space.

_____

_____

_____

Use specific details and examples in your response.

_____

_____

_____

_____

_____

_____

_____

_____

_____

_____

_____

_____

_____

_____

_____

_____

_____

_____

_____

_____

_____

_____

Ivy Global

# VR

## Section 1
## Verbal Reasoning

**40 Questions**

**Time: 20 minutes**

This section is divided into two parts that contain two different types of questions. As soon as you have completed Part One, answer the questions in Part Two. You may write in your test booklet. For each answer you select, fill in the corresponding circle on your answer document.

## PART ONE — SYNONYMS

Each question in Part One consists of a word in capital letters followed by four answer choices. Select the one word that is most nearly the same in meaning as the word in capital letters.

---

SAMPLE QUESTION:

CHARGE:

(A) release
(B) belittle
(C) accuse
(D) conspire

The correct answer is "accuse," so circle C is darkened.

Sample Answer

Ⓐ Ⓑ ● Ⓓ

---

## PART TWO — SENTENCE COMPLETION

Each question in Part Two is made up of a sentence with one blank. Each blank indicates that a word is missing. The sentence is followed by four answer choices. Select the word that will best complete the meaning of the sentence as a whole.

---

SAMPLE QUESTION:

It rained so much that the streets were -------.

(A) flooded
(B) arid
(C) paved
(D) crowded

The correct answer is "flooded," so circle A is darkened.

Sample Answer

● Ⓑ Ⓒ Ⓓ

---

**STOP. Do not go on until told to do so.**

**Ivy Global**

# VR

## PART ONE – SYNONYMS

**Directions:** Select the word that is most nearly the same in meaning as the word in capital letters.

1. IMPEDE
   - (A) increase
   - (B) ply
   - (C) block
   - (D) prepare

2. NOTORIOUS
   - (A) masculine
   - (B) gelatinous
   - (C) infamous
   - (D) numerous

3. EXUBERANT
   - (A) magical
   - (B) cheerful
   - (C) slippery
   - (D) exhausted

4. RIGID
   - (A) thorough
   - (B) direct
   - (C) cold
   - (D) inflexible

5. MOPE
   - (A) polish
   - (B) sleep
   - (C) pout
   - (D) attempt

6. EAGER
   - (A) thoughtful
   - (B) bored
   - (C) enthusiastic
   - (D) inspired

7. DREGS
   - (A) remnants
   - (B) coffee
   - (C) fighters
   - (D) surplus

8. PROBABLE
   - (A) soft
   - (B) likely
   - (C) distinct
   - (D) detestable

9. VARIABLE
   - (A) vertical
   - (B) capable
   - (C) colorful
   - (D) changeable

10. ANNUL
   - (A) record
   - (B) celebrate
   - (C) subtract
   - (D) void

*Go on to the next page* ➡

**Ivy Global**

11. MERCILESS

(A) thankless

(B) insecure

(C) ruthless

(D) aggressive

12. PUNGENT

(A) acrid

(B) unlikely

(C) peripheral

(D) wet

13. HUBRIS

(A) arrogance

(B) optimism

(C) shame

(D) indifference

14. DAWDLE

(A) draw

(B) hurry

(C) stall

(D) trip

15. IMMEDIATE

(A) newsworthy

(B) late

(C) prompt

(D) invisible

16. MOMENTOUS

(A) decayed

(B) damp

(C) invincible

(D) notable

17. SOLEMN

(A) miserable

(B) boring

(C) magnificent

(D) serious

18. SEIZE

(A) attack

(B) refuse

(C) capture

(D) count

19. MODERATE

(A) partisan

(B) measured

(C) warm

(D) careless

*Go on to the next page* ➜

# PART TWO – SENTENCE COMPLETION

**Directions:** Select the word that best completes the sentence.

20. Sydney wanted her assignment to be very ------, so she spent two weeks working to answer every question completely.

    (A) anxious
    (B) delectable
    (C) thorough
    (D) nimble

21. Stephanie gained a reputation as a ------ student by joining clubs, making friends, and always introducing herself to new students.

    (A) defensible
    (B) gregarious
    (C) hostile
    (D) sturdy

22. Because of their --------, Edmund Hilary and Tenzing Norgay persisted in challenging circumstances and became the first pair of climbers to successfully ascend Mount Everest.

    (A) hesitation
    (B) anxiety
    (C) apprehension
    (D) tenacity

23. Mr. Blackburn put peanuts on his window sill to ------ the squirrels, whose company he enjoyed.

    (A) entice
    (B) deceive
    (C) confound
    (D) offend

24. I wrote down the titles of my favorite books as I finished them, and over a few weeks I ------ a list to share with my reading group.

    (A) compiled
    (B) damaged
    (C) measured
    (D) polished

25. Walt Disney turned to television to ------ Disney Land even before it was built, creating anticipation and excitement in advance of its grand opening.

    (A) dignify
    (B) exchange
    (C) construct
    (D) promote

26. The film *O Brother, Where Art Thou?* was ------ based on Homer's Odyssey; while there were many parallels, it was largely a new work.

    (A) falsely
    (B) loosely
    (C) entirely
    (D) quickly

27. Becoming an Olympic athlete requires tremendous ----------, as you must train consistently and keep competing even after tough losses.

    (A) respect
    (B) organization
    (C) dedication
    (D) trepidation

*Go on to the next page* ➡

**Ivy Global**

28. Sections of the Appalachian Trail receive difficulty ratings for hikers; ------- should stay in the 1-4 range, leaving harder trails for more experienced hikers.

    (A) experts
    (B) adults
    (C) novices
    (D) climbers

29. Replicas sometimes ------- the original artwork so closely that only experts can tell them apart.

    (A) mitigate
    (B) confuse
    (C) repudiate
    (D) resemble

30. Jasper expressed his ------- to his collaborators by sending them each a small gift when the project was complete.

    (A) frustration
    (B) expectations
    (C) gratitude
    (D) anger

31. When police corruption is common, some citizens ------- the law, knowing that a small bribe can keep them out of trouble.

    (A) flout
    (B) uphold
    (C) enforce
    (D) impute

32. Conserving resources was ------- during World War I, as conservation was enforced by strict rationing laws.

    (A) undignified
    (B) permitted
    (C) compulsory
    (D) cursory

33. "Indorock" originated in the 1950s as a ------- of Indonesian and Western music, combining features of both styles.

    (A) conflict
    (B) charter
    (C) fusion
    (D) grounded

34. Even dogs that are normally docile can become ------- around their food, growling or even snapping at other dogs.

    (A) defensive
    (B) hoarse
    (C) poised
    (D) shabby

35. In a foreign lottery scam, the victim is ------- into paying a cash advance to claim a prize that doesn't exist.

    (A) arrested
    (B) bemused
    (C) assuaged
    (D) duped

36. Sailors have a number of traditional ------, including the beliefs that cats will bring good luck and that it is very bad luck to kill an albatross.

    (A) poems
    (B) superstitions
    (C) voyages
    (D) indiscretions

37. Katrina picked out a beautiful dress for her sister's wedding, but she had to ----it slightly for it to fit just right.

    (A) alter
    (B) design
    (C) create
    (D) reproduce

*Go on to the next page* →

38. Mrs. Baker wanted us to care about our work, so she had every student do an assignment on a topic that they --------- enjoyed

    (A) ironically

    (B) ostensibly

    (C) scarcely

    (D) sincerely

39. Many animals are becoming ---------- or extinct as their habitats are being destroyed.

    (A) abundant

    (B) endangered

    (C) domesticated

    (D) larger

40. The Companions were the ------- cavalry of the Macedonian army, so above all others they were given the best equipment, horses, and training.

    (A) elite

    (B) appalling

    (C) happiest

    (D) least

**STOP. Do not go on until told to do so.**   **STOP**

# Section 2
# Quantitative Reasoning

| 37 Questions | | Time: 35 minutes |
|---|---|---|

This section is divided into two parts that contain two different types of questions. As soon as you have completed Part One, answer the questions in Part Two. You may write in your test booklet. For each answer you select, remember to fill in the corresponding circle on your answer document.

Any figures that accompany the questions in this section may be assumed to be drawn as accurately as possible EXCEPT when it is stated that a particular figure is not drawn to scale. Letters such as $x, y,$ and $n$ stand for real numbers.

## PART ONE — WORD PROBLEMS

Each question in Part One consists of a word problem followed by four answer choices. You may write in your test booklet; however, you may be able to solve many of these problems in your head. Next, look at the four answer choices given and select the best answer.

---

SAMPLE QUESTION:

What is the value of the expression $3 + 7 \times (6 - 4)^2 - 8 \div 2$?

(A) 14

(B) 16

(C) 27

(D) 32

The correct answer is 27, so circle C is darkened.

Sample Answer

Ⓐ Ⓑ ● Ⓓ

---

*Go on to the next page* ➡

# QR

## PART TWO — QUANTITATIVE COMPARISONS

All questions in Part Two are quantitative comparisons between the quantities shown in Column A and Column B. Using the information given in each question, compare the quantity in Column A to the quantity in Column B, and choose one of these four answer choices:

    (A) The quantity in Column A is greater.

    (B) The quantity in Column B is greater.

    (C) The two quantities are equal.

    (D) The relationship cannot be determined from the information given.

---

SAMPLE QUESTIONS:

| Column A | Column B | Sample Answer |
|----------|----------|---------------|
| 5 | $\sqrt{25}$ | Ⓐ Ⓑ ● Ⓓ |

The quantity in Column A (5) is the same as the quantity in Column B (5), so circle C is darkened.

---

$$x = 6^2 - 3 \times 4$$

| Column A | Column B | Sample Answer |
|----------|----------|---------------|
| $x$ | 22 | ● Ⓑ Ⓒ Ⓓ |

The quantity in Column A (24) is greater than the quantity in Column B (22), so circle A is darkened.

---

**STOP.** Do not go on until told to do so. 🛑 **STOP**

1. Ivy is giving away rocks in the order of red, blue, yellow, gold, and silver. If Ivy keeps this color order and gives each of her friends 4 rocks, what color and order of rocks does she give to her 3rd friend?

   (A) red, blue, yellow, and gold

   (B) gold, silver, red, and blue

   (C) blue, yellow, gold, and silver

   (D) silver, red, blue, and yellow

2. If $b\bigstar = q \times \frac{3}{b} - b$, which expression is equivalent to $\frac{1}{5}\bigstar$?

   (A) $q\frac{1}{5}$

   (B) $q(15 - \frac{1}{5})$

   (C) $15q - \frac{1}{5}$

   (D) $15q - 1$

3. If Z is an integer less than -1, which of the following expressions has the largest value?

   (A) $-(Z + 24) - \frac{24}{Z^2}$

   (B) $-(Z - 24) - \frac{24}{-Z^2}$

   (C) $(Z + 24) - \frac{24}{Z^2}$

   (D) $(Z + 24) - \frac{24}{-Z^2}$

4. Li has 15 bookshelves that each measure 8 feet tall, 0.5 feet wide, and 4.5 feet long. She wants to store them in her closet, which measures 9 feet tall, 4 feet wide, and 5 feet long. How many bookshelves will she be able to fit inside the closet?

   (A) 4

   (B) 8

   (C) 10

   (D) 18

5. A family of $n$ people is sharing an amount of rice that costs a total of $p \times n$. John and his brother each eat a $1/4$ of the total amount of rice. The total cost of the rice they ate was $8.00. If each of the other family members splits the remaining rice equally and each has a portion that is $1/2$ the size of John's, what is the average cost of a serving of rice ($p$) per person in the family, rounded to the nearest penny?

   (A) $2.00

   (B) $2.67

   (C) $8.00

   (D) $16.02

6. A triangular block with a volume of 22.5 cm³ is placed into a rectangular box, as shown below.

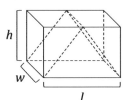

   If the box has a length ($l$) of 5 cm, a width ($w$) of 3 cm and a height ($h$) of 3 cm, what is the volume of the empty space remaining in the box?

   (A) $7\frac{1}{2}$ cm³

   (B) $22\frac{1}{2}$ cm³

   (C) $37\frac{1}{2}$ cm³

   (D) 198 cm³

*Go on to the next page* ➡

7.  A series of pools in a row are connected to each other in a water park. There are 5 pools and each pool is one half of the size of the pool before it.  If the largest pool is completely filled with $w$ gallons of water, how much water is needed to completely fill all 5 pools?

    (A) $w \times 2.5$ gallons

    (B) $w \times 0.5^5$ gallons

    (C) $w + w \times 0.5 + w \times 0.5^2 + w \times 0.5^3 + w \times 0.5^4$ gallons

    (D) $w \times 0.5 + w \times 0.5^2 + w \times 0.5^3 + w \times 0.5^4 + w \times 0.5^5$ gallons

8.  A cube is cut once horizontally and cut twice vertically, as shown by the dashed lines below, creating six rectangular pieces of equal size.

    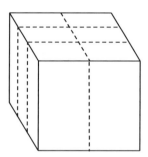

    If one face of the cube has an area of $9\text{cm}^2$, what is the volume of one of the six rectangular pieces?

    (A) $3\text{cm}^3$

    (B) $4.5\text{cm}^3$

    (C) $9\text{ cm}^3$

    (D) $27\text{cm}^3$

9.  Malcolm is rolling one $n$-sided number polygon twice. Each side of the polygon is inscribed with a number 1 to $n$, and each number is used only once. What is the probability that the sum of his rolls will equal $2n$?

    (A) $\frac{1}{n}$

    (B) $\left(\frac{1}{n}\right)^2$

    (C) $n$

    (D) $n^2$

10. If $\boxed{a} = \frac{4}{3a} + 8$ what is $\boxed{2}$?

    (A) $4\frac{2}{3}$

    (B) $8\frac{2}{3}$

    (C) $16\frac{2}{3}$

    (D) $32\frac{2}{3}$

11. Each bicycle stores one spare wheel and each car stores three bicycles. If one flatbed truck can carry four cars and three spare wheels, what is the total number of spare wheels that can be carried by three flatbed trucks?

    (A) 12

    (B) 24

    (C) 36

    (D) 45

*Go on to the next page* ➡

12. If $B$ is an odd integer and $P$ is an even integer, which of the following is true?

   (A) The product of the smallest prime factor of $P$ and the smallest prime factor of $B$ is always an odd integer.

   (B) $\frac{P}{B}$ is never an integer.

   (C) $\frac{B}{2}$ is an integer.

   (D) $P \times B$ is always an even integer.

13. A recycling machine breaks down computers and uses the parts to manufacture widgets. Its results are represented in a table.

| Computer(s) Recycled | Widgets Manufactured |
|---|---|
| 1 | $\frac{17}{3}$ |
| 3 | ? |
| 5 | $\frac{77}{3}$ |

   Based on the table, how many widgets will the machine create when it recycles three computers?

   (A) $\frac{32}{3}$

   (B) 15

   (C) $\frac{47}{3}$

   (D) 17

14. If it takes 3 people 2 minutes to move 8 flagstones, how many people are required to move 16 flagstones in 3 minutes?

   (A) 4

   (B) 6

   (C) 12

   (D) 14

15. Timmy writes $w$ words in a notebook on his first day. He writes again on the second day, adding 100% to the total number of words in his notebook. At the end of the week, he erases 50% of all the words written. How many words remain in his notebook?

   (A) $\frac{w}{2}$

   (B) $w$

   (C) $2w$

   (D) $4w$

16. Lorna rolls a six-sided number cube, labelled 1-6, twice. If she subtracts the value of her second roll from the value of her first, what is the probability that the difference will equal 3?

   (A) $\frac{1}{36}$

   (B) $\frac{1}{18}$

   (C) $\frac{1}{12}$

   (D) $\frac{1}{2}$

*Go on to the next page* ➡

17. The number of cars passing through an intersection during a five week period is shown below.

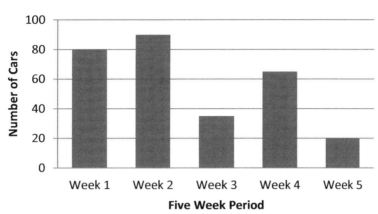

**Number of Cars at an Intersection**

Which of the following statements for this period is true?

(A) The mode number of cars at the intersection for the five week period is 55

(B) The median number of cars over the 5 week period is equal to the number of cars during week 3

(C) Over the course of the 5 week period, the range of the number of cars at the intersection was 70

(D) The number of cars steadily diminished over the course of the 5 week period

---

18. Two lines are graphed.

**Line A**

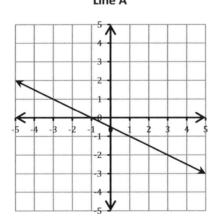

**Line B**

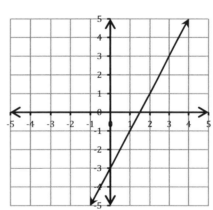

Which of the following statements is true?

(A) Line A is parallel to line B.

(B) Line A is perpendicular to line B.

(C) Line A is tangential to line B.

(D) Line A and line B both have negative slopes.

*Go on to the next page* ➜

19. Chen's backyard is one fourth the size of his neighbor's backyard. Both yards are squares. Chen is installing a picket fence along the border of his backyard. If the cost of installing a picket fence around Chen's neighbor's yard was $900, what is the cost of installing a picket fence around Chen's yard?

(A) $275

(B) $450

(C) $900

(D) $1800

20. A machine generates parts following the pattern shown in the table.

| Number of Hours of Production | Number of Parts Created |
|:---:|:---:|
| 2 | 3 |
| 4 | 9 |
| 6 | 27 |

How many hours of production are required for the machine to produce 81 parts?

(A) 7

(B) 8

(C) 9

(D) 12

21. Two nets are shown.

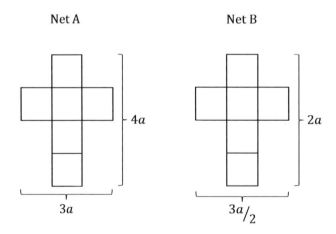

Note: *Figures not drawn to scale.*

When both nets are folded into three-dimensional objects, what will be the difference of the volume of object A minus the volume of object B?

(A) $\frac{a^3}{8}$

(B) $\frac{7}{8}a^3$

(C) $a^3$

(D) $8a^3$

*Go on to the next page* ➡

## PART TWO – QUANTITATIVE COMPARISONS

**Directions:** Using the information given in each question, compare the quantity in column A to the quantity in Column B. All questions in Part Two have these answer choices:

(A) The quantity in Column A is greater.

(B) The quantity in Column B is greater.

(C) The two quantities are equal.

(D) The relationship cannot be determined from the information given.

|  | Column A | Column B |
|---|---|---|
| 22. | $(5^1 - 1^5)^3$ | 125 |

A student graphs the line $3y = \frac{x}{2} + 3$

|  | Column A | Column B |
|---|---|---|
| 23. | The slope of the line | The y-intercept of the line divided by 6 |

A shaded rectangle is placed within a square as shown.

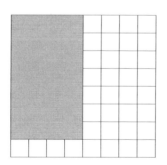

*Note: The area of each square grid is equal to 1.*

|  | Column A | Column B |
|---|---|---|
| 24. | The non-shaded area remaining in the square | 45 |

In Greentown every coin weighs 1 ounce regardless of its value. A shopkeeper in Greentown has $2.35 in her cash register, in quarters, dimes, and nickels.

*One quarter = $0.25, one dime = $0.10, one nickel = $0.05*

|  | Column A | Column B |
|---|---|---|
| 25. | The minimum weight possible of the coins in the shopkeeper's cash register | 8 ounces |

An object with eight equal sides, numbered 1-8, is rolled twice and the results are recorded.

|  | Column A | Column B |
|---|---|---|
| 26. | The probability that the sum of the rolls is equal to 15 | $\frac{3}{64}$ |

A triangle has a hypotenuse that is 5 inches long and a leg that is 4 inches long.

|  | Column A | Column B |
|---|---|---|
| 27. | The perimeter of the triangle in inches | 13 |

*Go on to the next page* ➡

---

**ANSWER CHOICES FOR ALL QUESTIONS ON THIS PAGE:**

(A) The quantity in Column A is greater.

(B) The quantity in Column B is greater.

(C) The two quantities are equal.

(D) The relationship cannot be determined from the information given.

---

Roland has 6 peaches, 9 grapes, and 5 apples. He randomly selects 1 peach, 1 grape, and 1 apple.

| Column A | Column B |
|---|---|
| 28. The probability that Roland will select a white peach, a green grape, and a red apple | $\dfrac{1}{270}$ |

---

One bag of marbles provides enough marbles for 5 kids.

| Column A | Column B |
|---|---|
| 29. The number of bags of marbles needed for 105 kids | The number of kids provided for with $4\frac{2}{5}$ bags of marbles |

---

The cost of a pencil is always 10% greater than the cost of an eraser.

| Column A | Column B |
|---|---|
| 30. The cost of a pencil if the cost of an eraser decreases by 10% | The original cost of an eraser |

---

| Column A | Column B |
|---|---|
| 31. The slope of the line perpendicular to the line with coordinates of $(-3,3)$ and $(3,-3)$ | 1 |

---

A sample of students is randomly selected from two classrooms. Their weekly study habits are surveyed.

| Classroom | English | History |
|---|---|---|
| Percent of classroom surveyed | 40% | 25% |
| People who study 1-5 hours per week | 10 | 20 |
| People who study 6+ hours per week | 25 | 10 |

| Column A | Column B |
|---|---|
| 32. The predicted number of people who study 6+ hours per week for the entire English class | The predicted number of people who study 1-5 hours per week for the entire History class |

*Go on to the next page* ➡

**ANSWER CHOICES FOR ALL QUESTIONS ON THIS PAGE:**

(A) The quantity in Column A is greater.
(B) The quantity in Column B is greater.
(C) The two quantities are equal.
(D) The relationship cannot be determined from the information given.

|  | Column A | Column B |
|---|---|---|
| 33. | Distance A | Distance A |

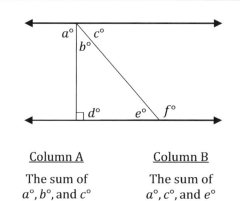

A deck of cards has 52 cards in total. There are 4 aces, 12 face cards, and 36 number cards. One card is picked and then replaced in the deck. The deck is shuffled and one more card is picked.

|  | Column A | Column B |
|---|---|---|
| 34. | The probability of picking two number cards | $\dfrac{1}{2}$ |

|  | Column A | Column B |
|---|---|---|
| 35. | $\dfrac{\sqrt{81}-3}{5-\sqrt{1+2\times 2^2}}$ | $-3$ |

|  | Column A | Column B |
|---|---|---|
| 36. | The sum of $a^\circ$, $b^\circ$, and $c^\circ$ | The sum of $a^\circ$, $c^\circ$, and $e^\circ$ |

William is running across the Port Mann Bridge, which is 4,200 feet long, He stops at four locations on the bridge to take pictures. The distance from the beginning of the bridge to each of these points is calculated in the table below.

| Stops Across the Port Mann Bridge | |
|---|---|
| **Stops on the Bridge** | **Distance from the Beginning of the Bridge** |
| A | 1,530 feet |
| B | 2,115 feet |
| C | 3,500 feet |
| D | 3,615 feet |

|  | Column A | Column B |
|---|---|---|
| 37. | The distance from William's *D* stop to the end of the bridge | The distance from William's *A* stop to William's *B* stop on the bridge |

**STOP. Do not go on until told to do so.**

**STOP**

# Section 3
# Reading Comprehension

This section contains six short reading passages. Each passage is followed by six questions based on its content. Answer the questions following each passage on the basis of what is <u>stated</u> or <u>implied</u> in that passage. You may write in your test booklet.

STOP. Do not go on
until told to do so.

**STOP**

# RC

Questions 1–6

1　　　In 1959, scientists in the Soviet Union
2　who were interested in the process by which
3　wolves became domesticated dogs initiated a
4　breeding experiment using silver foxes. The
5　experiment was led by Dmitri Belyaev, a
6　Russian scientist and academian.

7　　　Belyaev believed that in the ancestral
8　past of dogs, wolves with less fear of humans
9　were more likely to live near them and eat
10　scraps of their food. These wolves, he thought,
11　must have interbred, passing down their
12　tolerance of humans to their descendants, who
13　eventually became domestic dogs. To mimic
14　this process, he acquired a population of silver
15　foxes and bred only those that had "low flight
16　distance"—that is, the ones that he could get
17　quite close to before they ran away from him.

18　　　Since behavior is rooted in biology, by
19　choosing foxes that behaved in a certain way,
20　Belyaev was choosing foxes that shared certain
21　biological traits governing that behavior. After
22　only a few generations of foxes chosen for
23　breeding based on their "flight distance,"
24　Russian scientists observed notable changes in
25　the behavior of their fox population. By just the
26　tenth generation, Belyaev's foxes were not only
27　more comfortable around humans than their
28　wild forebears, but began actively seeking
29　human attention- whining to be petted, as dogs

30　do, and wagging their tails in response to a
31　human presence.

32　　　There were also changes in the physical
33　traits of the foxes. The color of their coats
34　changed from the regular gray, white, and
35　black pattern of wild silver foxes to a piebald
36　pattern, resembling that of many domestic
37　dogs. Many foxes were also born with floppy
38　ears, in contrast to the pointy ears of their wild
39　ancestors. These changes have been attributed
40　to various causes; some speculate that the
41　same physiological changes in the foxes which
42　resulted in the changes to their behavior also
43　cause changes to their physical appearance,
44　while others have suggested that they were
45　incidental changes, and simply occurred
46　because there was no longer the same selection
47　pressure as there had been in the wild to have
48　a particular coat pattern.

49　　　The descendants of Belyaev's original
50　experimental fox population are still alive
51　today, and the project continues; however,
52　since the collapse of the Soviet Union, the
53　project has had to seek alternative sources of
54　funding. One source of funding for the project
55　has been the sale of some foxes as pets, and it is
56　conceivable that one day owning a domestic
57　fox may be as commonplace as owning a cat or
58　dog.

*Go on to the next page* ➜

1.  This passage answers all of the following questions EXCEPT which one?

    (A) During which year did Belyaev begin his silver fox experiment?

    (B) What did Belyaev believe was the process by which wolves became dogs?

    (C) Why did Belyaev choose to use silver foxes for his experiment?

    (D) Are there any differences between the domesticated foxes and their wild ancestors?

2.  In line 45, the word "incidental" most nearly means

    (A) essential.

    (B) current.

    (C) chance.

    (D) pending.

3.  Based on information in the passage, we can conclude that if one of Belyaev's foxes ran away from him as soon as it noticed him, Belyaev would

    (A) sell it to the Department of Fur Animal Breeding.

    (B) not use it to breed the next generation of foxes.

    (C) lose track of it in the lab.

    (D) breed it with a fox that had equally high "flight" distance.

4.  This passage suggests that Belyaev's breeding experiment

    (A) has created foxes that are somewhat dog-like.

    (B) is unfair to the foxes.

    (C) is almost over.

    (D) failed to produce significant results.

5.  Which best describes the way the passage is organized?

    (A) An argument is given, followed by a counterargument.

    (B) A theory examined and then is disproven by contradicting evidence.

    (C) A hypothesis is described, followed by a verifying experiment.

    (D) A problem is presented but no solution is given.

6.  According to the passage, the causes of the physical changes in Belyaev's foxes

    (A) were a direct result of the changes observed in their behavior.

    (B) cannot be determined by scientists, because the original foxes are too different from their ancestors.

    (C) are not precisely known, although there are several possible explanations.

    (D) will eventually cause Belyaev's foxes to become indistinguishable from dogs.

*Go on to the next page* ➜

Questions 7-12

1       Sometimes geography can affect
2 language in surprising ways.  On the island of La
3 Gomera—one of the Canary Islands off the cost
4 of West Africa— deep ravines separate slivers of
5 mountain terrain and the people who live on it.
6 The ravines are too deep to be easily crossed,
7 and too wide for shouted words to carry across
8 them clearly. But the inhabitants of La Gomera
9 developed a unique way of communicating
10 across these deep ravines: an amazing whistled
11 speech called Silbo Gomero.  The sound of the
12 whistles can be heard clearly across the ravines,
13 allowing people to communicate in spite of the
14 long distances between them. This whistled
15 language is indigenous to the island, and its
16 existence has been documented since Roman
17 times.
18       The original whistled language was
19 developed by the original inhabitants of the
20 island, the Guanches. Though little is known
21 about the original language spoken by the
22 Guanches prior to Silbo Gomero, linguists
23 believe that it must have been very simple for it
24 to have been adopted into a whistled language.
25 Once the Guanches developed Silbo Gomero, it
26 spread to many other islands in the Canaries,
27 including el Hierro, Tenerife, and Gran Canaria.

28       The modern language of Silbo Gomero is
29 actually a dialect of Spanish. The Guanches
30 originally converted the sounds of their own
31 language into whistle-sounds, but eventually
32 applied that practice to the language of the
33 Spanish colonists. It is this whistled language
34 that the Spaniards themselves adopted.
35 Someone who speaks Silbo Gomero is often
36 called a silbador, or "whistler."
37       Silbo Gomero was adopted by the
38 Spanish settlers in the 16th century and
39 survived after the Guanches' population
40 dwindled. But with the advent of more modern
41 forms of communication, a simple telephone
42 could allow someone to communicate with
43 others across the ravines, or anywhere else,
44 without the aid of a whistled language. What was
45 once a language of geographical necessity had
46 become a cultural artifact.
47 People no longer needed to learn Silbo
48 Gomero, and so fewer people did- and this
49 unique means of communication was threatened
50 with extinction at the dawn of the 21st century.
51 But, having determined that this one-of-a-kind
52 language was a piece of intangible cultural
53 heritage worth preserving, the local government
54 added it to the school curriculum.

*Go on to the next page* ➜

7. The primary subject of this passage is

   (A) the geography of La Gomera.

   (B) the Spanish occupation of the Canary Islands.

   (C) Silbo Gomero, the whistled language of La Gomera.

   (D) languages that involve whistling and other non-vocal sounds.

8. In line 15, the word "indigenous" most nearly means

   (A) fashionable.

   (B) native.

   (C) ancient.

   (D) religious.

9. Silbo Gomero was developed by the inhabitants of La Gomera so they could

   (A) plot against the Spanish colonists.

   (B) communicate better in the local terrain.

   (C) communicate with Spanish settlers.

   (D) enhance La Gomera's unique culture.

10. It can be inferred that many modern speakers of Silbo Gomero

    (A) use it for coded communication.

    (B) also speak some of the original Guanches language.

    (C) learned the language for cultural reasons rather than as a necessity.

    (D) have little interest in preserving the language for future generations.

11. How did the original Spanish settlers acquire Silbo Gomero?

    (A) They learned it in the schools of La Gomera.

    (B) They were the original settlers of La Gomera and invented the language.

    (C) They picked up the whistled form of Spanish that the Guanches had invented.

    (D) They began whistling in order to communicate better with the Guanches.

12. It can be inferred that La Gomera's ravines

    (A) were detrimental to the family units of La Gomera

    (B) helped give rise to a new language

    (C) caused conflict among the inhabitants

    (D) confused the Spanish colonists

*Go on to the next page* ➡

Questions 13-18

The Paleozoic ocean was dominated by animals known as nautiloids. With over 2,500 species, these marine cephalopods were the main predators of the period, and were characterized by a tough external shell. In many species, the shell served not only as a form of protection, but also as a form of buoyancy control. The modern nautilus, for example—one of few surviving nautiloids—has a shell containing air-filled pockets, which help it to maintain neutral buoyancy in water. While there used to be many types of shell shapes and forms, today there is only the spiral-shaped shell of the modern nautilus.

Much of what we know about extinct nautiloids actually comes from studying the modern nautilus. As one of only a few species of nautiloids that is still around today, nautili share many characteristics with their extinct ancestors. For example, the modern nautilus is also a predator, using its beak-like jaws to feed on crustaceans. The modern nautilus also uses the same mechanism for movement as its ancestors: jet propulsion. When the nautilus wants to move in a certain direction, it points an interior funnel in the desired direction and expels water from it, propelling it forward. The combination of its air-filled pockets and jet propulsion allows the nautilus to move easily through the ocean.

Unlike the nautilus, many other modern cephalopods lack an external shell, but the shell usually isn't completely absent. Instead, modern cephalopods often possess an internal shell. In cuttlefish this shell is called the cuttlebone and, like the shell of the nautilus, contains gas-filled pockets that help the cuttlefish to maintain buoyancy. It is this cuttlebone that distinguishes cuttlefish from other squid species, which they closely resemble. Squid have lost their ancestral shells entirely over the course of their evolution; they now only have a pen, a small internal structure where muscles attach. Since they lack a shell with gas pockets, squid species must use other physical traits to maintain neutral buoyancy, such as producing internal liquid ammonia that is lighter than water.

*Go on to the next page* ➜

13. In this passage, the author's main purpose is to

    (A) entertain.

    (B) speculate.

    (C) inform.

    (D) inquire.

14. Nautilus shells contain gas-filled pockets

    (A) for the storage of food.

    (B) for buoyancy control.

    (C) to eliminate waste.

    (D) for protection from predators.

15. In line 39, the word "distinguishes" most nearly means

    (A) differentiates.

    (B) honors.

    (C) poses.

    (D) outlines.

16. Based on the context of the passage, the word "cephalopod" (line 3) most likely refers to

    (A) any animal with a shell.

    (B) any marine predator.

    (C) a subset of nautiloids, some of which survive in the modern day.

    (D) a broader category of animals which includes the nautiloids.

17. It can be inferred from the passage that most nautiloids

    (A) possessed internal shells.

    (B) hunted other nautiloids.

    (C) are now extinct.

    (D) could not swim.

18. In line 27, the word "expels" most nearly means

    (A) tricks.

    (B) entraps.

    (C) ejects.

    (D) inhales.

*Go on to the next page* ➡

Questions 19-24

1　　　The air out there was different from
2　home; the air of home was cool and humid, but
3　here the hot, dry air pulled the moisture from
4　your skin.  The trees were different, too –
5　stunted things, with short, gnarly bodies, and
6　only sparse needles for their foliage.  The
7　ground was parched, and the rocks were not
8　the familiar greys and greens of the moist and
9　mossy boulders of home, but yellow and
10　orange, and dotted here and there with lichens
11　of black, and white, and red.  We hiked for a
12　little more than an hour in that alien landscape,
13　and then we came to the cliff which had been
14　our destination.
15　　　We stood together at the top of the cliff,
16　enjoying the gentle breeze. A hawk hovered in
17　the distance, riding the updrafts. In the vast
18　expanse before us, the only sound was the
19　wind. We spoke in whispers, and she said, "It's
20　so quiet."
21　　　"I know," came my reply. Somehow those
22　words didn't seem like enough, so I added, "I
23　bet if I shouted, it would echo for miles."
24　　　Turning to me with a mischievous
25　expression, she asked, "Why don't you?"
26　　　I thought about it. Why not? It didn't
27　seem like there would be anything wrong with

28　shouting, and there was nobody around who
29　would stop me or complain that I had. I also
30　thought that it could be fun to make such a
31　sound, and to hear my voice echo back from the
32　canyon. But the most pressing reason, although
33　I am ashamed to admit it, was that it seemed as
34　though I had been challenged. And so, with my
35　ego at stake, I resolved to let out a resounding
36　cry and make the canyon echo with my voice.
37　But as I took a breath, something restrained
38　me.
39　　　There was a sacred quality in the vast
40　depth of the silence, and it affected me. An
41　aversion to blasphemy welled up inside me,
42　and I could not compel myself to shatter the
43　peace of the moment. I exhaled quietly, and as
44　my breath mingled with the passing breeze I
45　confessed, "I don't think I should. It seems
46　wrong."
47　　　"I know," she said, and we stood there a
48　while longer without speaking. Eventually, we
49　left the silence of the cliff and headed back to
50　the trail; but the silence never left me—not
51　entirely. In a peaceful moment, I can still hear
52　it—and I still can't bring myself to break it.

*Go on to the next page* ➡

19. Why did the narrator refrain from shouting?

    (A) He didn't want to disturb a peaceful moment.

    (B) He was embarrassed to think that someone might hear him.

    (C) He was afraid that he would fail to live up to a challenge.

    (D) He was concerned that he might frighten the hawk.

20. Based on the context of the passage, "riding the updrafts" (line 17) probably means that the hawk was

    (A) hunting its prey

    (B) diving from the sky

    (C) calling to its mate

    (D) gliding on the wind

21. What does the narrator mean when he says "the silence never left me" (line 60)?

    (A) He was struck deaf.

    (B) He is able to ignore loud noises by remembering the silence.

    (C) He is still affected by the memory of the silence.

    (D) He is now attracted to quiet places.

22. In line 12, the word "alien" most nearly means

    (A) beautiful.

    (B) extraterrestrial.

    (C) unfamiliar.

    (D) deserted.

23. Which word best describes the narrator's attitude towards the silence of the cliff?

    (A) reverent

    (B) resentful

    (C) submissive

    (D) confused

24. It can be inferred that the narrator

    (A) hates hiking.

    (B) only went to the cliff to impress his friend.

    (C) is not originally from the area he is describing.

    (D) is scared of loud noises.

*Go on to the next page* ➡

Questions 25-30

1     Falconry—the practice of hunting with
2    trained birds of prey—was for many centuries
3    one of the main sports of the richer classes. The
4    time, money, and hunting space that the sport
5    required essentially ensured that only the
6    noble classes would be able to participate.
7    Since many more efficient methods of hunting
8    have always existed, falconry has probably
9    always been considered pure sport rather than
10   a practical method of hunting. In this way,
11   falconry became a status symbol for wealth and
12   nobility; the lower classes could not afford to
13   pursue inefficient food-gathering practices.
14     Falconry is quite ancient. It was
15   introduced into England from continental
16   Europe about A.D. 860, and from that time to
17   the middle of the 17th century, falconry excited
18   more enthusiasm than any other English sport,
19   even fox-hunting. Stringent laws, notably
20   during the reigns of William the Conqueror,
21   Edward III, Henry VIII and Elizabeth I, were
22   passed from time to time to regulate falconry.
23   Different species of falcon and hawk were

24   allotted to men according to rank and station—
25   for instance, to the emperor the eagle and
26   vulture, to royalty the jerfalcons, to an earl the
27   peregrine, to a yeoman the goshawk, and to a
28   servant the useless kestrel.
29     Falconry remained very popular until the
30   17th century, at which point guns became the
31   preferred tool for hunting. Falconry continued
32   to decline until it had a sudden resurgence
33   during the late 19th and early 20th centuries. It
34   was during this resurgence that falconry came
35   to North America, where Colonel R. Luff
36   Meredith helped to establish falconry as an
37   American sport.
38     In modern times, technology and
39   advances in veterinary medicine have
40   expanded the range of the sport. For example,
41   by attaching radio transmitters to the birds,
42   falconers can pursue prey and engage in styles
43   of flight that previously would have resulted in
44   the loss of the falconry bird. Modern veterinary
45   practices have also extended the life span of the
46   birds.

*Go on to the next page* ➡

25. The main purpose of this passage is to

    (A) criticize the inefficient practice of using falcons to capture game.

    (B) provide some historical information about falconry.

    (C) argue that falconry is the best sport.

    (D) rank varieties of falcon and hawk.

26. As it is used in the passage, "pure sport" (line 9) is probably

    (A) a sport that only the wealthy engage in.

    (B) a sport that is favored and regulated by British monarchs.

    (C) a sport that is engaged in for entertainment and not out of necessity.

    (D) a very popular sport.

27. According to the passage, falconry most likely spread to England

    (A) in the middle of the 17th century.

    (B) during the reign of Queen Elizabeth.

    (C) around A.D. 860.

    (D) in order to help identify rank.

28. The passage suggests that fox-hunting

    (A) has been extremely popular in England.

    (B) is a cruel sport.

    (C) is the most effective way of capturing game.

    (D) is older than falconry.

29. Which of these puts the falcons and hawks in correct order of rank, from lowest to highest?

    (A) kestrel, vulture, goshawk, peregrine

    (B) eagle, peregrine, kestrel, jerfalcon

    (C) eagle, vulture, goshawk, peregrine

    (D) kestrel, peregrine, jerfalcon, eagle

30. In line 19, the word "stringent" most nearly means

    (A) flexible.

    (B) restrictive.

    (C) out-dated.

    (D) unnecessary.

*Go on to the next page* ➡

Questions 31-36

1      Rapid industrialization in China over
2 past decades has led to dramatic increases in
3 pollution. China's industrial revolution did not
4 begin until the middle of the 20th century, far
5 after western industrialization, but it occurred
6 at a pace that far exceeded that of the western
7 process. As a result, China leapt into the
8 industrial world in only a single generation.
9 While this process brought rapid economic
10 growth, it also left China with a large industrial
11 sector and few environmental protections.
12      Chinese environmental officials are now
13 raising the same concern that has worried
14 environmental activists for years: that severe
15 pollution has led to a rise of so-called "cancer
16 villages." Activists and some journalists have
17 been using this term for several years to
18 describe villages with high cancer rates which
19 are located close to contaminated waterways,
20 industrial parks, or construction sites.
21      A report issued this week by China's
22 Environment Ministry specifically mentions
23 "cancer villages," blaming the problem on
24 severe water and air pollution. It is thought to
25 be one of the first times the term has been used

26 by government officials. Official statistics
27 indicate that China has about 1,700 water
28 pollution accidents each year and that up to 40
29 percent of the country's rivers are seriously
30 polluted.
31      Water researcher Zhao Feihong at the
32 Beijing Healthcare Association said last month
33 that of the more than 100 rivers in Beijing only
34 two or three can be used for tap water. "The
35 rest of the rivers, if they have not dried up, are
36 polluted by discharge," she said. She felt that
37 the increased reporting from government
38 officials on water pollution was a positive
39 development, but that citizens would benefit
40 from even more frequent disclosure of any
41 environmental issues.
42      Air pollution is also a serious concern.
43 During the last week of January, smog hung
44 over cities and towns from Liaoning in the
45 north to as far south as Guangdong, and air
46 pollution reached unhealthy levels for long
47 periods of time. Chinese officials blamed
48 industrial activity, construction, and the
49 widespread use of coal for heat.

*Go on to the next page* ➡

31. It can be inferred from the passage that heavy pollution

    (A) occurs mainly around small villages.

    (B) causes an increase in cancer rates.

    (C) is only a problem in China.

    (D) increases the demand for heating coal.

32. The passage was most likely taken from

    (A) a newspaper.

    (B) an encyclopedia.

    (C) a diary.

    (D) a letter.

33. The passage discusses all of the following as possible causes for high rates of cancer in "cancer villages" EXCEPT

    (A) water pollution.

    (B) pollutants from construction.

    (C) unhealthy lifestyle choices.

    (D) air pollution.

34. What would the author most likely discuss next?

    (A) the Chinese medical system

    (B) the various ministries in the Chinese government

    (C) why some rivers cannot be used for tap water

    (D) possible solutions for the problem of "cancer villages"

35. The primary purpose of the passage is to

    (A) recount China's industrial revolution.

    (B) discuss China's pollution and its effects on health.

    (C) describe Beijing's polluted rivers.

    (D) explain the role of China's environmental officials.

36. According to the passage, Chinese environmental officials are discussing concerns about "cancer villages"

    (A) long after environmental groups noticed the problem.

    (B) together with environmental activists and village leaders.

    (C) only after intense pressure by protest groups.

    (D) in hopes of drawing attention to a new and surprising problem.

STOP. Do not go on until told to do so.

**STOP**

# SECTION 4

# Mathematics Achievement

Each question is followed by four suggested answers. Read each question and then decide which one of the four suggested answers is best.

Find the row of spaces on your answer document that has the same number as the question. In this row, mark the space having the same letter as the answer you have chosen. You may write in your test booklet.

---

SAMPLE QUESTION:

Sample Answer

If $a = 3$, what is the value $a^2 + (3 \times 4) \div 6$?

Ⓐ ● Ⓒ Ⓓ

(A) 3.5

(B) 11

(C) 14.5

(D) 20

The correct answer is 11, so circle B is darkened.

---

STOP. Do not go on until told to do so.

**STOP**

1.  Machines $A$ and $B$ produce boxes at the same rate, but machine $A$ breaks down three times quicker than machine $B$. If machine $B$ can produce $P$ boxes before it breaks down, approximately how many boxes can machine $A$ produce before it breaks down?

    (A) $25\% \times P$

    (B) $33\% \times P$

    (C) $100\% \times P$

    (D) $300\% \times P$

2.  A cube has a side length of $x$ and is cut into four pieces diagonally as shown.

    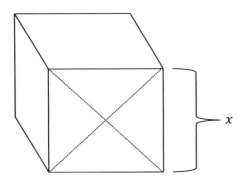

    What is the volume of one of these four sections?

    (A) $\frac{x^2}{4}$

    (B) $\frac{x^3}{4}$

    (C) $x^2$

    (D) $x^3$

3.  If $A = \cap \times 3$ and $Q = A \div 3$, which expression below is correct?

    (A) $Q = \cap$

    (B) $Q = A \times 3$

    (C) $A = Q \times \cap$

    (D) $A = Q \div 3$

4.  At 80% capacity, five houses can hold 100 people. How many people can 3 houses hold at 100% capacity?

    (A) 50

    (B) 75

    (C) 100

    (D) 125

5.  A mother needs to buy 2 boxes of baby wipes at \$9.00 each. There is a fee of \$5.00 for door-to-door delivery and a tax of 15% calculated after the delivery cost has been added. What is the total cost of the order?

    (A) \$20.70

    (B) \$23.00

    (C) \$25.70

    (D) \$26.45

6.  If $A = \pi r^2$ and $r = {}^d/_2$ than what is $A$ when $d$ is 4 centimeters?

    (A) $\frac{1}{4}\pi$ cm$^2$

    (B) $\frac{1}{2}\pi$ cm$^2$

    (C) $4\pi$ cm$^2$

    (D) $16\pi$ cm$^2$

7.  What is the difference of $6254 - 8926$?

    (A) -2672

    (B) -2662

    (C) -2640

    (D) -2336

*Go on to the next page* ➡

# MA

*Questions 8-9 use the following graph.*

The number of births in Newville from 2009 to 2013 is shown on the graph below.

**Births in Newville**

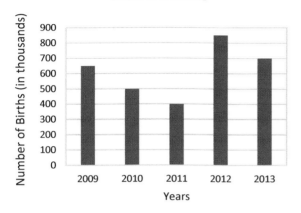

8.  What is the median number of births per year in Newville?

    (A) 400,000

    (B) 500,000

    (C) 650,000

    (D) 700,000

9.  What is the range of the number of births per year in Newville?

    (A) 4,500

    (B) 50,000

    (C) 300,000

    (D) 450,000

10. Norman is rolling two six-sided number cubes, numbered 1-6, and then multiplying the numbers together. What is the probability that the product of his rolls will be 12?

    (A) $\frac{1}{36}$

    (B) $\frac{1}{18}$

    (C) $\frac{1}{9}$

    (D) $\frac{1}{6}$

11. Giovanni writes one note for each of his two friends in the first period of school. His friends, in turn, each write notes for two of their friends in the second period. If this pattern continues until the fourth period of the school day, how many notes will be written in total?

    (A) 2

    (B) 16

    (C) 30

    (D) 64

12. If $g \times a = d$ and $e = \frac{g}{b} \div a$, which expression is equal to $d$?

    (A) $\frac{1}{b}$

    (B) $ga^2$

    (C) $eba^2$

    (D) $\frac{g}{ba}$

13. If $6A = 4\mathbf{O}$ and $\mathbf{O} = -3$, what is the value of $A$?

    (A) $-12$

    (B) $-2$

    (C) $\frac{3}{2}$

    (D) 4

*Go on to the next page* ➡

14. Figure *CD* is made from joining shapes *D* and *C*.

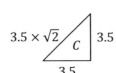 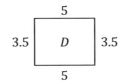 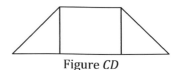

If *C* is a triangle and *D* is a rectangle, what is the perimeter of Figure *CD*?

(A) $23.5 + 3.5 \times \sqrt{2}$

(B) $17 + 7 \times \sqrt{2}$

(C) $31 + 7 \times \sqrt{2}$

(D) $34 + 7 \times \sqrt{2}$

---

15. If the ratio of $Y : 4$ is the same as $132 : 44$, what is the value of $Y$?

(A) 8

(B) 12

(C) 16

(D) 32

16. James bought a box of 72 cookies. He first gave $1/2$ of the cookies to his brother, and then gave $1/3$ of the remaining cookies to his sister. If James gives 4 cookies to his mother, how many cookies will he have remaining in the box?

(A) 4

(B) 8

(C) 12

(D) 20

17. If a trapezoid has a base, *b*, of 2 centimeters, a top, *t*, of 6 centimeters, and a height, *h*, of 2 centimeters, what is the area of the trapezoid? Note: Area of a trapezoid $= \frac{1}{2}(b + t)h$

(A) 8 cm²

(B) 10 cm²

(C) 12 cm²

(D) 16 cm²

18. Fang is playing in a video game tournament, and has lost 3 games. Players receive a score of 0 for each game they lose, and a score of 1 for each game they win. With 5 games remaining, what is the minimum number of games that Fang must win if he wants his median score to be 1?

(A) 0

(B) 3

(C) 4

(D) 5

*Go on to the next page* ➡

19. Jarred has a bin of 9 socks with 3 red socks, 4 blue socks, 1 black sock, and 1 white sock. He selects one sock, puts it back and then selects one more. What is the probability that he will pick one red sock and then one black sock?

    (A) $\frac{1}{27}$

    (B) $\frac{1}{9}$

    (C) $\frac{1}{3}$

    (D) $\frac{4}{9}$

20. Which of the following is closest to $0.167 \times 19$?

    (A) $\frac{1}{3}$ of 10

    (B) $\frac{1}{6}$ of 40

    (C) $\frac{1}{16}$ of 40

    (D) $\frac{1}{3}$ of 20

21. The figure below shows a square with a side length of 5 inches and two identical rectangles whose areas are each 10 inches².

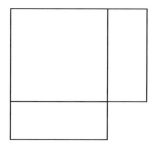

    What is the perimeter of the entire figure?

    (A) 18 inches

    (B) 28 inches

    (C) 38 inches

    (D) 48 inches

22. Carl can drink 2 cups of milk in 2 minutes. If the rest of Carl's family can drink at the same rate, how many cups can the family of four drink in 3 minutes?

    (A) 2

    (B) 3

    (C) 6

    (D) 12

23. There are 48 butterflies in a box, and boxes of butterflies are stacked in a warehouse. If the ratio of boxes in the warehouse to butterflies in a box is 1:8, how many butterflies are in the whole warehouse?

    (A) 44

    (B) 88

    (C) 288

    (D) 384

24. In the figure below, a triangle is on top of two squares with side lengths of 6.

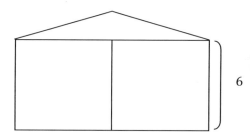

    If the height of the entire figure is 10, what is its area?

    (A) 48

    (B) 60

    (C) 96

    (D) 120

*Go on to the next page* ➡

*Questions 25-26 refer to the chart below:*

John runs a 10 mile race. His time per mile as recorded at the end of each mile is shown on a line graph.

**Race Time Per Mile**

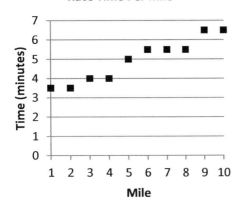

25. How many minutes does it take John to run the entire race?

(A) 6.5

(B) 48.5

(C) 49.5

(D) 50.0

26. Which of the following statements is true?

(A) John's average (mean) time per mile was greater than his median time per mile.

(B) John's median time was between 5 minutes and 5.5 minutes.

(C) John's speed increased over the course of the race.

(D) The mode for John's time per mile was 5 minutes.

27. A cement truck carries 216 cubic yards of mixed cement. A hole with a volume of 1620 cubic feet needs to be filled with cement. If the cement truck pours at a rate of 20 cubic yards per minute, how many minutes will it take for the pool to be entirely full?

1 cubic yard=27 cubic feet

(A) 1 minute

(B) 2 minutes

(C) 3 minutes

(D) 4 minutes

28. On a set of blueprints for a house, 4 cm is equal to 3 meters. If the height of the house measures 12 cm on the blueprints, what is the actual height of the house?

(A) 6 meters

(B) 9 meters

(C) 16 meters

(D) 32 meters

29. Which is equivalent to the following expression?

$$3 \times \left(\frac{1}{2} - \frac{1}{3}\right) + \frac{3x}{12} = y$$

(A) $x = -2(2y + 1)$

(B) $x = -\frac{y}{4} + \frac{1}{2}$

(C) $x = 4\left(y - \frac{7}{6}\right)$

(D) $x = \frac{3}{2} + \frac{y}{4}$

*Go on to the next page* ➡

30. A flag pole is one third the height of an adjacent building, which is 16 meters tall. If a sapling is two eighths of the height of the flag pole, then how tall is it?

    (A) $\frac{1}{3}$ meters

    (B) $\frac{2}{3}$ meters

    (C) 1 meter

    (D) $\frac{4}{3}$ meters

31. What is the smallest prime factor of 143?

    (A) 1

    (B) 7

    (C) 11

    (D) 13

32. The number of bicycles produced during the months of June to November is shown on a graph.

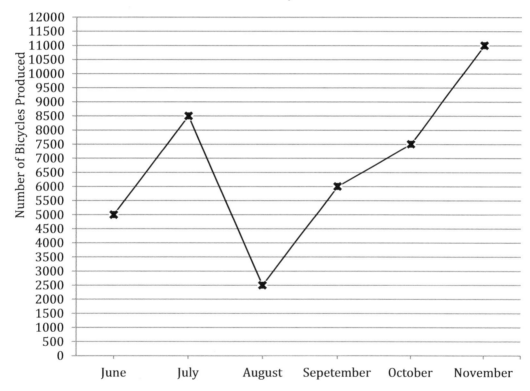

BICYCLES PRODUCED FROM JUNE TO NOVEMBER

Which month showed the greatest percent increase in production from the month before?

(A) July

(B) September

(C) October

(D) November

*Go on to the next page* ➡

33. The sum of three consecutive integers is -9. What is the largest of the three integers?

    (A) -9
    (B) -6
    (C) -4
    (D) -2

34. If $\frac{\triangleleft}{3} = \square \times 4$ and $\square = 2$, what is the value of $\triangleleft$?

    (A) $\frac{1}{12}$
    (B) $\frac{1}{6}$
    (C) $\frac{1}{3}$
    (D) 24

35. Jordan has to decide between 5 different suits, 6 different hats, and 2 different pairs of socks. If he wants to select one outfit that has one suit, one hat, and one pair of socks, how many choices does he have?

    (A) 13
    (B) 30
    (C) 60
    (D) 120

36. For any numbers $l$ and $k$, $\frac{l}{k} \times 2 = k + 4$. Which expression represents the value of $l \times 3$?

    (A) $k \times 3$
    (B) $\frac{3k^2}{2} + 6k$
    (C) $\frac{3}{2}(k^2 + 2k)$
    (D) $3(5k)$

37. What is the closest value to $\sqrt{78}$?

    (A) 6
    (B) 7
    (C) 8
    (D) 9

38. 40% of $c$ is equal to $r$. What is 15% of $r$, in terms of $c$?

    (A) $0.006c$
    (B) $0.06c$
    (C) $0.325c$
    (D) $0.75c$

39. Jarred is rolling one six-sided number cube, numbered 1-6, twice. If the first number rolled is the numerator and the second number rolled is the denominator, what is probability that the quotient of the two rolls is 2?

    (A) $\frac{1}{36}$
    (B) $\frac{1}{18}$
    (C) $\frac{1}{12}$
    (D) $\frac{1}{9}$

**STOP. Do not go on until told to do so.** STOP

40. Rashmi works for a computer company. The profit for the company, $P$, relates to the number of jobs, $J$, that she completes as per the equation below:

$$P = J \times \$200 - \$400$$

What does this formula indicate?

(A) For every project completed, the company gains $400.

(B) If no projects are completed, the company will not pay Rashmi.

(C) If Rashmi completes more than two projects for the company, the company will have a positive profit.

(D) Regardless of how many projects Rashmi completes, the company will gain profit from her work.

41. The circumference of a circle touches the points (-1,-1) and (1,1) on a graph.

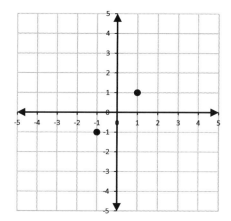

What is one other point on this graph that the circumference of this circle touches?

(A) (1,-2)

(B) (-1,2)

(C) (1,0)

(D) (1,-1)

42. In the coordinate plane below, if $\triangle ABC$ were reflected along the $x$ axis, what would be the new coordinates for point $B$?

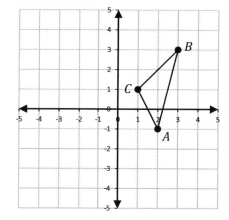

(A) (3,-3)

(B) (-3,3)

(C) (3,-2)

(D) (3,2)

43. $A = \dfrac{2}{(5-2)} \times \dfrac{4}{5} \times 3 - \dfrac{2(3+2)}{4}$

What is the value of $A$?

(A) $-\dfrac{17}{5}$

(B) $-\dfrac{9}{10}$

(C) $\dfrac{9}{10}$

(D) $\dfrac{23}{10}$

*Go on to the next page* ➡

44. Sasha is driving to Washington from Portland and must pass through four towns on her drive. The distances between each of these towns is represented in the table below.

| DISTANCE BETWEEN TOWNS | |
|---|---|
| Portland to Evanston | 805 miles |
| Evanston to Rawlins | 208 miles |
| Rawlins to Davenport | 944 miles |
| Davenport to Washington | 843 miles |

If Sasha is halfway between Rawlins and Davenport, which of the following is true?

(A) The total distance from Portland to Washington is 3,000 miles

(B) Sasha has 1,787 miles remaining to drive to Washington

(C) The distance from Portland to Rawlins is half the distance from Portland to Washington

(D) Sasha has driven more than half of the trip from Portland to Washington.

45. A trading card costs $3.00, and there is a 15% tax. Yun has a ten dollar bill and a five dollar bill. If Yun purchases three trading cards, how much change will he receive?

(A) $3.00

(B) $4.65

(C) $5.10

(D) $6.00

46. Continue the pattern:

(A)

(B)

(C)

(D)

47. Mama's Popcorn is estimating its profitability from sales. The cost to produce one bag of popcorn is $1.50 and each bag of popcorn sells for $4.00. The cost to set up in the market is $250.00 per day. If Mama's Popcorn expects to sell 150 bags of popcorn in a day, what will be its profit for the day after it pays all expenses?

(A) $125.00

(B) $225.00

(C) $250.00

(D) $600.00

**STOP. Do not go on until told to do so.**

# Essay Topic Sheet

The directions for the Essay portion of the ISEE are printed in the box below. Use the pre-lined pages on pages 170-171 for this part of the Practice Test.

---

You will have 30 minutes to plan and write an essay on the topic printed on the other side of this page. **Do not write on another topic. An essay on another topic is not acceptable.**

The essay is designed to give you an opportunity to show how well you can write. You should try to express your thoughts clearly. How well you write is much more important than how much you write, but you need to say enough for a reader to understand what you mean.

You will probably want to write more than a short paragraph. You should also be aware that a copy of your essay will be sent to each school that will be receiving your test results. You are to write only in the appropriate section of the answer sheet. Please write or print so that your writing may be read by someone who is not familiar with your handwriting.

You may make notes and plan your essay on the reverse side of the page. Allow enough time to copy the final form onto your answer sheet. You must copy the essay topic onto your answer sheet, on page 170, in the box provided.

Please remember to write only the final draft of the essay on pages 170-171 of your answer sheet and to write it in blue or black pen. Again, you may use cursive writing or you may print. Only pages 170-171 will be sent to the schools.

---

*Directions continue on the next page.*

**REMINDER:** Please write this essay topic on the first few lines of the first page of your essay sheet.

**Essay Topic**

Tell us about someone who has had a major influence on the way that you think about the world, and explain how he or she has influenced your thinking.

- Only write on this essay question
- Only pages 170 and 171 will be sent to the schools
- Only write in blue or black pen

# NOTES

_____

_____

_____

_____

_____

_____

_____

_____

_____

_____

_____

_____

_____

_____

_____

_____

_____

_____

_____

_____

**Ivy Global**

# PRACTICE TEST 5

UPPER LEVEL

# HOW TO TAKE THIS PRACTICE TEST

To simulate an accurate testing environment, sit at a desk in a quiet location free of distractions—no TV, computers, phones, music, or noise—and clear your desk of all materials except pencils and erasers. Remember that no calculators, rulers, protractors, dictionaries, or other aids are allowed on the ISEE.

Give yourself the following amounts of time for each section:

| SECTION | SUBJECT | TIME LIMIT |
|---|---|---|
| 1 | Verbal Reasoning | 20 minutes |
| 2 | Quantitative Reasoning | 35 minutes |
| 5 minute break | | |
| 3 | Reading Comprehension | 35 minutes |
| 4 | Mathematics Achievement | 40 minutes |
| 5 minute break | | |
| 5 | Essay | 30 minutes |

Have an adult help you monitor your time, or use a watch and time yourself. Only give yourself the allotted time for each section; put your pencil down when your time is up.

Follow the instructions carefully. As you take your test, bubble your answers into the answer sheets provided. Use the test booklet as scratch paper for notes and calculations. Remember that you are not granted time at the end of a section to transfer your answers to the answer sheet, so you must do this as you go along.

When you are finished, check your answers against the answer keys provided. Then, score your exam using the directions at the end of the book.

Note: students with diagnosed learning disabilities who apply for testing with accommodations may receive extra time, or may be allowed to use certain assistive devices during the ISEE. For more information, visit http://erblearn.org/parents/admission/isee/accommodations.

# Ivy Global

# ISEE
## UPPER LEVEL TEST 1

---

**MARKING INSTRUCTIONS**

- Use a #2 or HB pencil only on pages 216 and 217.
- Use a ballpoint pen for your essay on pages 218 and 219.
- Make dark marks that completely fill the circle.
- Erase clearly any mark you wish to change.
- Make no stray marks on this form.
- Do not fold or crease this form.

| Correct Mark | Incorrect Marks |
|:---:|:---:|
| ● | ⊗ ◔ ✓ ◑ ↺ |

---

**1 VERBAL REASONING**

| | | |
|---|---|---|
| 1 Ⓐ Ⓑ Ⓒ Ⓓ | 15 Ⓐ Ⓑ Ⓒ Ⓓ | 29 Ⓐ Ⓑ Ⓒ Ⓓ |
| 2 Ⓐ Ⓑ Ⓒ Ⓓ | 16 Ⓐ Ⓑ Ⓒ Ⓓ | 30 Ⓐ Ⓑ Ⓒ Ⓓ |
| 3 Ⓐ Ⓑ Ⓒ Ⓓ | 17 Ⓐ Ⓑ Ⓒ Ⓓ | 31 Ⓐ Ⓑ Ⓒ Ⓓ |
| 4 Ⓐ Ⓑ Ⓒ Ⓓ | 18 Ⓐ Ⓑ Ⓒ Ⓓ | 32 Ⓐ Ⓑ Ⓒ Ⓓ |
| 5 Ⓐ Ⓑ Ⓒ Ⓓ | 19 Ⓐ Ⓑ Ⓒ Ⓓ | 33 Ⓐ Ⓑ Ⓒ Ⓓ |
| 6 Ⓐ Ⓑ Ⓒ Ⓓ | 20 Ⓐ Ⓑ Ⓒ Ⓓ | 34 Ⓐ Ⓑ Ⓒ Ⓓ **Lower Level Ends** |
| 7 Ⓐ Ⓑ Ⓒ Ⓓ | 21 Ⓐ Ⓑ Ⓒ Ⓓ | 35 Ⓐ Ⓑ Ⓒ Ⓓ |
| 8 Ⓐ Ⓑ Ⓒ Ⓓ | 22 Ⓐ Ⓑ Ⓒ Ⓓ | 36 Ⓐ Ⓑ Ⓒ Ⓓ |
| 9 Ⓐ Ⓑ Ⓒ Ⓓ | 23 Ⓐ Ⓑ Ⓒ Ⓓ | 37 Ⓐ Ⓑ Ⓒ Ⓓ |
| 10 Ⓐ Ⓑ Ⓒ Ⓓ | 24 Ⓐ Ⓑ Ⓒ Ⓓ | 38 Ⓐ Ⓑ Ⓒ Ⓓ |
| 11 Ⓐ Ⓑ Ⓒ Ⓓ | 25 Ⓐ Ⓑ Ⓒ Ⓓ | 39 Ⓐ Ⓑ Ⓒ Ⓓ |
| 12 Ⓐ Ⓑ Ⓒ Ⓓ | 26 Ⓐ Ⓑ Ⓒ Ⓓ | 40 Ⓐ Ⓑ Ⓒ Ⓓ **Middle/Upper Level Ends** |
| 13 Ⓐ Ⓑ Ⓒ Ⓓ | 27 Ⓐ Ⓑ Ⓒ Ⓓ | |
| 14 Ⓐ Ⓑ Ⓒ Ⓓ | 28 Ⓐ Ⓑ Ⓒ Ⓓ | |

## 2 QUANTITATIVE REASONING

| | | | |
|---|---|---|---|
| 1 Ⓐ Ⓑ Ⓒ Ⓓ | 15 Ⓐ Ⓑ Ⓒ Ⓓ | 29 Ⓐ Ⓑ Ⓒ Ⓓ | |
| 2 Ⓐ Ⓑ Ⓒ Ⓓ | 16 Ⓐ Ⓑ Ⓒ Ⓓ | 30 Ⓐ Ⓑ Ⓒ Ⓓ | |
| 3 Ⓐ Ⓑ Ⓒ Ⓓ | 17 Ⓐ Ⓑ Ⓒ Ⓓ | 31 Ⓐ Ⓑ Ⓒ Ⓓ | |
| 4 Ⓐ Ⓑ Ⓒ Ⓓ | 18 Ⓐ Ⓑ Ⓒ Ⓓ | 32 Ⓐ Ⓑ Ⓒ Ⓓ | |
| 5 Ⓐ Ⓑ Ⓒ Ⓓ | 19 Ⓐ Ⓑ Ⓒ Ⓓ | 33 Ⓐ Ⓑ Ⓒ Ⓓ | |
| 6 Ⓐ Ⓑ Ⓒ Ⓓ | 20 Ⓐ Ⓑ Ⓒ Ⓓ | 34 Ⓐ Ⓑ Ⓒ Ⓓ | |
| 7 Ⓐ Ⓑ Ⓒ Ⓓ | 21 Ⓐ Ⓑ Ⓒ Ⓓ | 35 Ⓐ Ⓑ Ⓒ Ⓓ | |
| 8 Ⓐ Ⓑ Ⓒ Ⓓ | 22 Ⓐ Ⓑ Ⓒ Ⓓ | 36 Ⓐ Ⓑ Ⓒ Ⓓ | |
| 9 Ⓐ Ⓑ Ⓒ Ⓓ | 23 Ⓐ Ⓑ Ⓒ Ⓓ | 37 Ⓐ Ⓑ Ⓒ Ⓓ **Middle/Upper Level Ends** | |
| 10 Ⓐ Ⓑ Ⓒ Ⓓ | 24 Ⓐ Ⓑ Ⓒ Ⓓ | 38 Ⓐ Ⓑ Ⓒ Ⓓ **Lower Level Ends** | |
| 11 Ⓐ Ⓑ Ⓒ Ⓓ | 25 Ⓐ Ⓑ Ⓒ Ⓓ | | |
| 12 Ⓐ Ⓑ Ⓒ Ⓓ | 26 Ⓐ Ⓑ Ⓒ Ⓓ | | |
| 13 Ⓐ Ⓑ Ⓒ Ⓓ | 27 Ⓐ Ⓑ Ⓒ Ⓓ | | |
| 14 Ⓐ Ⓑ Ⓒ Ⓓ | 28 Ⓐ Ⓑ Ⓒ Ⓓ | | |

## 4 MATHEMATICS ACHIEVEMENT

| | | |
|---|---|---|
| 1 Ⓐ Ⓑ Ⓒ Ⓓ | 18 Ⓐ Ⓑ Ⓒ Ⓓ | 35 Ⓐ Ⓑ Ⓒ Ⓓ |
| 2 Ⓐ Ⓑ Ⓒ Ⓓ | 19 Ⓐ Ⓑ Ⓒ Ⓓ | 36 Ⓐ Ⓑ Ⓒ Ⓓ |
| 3 Ⓐ Ⓑ Ⓒ Ⓓ | 20 Ⓐ Ⓑ Ⓒ Ⓓ | 37 Ⓐ Ⓑ Ⓒ Ⓓ |
| 4 Ⓐ Ⓑ Ⓒ Ⓓ | 21 Ⓐ Ⓑ Ⓒ Ⓓ | 38 Ⓐ Ⓑ Ⓒ Ⓓ |
| 5 Ⓐ Ⓑ Ⓒ Ⓓ | 22 Ⓐ Ⓑ Ⓒ Ⓓ | 39 Ⓐ Ⓑ Ⓒ Ⓓ |
| 6 Ⓐ Ⓑ Ⓒ Ⓓ | 23 Ⓐ Ⓑ Ⓒ Ⓓ | 40 Ⓐ Ⓑ Ⓒ Ⓓ |
| 7 Ⓐ Ⓑ Ⓒ Ⓓ | 24 Ⓐ Ⓑ Ⓒ Ⓓ | 41 Ⓐ Ⓑ Ⓒ Ⓓ |
| 8 Ⓐ Ⓑ Ⓒ Ⓓ | 25 Ⓐ Ⓑ Ⓒ Ⓓ | 42 Ⓐ Ⓑ Ⓒ Ⓓ |
| 9 Ⓐ Ⓑ Ⓒ Ⓓ | 26 Ⓐ Ⓑ Ⓒ Ⓓ | 43 Ⓐ Ⓑ Ⓒ Ⓓ |
| 10 Ⓐ Ⓑ Ⓒ Ⓓ | 27 Ⓐ Ⓑ Ⓒ Ⓓ | 44 Ⓐ Ⓑ Ⓒ Ⓓ |
| 11 Ⓐ Ⓑ Ⓒ Ⓓ | 28 Ⓐ Ⓑ Ⓒ Ⓓ | 45 Ⓐ Ⓑ Ⓒ Ⓓ |
| 12 Ⓐ Ⓑ Ⓒ Ⓓ | 29 Ⓐ Ⓑ Ⓒ Ⓓ | 46 Ⓐ Ⓑ Ⓒ Ⓓ |
| 13 Ⓐ Ⓑ Ⓒ Ⓓ | 30 Ⓐ Ⓑ Ⓒ Ⓓ **Lower Level Ends** | 47 Ⓐ Ⓑ Ⓒ Ⓓ **Middle/Upper Level Ends** |
| 14 Ⓐ Ⓑ Ⓒ Ⓓ | 31 Ⓐ Ⓑ Ⓒ Ⓓ | |
| 15 Ⓐ Ⓑ Ⓒ Ⓓ | 32 Ⓐ Ⓑ Ⓒ Ⓓ | |
| 16 Ⓐ Ⓑ Ⓒ Ⓓ | 33 Ⓐ Ⓑ Ⓒ Ⓓ | |
| 17 Ⓐ Ⓑ Ⓒ Ⓓ | 34 Ⓐ Ⓑ Ⓒ Ⓓ | |

## 3 READING COMPREHENSION

| | | |
|---|---|---|
| 1 Ⓐ Ⓑ Ⓒ Ⓓ | 15 Ⓐ Ⓑ Ⓒ Ⓓ | 29 Ⓐ Ⓑ Ⓒ Ⓓ |
| 2 Ⓐ Ⓑ Ⓒ Ⓓ | 16 Ⓐ Ⓑ Ⓒ Ⓓ | 30 Ⓐ Ⓑ Ⓒ Ⓓ |
| 3 Ⓐ Ⓑ Ⓒ Ⓓ | 17 Ⓐ Ⓑ Ⓒ Ⓓ | 31 Ⓐ Ⓑ Ⓒ Ⓓ |
| 4 Ⓐ Ⓑ Ⓒ Ⓓ | 18 Ⓐ Ⓑ Ⓒ Ⓓ | 32 Ⓐ Ⓑ Ⓒ Ⓓ |
| 5 Ⓐ Ⓑ Ⓒ Ⓓ | 19 Ⓐ Ⓑ Ⓒ Ⓓ | 33 Ⓐ Ⓑ Ⓒ Ⓓ |
| 6 Ⓐ Ⓑ Ⓒ Ⓓ | 20 Ⓐ Ⓑ Ⓒ Ⓓ | 34 Ⓐ Ⓑ Ⓒ Ⓓ |
| 7 Ⓐ Ⓑ Ⓒ Ⓓ | 21 Ⓐ Ⓑ Ⓒ Ⓓ | 35 Ⓐ Ⓑ Ⓒ Ⓓ |
| 8 Ⓐ Ⓑ Ⓒ Ⓓ | 22 Ⓐ Ⓑ Ⓒ Ⓓ | 36 Ⓐ Ⓑ Ⓒ Ⓓ **Middle/Upper Level Ends** |
| 9 Ⓐ Ⓑ Ⓒ Ⓓ | 23 Ⓐ Ⓑ Ⓒ Ⓓ | |
| 10 Ⓐ Ⓑ Ⓒ Ⓓ | 24 Ⓐ Ⓑ Ⓒ Ⓓ | |
| 11 Ⓐ Ⓑ Ⓒ Ⓓ | 25 Ⓐ Ⓑ Ⓒ Ⓓ **Lower Level Ends** | |
| 12 Ⓐ Ⓑ Ⓒ Ⓓ | 26 Ⓐ Ⓑ Ⓒ Ⓓ | |
| 13 Ⓐ Ⓑ Ⓒ Ⓓ | 27 Ⓐ Ⓑ Ⓒ Ⓓ | |
| 14 Ⓐ Ⓑ Ⓒ Ⓓ | 28 Ⓐ Ⓑ Ⓒ Ⓓ | |

**Ivy Global**

STUDENT NAME _____ GRADE APPLYING FOR _____

Use a blue or black ballpoint pen to write the final draft of your essay on this sheet.

You must write your essay topic in this space.

_____

_____

_____

Use specific details and examples in your response.

_____

_____

_____

_____

_____

_____

_____

_____

_____

_____

_____

_____

_____

_____

_____

_____

_____

_____

_____

_____

_____

_____

_____

_____

_____

Ivy Global

# Section 1
# Verbal Reasoning

| 40 Questions | Time: 20 minutes |

This section is divided into two parts that contain two different types of questions. As soon as you have completed Part One, answer the questions in Part Two. You may write in your test booklet. For each answer you select, fill in the corresponding circle on your answer document.

## PART ONE — SYNONYMS

Each question in Part One consists of a word in capital letters followed by four answer choices. Select the one word that is most nearly the same in meaning as the word in capital letters.

---

SAMPLE QUESTION:                                    Sample Answer

CHARGE:                                              Ⓐ Ⓑ ● Ⓓ

(A) release

(B) belittle

(C) accuse

(D) conspire

The correct answer is "accuse," so circle C is darkened.

---

*Go on to the next page* ➜

## PART TWO — SENTENCE COMPLETION

Each question in Part Two is made up of a sentence with one blank. Each blank indicates that a word or phrase is missing. The sentence is followed by four answer choices. Select the word or phrase that will best complete the meaning of the sentence as a whole.

---

SAMPLE QUESTIONS:                                                   <u>Sample Answer</u>

It rained so much that the streets were -------.                   ● Ⓑ Ⓒ Ⓓ

(A) flooded

(B) arid

(C) paved

(D) crowded

The correct answer is "flooded," so circle A is darkened.

The house was so dirty that it took -------.                       Ⓐ Ⓑ Ⓒ ●

(A) less than ten minutes to wash it.

(B) four months to demolish it.

(C) over a week to walk across it.

(D) two days to clean it.

The correct answer is "two days to clean it," so circle D is darkened.

---

STOP. Do not go on
until told to do so.

**Directions:** Select the word that is most nearly the same in meaning as the word in capital letters.

1. VANITY

(A) conceit

(B) greed

(C) ruthlessness

(D) imagination

2. IMMACULATE

(A) shackled

(B) warranted

(C) indigo

(D) flawless

3. TURBULENT

(A) stormy

(B) breathless

(C) jumbled

(D) obnoxious

4. LADEN

(A) upheld

(B) submerged

(C) burdened

(D) broken

5. EXPEDITE

(A) construct

(B) hurry

(C) incite

(D) record

6. ETERNAL

(A) ephemeral

(B) internal

(C) final

(D) infinite

7. BOLSTER

(A) demolish

(B) invite

(C) support

(D) lock

8. APPLICABLE

(A) submissive

(B) appropriate

(C) open

(D) apprehensive

9. EXPEDITIOUS

(A) quick

(B) jumpy

(C) nervous

(D) prior

10. DIPLOMAT

(A) governor

(B) ambassador

(C) ally

(D) friend

11. PLUMMET

(A) indicate

(B) celebrate

(C) fall

(D) hasten

12. FRAUD

(A) deterrent

(B) propaganda

(C) coercion

(D) deception

*Go on to the next page* ➡

13. DEDUCE

   (A) lessen

   (B) tutor

   (C) infer

   (D) demote

14. SWINDLE

   (A) open

   (B) invent

   (C) impoverish

   (D) cheat

15. INVISIBLE

   (A) silent

   (B) unseen

   (C) secure

   (D) unpredictable

16. JEER

   (A) mock

   (B) praise

   (C) annoy

   (D) activate

17. FRIVOLOUS

   (A) enjoyable

   (B) silly

   (C) outrageous

   (D) unseemly

18. EVADE

   (A) depart

   (B) defend

   (C) dislike

   (D) escape

19. SPRUCE

   (A) cleanliness

   (B) evergreen

   (C) broom

   (D) virtue

*Go on to the next page* ➡

## PART TWO – SENTENCE COMPLETION

**Directions:** Select the word that best completes the sentence.

20. While many actors are melodramatic in their portrayals of characters, Morgan Freeman is known for his more -------- acting technique.

    (A) noisy

    (B) enthusiastic

    (C) subtle

    (D) excruciating

21. The sloth received its name for its -------- movements; it can take an hour for it to move a few feet.

    (A) shaky

    (B) rapid

    (C) vicious

    (D) languid

22. The mechanic's repairs were only ---------; the car looked much better, but the engine still wouldn't start.

    (A) ingenious

    (B) unoriginal

    (C) superficial

    (D) simplistic

23. Mules have a reputation for -------- behavior, but they're actually quite compliant when treated properly.

    (A) jubilant

    (B) bored

    (C) focused

    (D) obstinate

24. The beginning of the flu is usually marked by --------; patients are tired and unable to get out of bed.

    (A) fervor

    (B) fatigue

    (C) dread

    (D) amusement

25. Although Bob was very --------, he still lacked the practical knowledge to take proper care of himself.

    (A) childish

    (B) sublime

    (C) pragmatic

    (D) intelligent

26. Because our debate club picks very -------- topics, we often have heated debates.

    (A) unknown

    (B) contentious

    (C) delightful

    (D) lighthearted

27. James Crawford's famous song "Jock-a-mo" had an -------- beat, which induced listeners to clap and move along with the music.

    (A) airy

    (B) intangible

    (C) uncouth

    (D) infectious

*Go on to the next page* ➜

28. Since she is usually interested in studying chemistry, Christine's -------- attitude toward the chemistry professor's presentation was surprising.

    (A) inane
    (B) engaged
    (C) apathetic
    (D) graceful

29. The -------- play of accident-prone children often stands in sharp contrast to the vigilance of their careful parents.

    (A) quiet
    (B) heedless
    (C) uninterrupted
    (D) obnoxious

30. When trekking through the desert, it is important to carry some form of liquid to -------- one's inevitable thirst.

    (A) foster
    (B) kick
    (C) brew
    (D) quench

31. The Salem witch trials led to the unfair -------- of many innocent people whose only indictments were the words of confused or dishonest witnesses.

    (A) persecution
    (B) release
    (C) competition
    (D) transformation

32. Though many people find Brussels sprouts quite a -------- vegetable, others find them -------- and refuse to eat them.

    (A) savory...average
    (B) horrendous...annoying
    (C) tasty...repugnant
    (D) starchy...arcane

33. In some circles, George Orwell has been -------- as a prophet for -------- the real-world rise of mass surveillance in his dark, fictional novel, *1984*.

    (A) derided...preventing
    (B) promoted...endorsing
    (C) hailed...predicting
    (D) negated...anticipating

34. I hoped to -------- the rock wall with relative ease, but a bad ankle sprain at the start forced me to -------- my goal.

    (A) scale...achieve
    (B) ascend...abandon
    (C) trek...improve
    (D) ply...enervate

35. Some worry that social networking sites are -------- to our social lives, and find it -------- that many people have more virtual friends than real ones.

    (A) hazardous...relaxing
    (B) detrimental...unnerving
    (C) beneficial...exciting
    (D) fortunate...scary

36. Though the original Model T Fords were -------- by comparison with modern cars, they were actually more -------- than some cars of the early 1970s.

    (A) wasteful...efficient
    (B) sleek...stylish
    (C) flat...ineffective
    (D) unattractive...resourceful

*Go on to the next page* ➡

37. Though Ben Stiller movies are usually -------- and easy to follow, his latest film proved to be dreary and --------.

    (A) depressing...unfathomable

    (B) hilarious...visible

    (C) old-fashioned...paranoid

    (D) amusing...opaque

38. William Shakespeare often -------- new phrases and even new words in his work, earning him a reputation as a bold and -------- writer.

    (A) coined...innovative

    (B) faked...productive

    (C) created...loathsome

    (D) analyzed...barbarous

39. Many people claim they don't eat -------- food because it doesn't taste good; they would prefer the food they eat be both healthy and --------.

    (A) perilous...delicious

    (B) nutritious...appetizing

    (C) innocent...unappealing

    (D) excessive...reliable

40. While Sarah viewed snow days as a -------- when they secured her a day out of school, they became more of a -------- when they interfered with her travel plans.

    (A) blessing...chance

    (B) horror...farce

    (C) boon...hindrance

    (D) byproduct...task

**STOP. Do not go on until told to do so.** **STOP**

# Section 2
# Quantitative Reasoning

Each question is followed by four suggested answers. Read each question and then decide which one of the four suggested answers is best.

Find the row of spaces on your answer document that has the same number as the question. In this row, mark the space having the same letter as the answer you have chosen. You may write in your test booklet.

---

SAMPLE QUESTIONS:           <u>Sample Answer</u>

What is the value of the expression $(4 + 6) \div 2$?      Ⓐ Ⓑ ● Ⓓ

(A) 2

(B) 4

(C) 5

(D) 7

The correct answer is 5, so circle C is darkened.

A square has an area of 25cm². What is the length of one of its      Ⓐ ● Ⓒ Ⓓ
sides?

(A) 1 cm

(B) 5 cm

(C) 10 cm

(D) 25 cm

The correct answer is 5, so circle B is darkened.

---

*Go on to the next page* ➜

**2**

## PART TWO — QUANTITATIVE COMPARISONS

All questions in Part Two are quantitative comparisons between the quantities shown in Column A and Column B. Using the information given in each question, compare the quantity in Column A to the quantity in Column B, and choose one of these four answer choices:

(A) The quantity in Column A is greater.

(B) The quantity in Column B is greater.

(C) The two quantities are equal.

(D) The relationship cannot be determined from the information given.

---

SAMPLE QUESTIONS:

| Column A | Column B | Sample Answer |
|----------|----------|---------------|
| 5 | $\sqrt{25}$ | Ⓐ Ⓑ ● Ⓓ |

The quantity in Column A (5) is the same as the quantity in Column B (5), so circle C is darkened.

---

$$x = 6^2 - 3 \times 4$$

| Column A | Column B | Sample Answer |
|----------|----------|---------------|
| $x$ | 22 | ● Ⓑ Ⓒ Ⓓ |

The quantity in Column A (24) is greater than the quantity in Column B (22), so circle A is darkened.

---

**STOP. Do not go on until told to do so.**  **STOP**

**Ivy Global**

# QR

## PART ONE – WORD PROBLEMS

**Directions:** Choose the best answer from the four choices given.

1. The formula for a cylinder's volume is $V = \pi r^2 h$, where $r$ is the cylinder's radius and $h$ is the cylinder's height. If a cylinder has a radius equal to its height $h$, what is the cylinder's volume in terms of its height?

    (A) $4\pi h$

    (B) $\pi h^3$

    (C) $2\pi h^3$

    (D) $16\pi h^3$

2. The diagram below shows a 12" long piece of paper that Samantha folded in half. She made one cut so that when she unfolded the paper, a perfect circle had been cut out.

    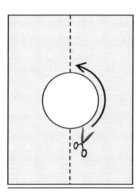

    If the circle's diameter measures $\frac{1}{3}$ of the length of the paper, what was the length of the cut she made?

    (A) 2 in.

    (B) 4 in.

    (C) $2\pi$ in.

    (D) $3\pi$ in.

3. The irregular polygon below has sides of unequal lengths.

    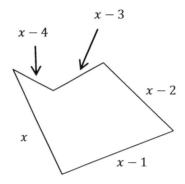

    If the polygon's total perimeter is 20, what is the value of $x$?

    (A) 6

    (B) 5

    (C) 4

    (D) 2

4. If $y^{-2} = (x - 2)^{\frac{1}{2}}$, then which expression is equal to $x$?

    (A) $y^2 + 2$

    (B) $\frac{2}{y^4}$

    (C) $2 - y^{-2}$

    (D) $\frac{1}{y^4} + 2$

5. Which of the following expressions is equivalent to $\left(\frac{2^4}{4^2}\right)^2$ ?

    (A) $(2)^{\frac{1}{2}}$

    (B) $4^0$

    (C) $(2)^{-\frac{1}{2}}$

    (D) $4^{-2}$

*Go on to the next page* ➡

6. If the sum of all integers from 600 to 800, inclusive, is $w$, what is the average value of all of these integers?

   (A) $\frac{w}{201}$

   (B) $\frac{w^2}{101 \times 100}$

   (C) $(w - 101)^2$

   (D) $201 \times w$

7. The rectangle below has an area of $7m^2$.

   | | |
   |---|---|
   | $Area = 7m^2$ | Note: figure not to scale. |

   If all sides of the rectangle are integers, which of the following could be the perimeter of the rectangle?

   (A) 49

   (B) 28

   (C) 16

   (D) 12

8. Luisa is thinking of a prime number that is greater than 8 and less than 30. If Elizabeth randomly guesses one number that fits this description, what is her probability of guessing Luisa's number?

   (A) $\frac{1}{29}$

   (B) $\frac{1}{22}$

   (C) $\frac{1}{9}$

   (D) $\frac{1}{6}$

9. Franklin was simmering 10 cups of soup at a constant temperature of 95°F. He then added 2 cups of broth, which had a temperature of 95°F. Which graph best represents the temperature of his soup as a function of time?

   (A)
   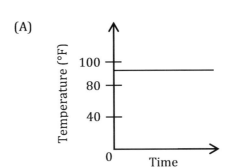

   (B)
   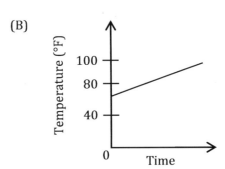

   (C)
   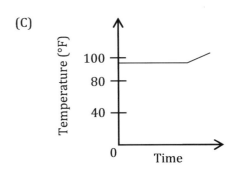

   (D)
   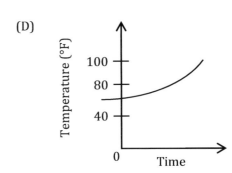

*Go on to the next page* ➡

10. If $5 :: 8 = 5^2 - 8$, what is the value of $7 :: 3$?

    (A) 21

    (B) 40

    (C) 46

    (D) 49

11. The two triangles below are similar. Triangle $B$'s sides are proportionally $\frac{2}{3}$ the length of Triangle $A$'s.

    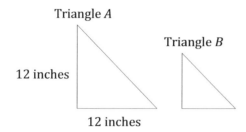

    What is the ratio of Triangle $A$'s area to Triangle $B$'s area?

    (A) 3 to 5

    (B) 2 to 1

    (C) 2 to 3

    (D) 9 to 4

12. The stem-and-leaf plot below shows the results of 20 students' test scores in Mrs. Louis's class.

    | 10 | 0 0 |
    |----|-----|
    | 9  | 9 8 8 5 2 |
    | 8  | 9 7 6 4 4 4 3 0 |
    | 7  | 3 3 2 1 0 |

    Mrs. Louis decided to boost the students' test scores by increasing each score by 10%. What was the range of the data after this boost?

    (A) 27

    (B) 30

    (C) 33

    (D) 84

13. If $u$ is a positive integer and $(t + u)^2 = t^2 + 26t + u^2$, what is the value of $u$?

    (A) 3

    (B) 13

    (C) 26

    (D) 169

14. The variables $a$ and $b$ are both positive integers. If $a > b$ and $ab = 9$, what is the value of $a^2 - b^2$?

    (A) 80

    (B) 9

    (C) 0

    (D) -80

15. The shaded right triangle is attached to a square by its hypotenuse, as shown in the figure below. The perimeter of the square is $x$ cm.

    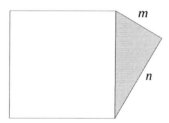

    What is the value of $m^2 + n^2$?

    (A) $x - 4$

    (B) $x^2 \times 4$

    (C) $\left(\frac{x}{4}\right)^2$

    (D) $\left(\frac{x}{16}\right)^2$

16. A square has an area of $A$. If the length of each side is decreased by 50%, what is the square's new area, in terms of $A$?

    (A) $4A$

    (B) $2A$

    (C) $\frac{1}{2}A$

    (D) $\frac{A}{4}$

*Go on to the next page* ➡

17. Use the chart below to answer the question.

**Quiz Scores**

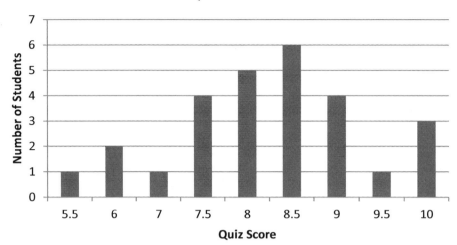

One student's quiz has not yet been graded. Which of the following quiz grades would cause the data's median to change the most?

(A) 7.5

(B) 8.5

(C) 9.5

(D) 10

---

18. Use the graph below to answer the question.

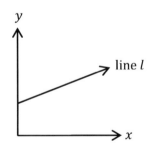

Line $k$ is perpendicular to line $l$. Line $k$'s slope could NOT be which of the following type of number?

(A) A composite number

(B) A positive integer

(C) A prime number

(D) A rational number

19. Which of the following expressions is equivalent to the expression $x^2 - 4$?

(A) $(x + \sqrt{2})(x - \sqrt{2})$

(B) $(x + 2)(x - 2)$

(C) $(x - \sqrt{2})^2$

(D) $(x + 2i)(x - 2i)$

*Go on to the next page* ➡

20. A cube is shown.

Which of the figures is a possible net for the cube?

(A)

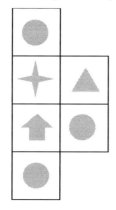

(C)

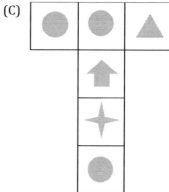

(B)

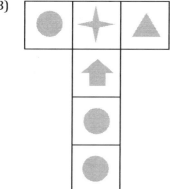

(D)

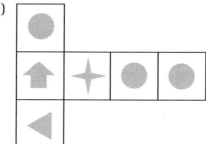

*Go on to the next page* ➡

## PART TWO – QUANTITATIVE COMPARISONS

**Directions:** Using the information given in each question, compare the quantity in column A to the quantity in Column B. All questions in Part Two have these answer choices:

(A) The quantity in Column A is greater.

(B) The quantity in Column B is greater.

(C) The two quantities are equal.

(D) The relationship cannot be determined from the information given.

---

The two rectangles shown below are similar.

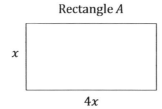

Rectangle A           Rectangle B

*Note: figure not to scale*

|  | Column A | Column B |
|---|---|---|
| 21. | The area of rectangle $B$ | $8x^2$ |

---

The diagram below shows the results of a survey that asked 860 people about their pets.

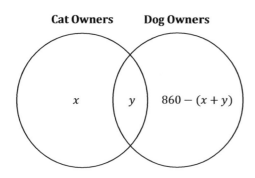

| | Column A | Column B |
|---|---|---|
| 22. | The number of people who own a cat | The number of people who own a dog |

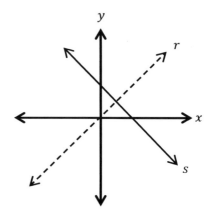

Line $r$ is the graph of $2x + b$. Line $s$ is perpendicular to line $r$.

| | Column A | Column B |
|---|---|---|
| 23. | $-2$ | The slope of line $s$ |

*Go on to the next page* ➡

---

**ANSWER CHOICES FOR ALL QUESTIONS ON THIS PAGE:**

(A) The quantity in Column A is greater.

(B) The quantity in Column B is greater.

(C) The two quantities are equal.

(D) The relationship cannot be determined from the information given.

---

|  | Column A | Column B |
|---|---|---|
| 24. | $25 \times 20$ | $26 \times 19$ |

|  | Column A | Column B |
|---|---|---|
| 25. | The sum of all prime numbers greater than 35 and less than 43 | The sum of all prime numbers less than 23. |

$$[\spadesuit]p = 2(p - 3) - 5$$

|  | Column A | Column B |
|---|---|---|
| 26. | $[\spadesuit]2$ | $-3$ |

|  | Column A | Column B |
|---|---|---|
| 27. | 30% of 20 | 20% of 30 |

$y$ is a positive integer whole number

|  | Column A | Column B |
|---|---|---|
| 28. | $y^2$ | $\left(\dfrac{1}{y}\right)^{-3}$ |

The circular target below has a diameter of 8 feet. A square section of the target with side lengths of $\sqrt{\pi}$ feet has been shaded in.

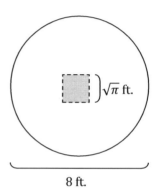

8 ft.

A beanbag that has been randomly tossed lands on the circular target.

|  | Column A | Column B |
|---|---|---|
| 29. | The probability that the beanbag lands within the shaded square | $\dfrac{1}{16}$ |

---

Pete has ten carrots and one piece of celery in his lunch. He is randomly selecting vegetables to eat one at a time.

|  | Column A | Column B |
|---|---|---|
| 30. | The probability that he eats one carrot and then the piece of celery | The probability that he eats the piece of celery and then one carrot |

*Go on to the next page* ➡

---

**ANSWER CHOICES FOR ALL QUESTIONS ON THIS PAGE:**

(A) The quantity in Column A is greater.

(B) The quantity in Column B is greater.

(C) The two quantities are equal.

(D) The relationship cannot be determined from the information given.

---

Two cylinders are shown below. Cylinder *B* is twice as tall as Cylinder *A*, but is one-half as wide. The formula for the volume of a cylinder is $V = \pi r^2 h$.

Cylinder *A*     Cylinder *B*

*Note: Figures not drawn to scale.*

|    | Column A | Column B |
|----|----------|----------|
| 31. | The volume of Cylinder *A* | The volume of Cylinder *B* |

---

$$x^3 - 12x^2 + 35x = 0$$

|    | Column A | Column B |
|----|----------|----------|
| 32. | $x$ | 4 |

---

6% of the audience members, or 10 people, enjoyed a certain play.

|    | Column A | Column B |
|----|----------|----------|
| 33. | The total number of audience members | 100 |

---

Use the figure below to answer the question.

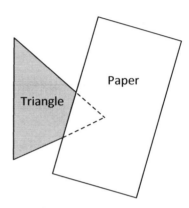

A triangle is partially covered by a piece of paper so that only the shaded portion is visible.

|    | Column A | Column B |
|----|----------|----------|
| 34. | The sum of the interior angles of the original triangle | The sum of the interior angles of the shaded region |

---

|    | Column A | Column B |
|----|----------|----------|
| 35. | The surface area of a 10 cm × 10 cm × 10 cm cube | The surface area of a 10 cm × 5 cm × 20 cm rectangular prism |

---

$$(e^2 + f^2) = 13 \text{ and } ef = 6$$

|    | Column A | Column B |
|----|----------|----------|
| 36. | $(e + f)^2$ | $2ef$ |

---

*Go on to the next page* ➜

**ANSWER CHOICES FOR ALL QUESTIONS ON THIS PAGE:**

    (A) The quantity in Column A is greater.

    (B) The quantity in Column B is greater.

    (C) The two quantities are equal.

    (D) The relationship cannot be determined from the information given.

Use the histogram below to answer the question.

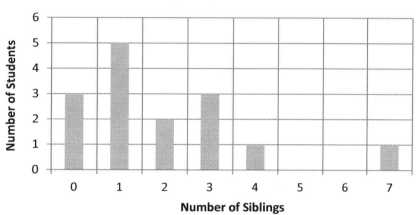

**Number of Siblings in 15 Students' Families**

| | Column A | | Column B |
|---|---|---|---|
| 37. | The median of the data. | | The mode of the data. |

# Section 3
# Reading Comprehension

This section contains six short reading passages. Each passage is followed by six questions based on its content. Answer the questions following each passage on the basis of what is <u>stated</u> or <u>implied</u> in that passage. You may write in your test booklet.

STOP. Do not go on
until told to do so. **STOP**

Ivy Global

Questions 1–6

As a child, I had the good fortune to be given all the spare parts and broken devices that I could have desired, which were the surpluses of my father's business. To a curious child, of course, nearly any object can become an object of play- but the complex and interesting things that were cast off from my father's shop were exceptional toys, and superb materials for experimentation.

It won't be a surprise that I began my experiments mainly by disassembling things and leaving them in a pile. After a while, I began to have some luck in putting things back together. But since the devices were broken already when I received them, there was little I could do to confirm the soundness of my work but to see that they looked right, and perhaps to spin with my finger what should properly be spun by a motor. Then came a day when I cracked open a simple electric motor which had been extracted from a fan brought in for repair: the motor wouldn't run, was deemed dead, and was handed off to me for my play. I had opened up similar devices before, and had a vague idea of their operation, although I did not know the names of all the parts as I do now.

An electric motor contains several magnets arranged around a central rotor, which holds an electromagnet. At the base of the rotor is a "commutator," which is a sort of spinning switch. Several metal brushes make contact with the commutator, and complete a circuit which powers the electromagnet on the rotor. When powered, the electromagnet is alternately repelled and attracted by the magnets around it. The rotor is thus kept in constant motion so long as the electromagnet is supplied with electricity.

In the motor which I had just opened, one of the metallic brushes which make contact with the commutator (and thereby supply power to the electromagnet in the rotor and make the whole process work) had somehow come to be bent away from its intended position. Because of the dislocation of this vital component, the circuit could not be completed and the electromagnet could not receive power. All there was for me to do was to bend the brush back into place, and attach the motor to a battery- and it whirred to life there in front of me! I excitedly presented the work to my father, was congratulated, and was rewarded with an apple tart and an invitation thereafter to come and help out in the shop with simple repairs.

*Go on to the next page* ➜

1. Which sentence best summarizes this passage?

   (A) An electric motor has a part called a "commutator," which is a very important part that is necessary for the motor to function.

   (B) Although the narrator needed to repair an electric motor, he was frustrated because he only had broken devices to work with.

   (C) The narrator was allowed to play with broken machines as a child, and after fixing an electric motor was given congratulations and rewards.

   (D) The passage lists the parts of electric motors, and provides basic instructions for repairing them when damaged.

2. Based on the passage, we can conclude that an electromagnet

   (A) needs to be supplied with electricity in order to function properly.

   (B) is a component used to power fans.

   (C) will continue to spin out of control if its circuit is broken.

   (D) is a very valuable component which should not be lightly discarded.

3. As it is used in line 45, "dislocation" most nearly means

   (A) annihilation

   (B) misplacement

   (C) circulation

   (D) correction

4. The role of the metallic brushes in an electric motor is to

   (A) hold the commutator firmly in place.

   (B) keep the internal components clean.

   (C) complete a circuit in the motor.

   (D) safely discharge excess electricity.

5. Based on information in the passage, which of the following statements about the narrator's father is most likely to be true?

   (A) The narrator's father was too busy to pay much attention to his son, and so the narrator was left to play alone.

   (B) The narrator's father spent much of his free time teaching his son to repair broken machinery.

   (C) The narrator's father was too poor to afford real toys, so he gave his son junk to play with instead.

   (D) The narrator's father operated a business which repaired a lot of broken mechanical devices.

6. The purpose of the third paragraph is to

   (A) tell the story of how the narrator fixed an electric motor.

   (B) explain how the narrator came to possess and electric motor.

   (C) add details which help to support the narrator's argument.

   (D) describe how an electric motor operates.

*Go on to the next page* ➡

1       It is common today to read about the
2   revolutionary nature of the Internet.  It doesn't
3   take much exposure to the claims of the tech
4   crowd to see that just about every aspect of our
5   lives has purportedly been changed
6   fundamentally and forever by the advent of the
7   Web. But how fundamental have the changes
8   brought about by the Internet really been?
9       The first thing one should know when
10  considering the proposition that the Internet
11  has changed the world is that, as of 2012,
12  Internet users only make up a little more than a
13  third of the world population.   However
14  revolutionary the changes may be for that
15  networked minority, most of the world
16  continues to drudge on without the Web.
17      And to those of us who are online, much
18  of what the Internet brings is not clearly new,
19  and some of it is not even clearly useful.  Online
20  shopping is only a quicker, more convenient
21  version of mail-order shopping. Searching for
22  information online is a quicker version of
23  searching a library, but the credibility of online
24  sources is often questionable. Communicating
25  online is hardly an improvement at all over

26  previous technologies: it may be nearly instant,
27  but so are phone calls and radio
28  communication- and they've been around for a
29  century!  And online communication certainly
30  doesn't provide a clear benefit to our social
31  lives: studies suggest that as we make more
32  and more friends online, we have fewer and
33  fewer in real life- and real friends are worth far
34  more than nominal Internet "friends."
35      The Internet is certainly a convenience,
36  which enables us to do more quickly many of
37  the things which we have always done, without
38  so much as leaving our chairs.  But it is not
39  without its downsides, and ultimately it is still
40  only a convenience:  it is not the end of human
41  progress, the final stage of history, or the
42  zenith of human achievement. The sense of the
43  all-encompassing importance of the Internet is
44  merely a symptom of our newfound reliance on
45  this great modern convenience, and will seem
46  as quaint and misguided to our descendants as
47  the industrial-age fantasy that industrialization
48  would free humanity from the demands of
49  labor, to live in endless leisure and abundance.

*Go on to the next page* ➜

7. The main purpose of this passage is to

    (A) persuade the reader that the Internet isn't actually a revolutionary invention.

    (B) provide an unbiased overview of how the Internet has affected our lives.

    (C) opine that online friends are not worth as much as real friends.

    (D) discuss pre-internet technologies that had functions now carried out by the Internet.

8. The passage implies that information in a library

    (A) is easier to access than online information.

    (B) is actually about as easy to search through as online information.

    (C) is more credible than information on the Internet.

    (D) is less likely to have a negative impact on your social life.

9. Lines 29-34 suggest that online friendships

    (A) are more numerous than in-person friendships.

    (B) are only beneficial to certain types of people.

    (C) shouldn't be considered as real friendships.

    (D) often cause harm to your in-person friendships.

10. Which of the following sentences restates one of the author's main points?

    (A) It's unfair to most of the world to use the Internet as a primary form of communication.

    (B) Many of the things we do on the Internet can also be done without the Internet.

    (C) People who spend too much time online will lose all of their friends.

    (D) Although it's convenient, the Internet is not as revolutionary as industrialization.

11. Which best describes the organization of this passage?

    (A) A question is posed, some evidence is discussed, and a conclusion is clearly stated only after providing evidence.

    (B) A fact is stated, some questions are asked about the fact, and answers are provided to each question in turn.

    (C) The passage offers evidence on two sides of an issue, leaving it to the reader to draw their own conclusions.

    (D) The passage provides evidence in favor of one side of an argument, without considering any counter-evidence.

12. As it is used in line 5, the word "purportedly" most nearly means

    (A) undeniably.

    (B) supposedly.

    (C) unfortunately.

    (D) similarly.

*Go on to the next page* ➜

Questions 13–18

1    Scrimshaw is an art of creating delicate
2    engravings on the teeth and bones of whales, or
3    the tusks of walruses, and the artisan who
4    practices scrimshaw is called a scrimshander.
5        The practice began on whaling ships
6    between 1745 and 1759.  It derived from the
7    practice of creating common tools on-board the
8    ship using the bones of whales, which were
9    abundant and easily accessible on whaling
10   ships.  Whalers had more free time than other
11   sailors of the period - and so, at times when
12   others might have been working, whalers
13   needed a hobby.  Using simple needles, they
14   began to etch designs and pictures into the
15   teeth and bones of whales, and to highlight
16   their engravings with dark pigments- often
17   soot, or tobacco juice.
18       The practice of scrimshaw expanded as
19   the market for whale teeth grew, reaching its
20   peak in the middle of the 19th century.  The
21   market declined as the whaling industry waned
22   in the latter part of the 1800s, and in 1976 an
23   international treaty called the Convetion on
24   International Trade in Endangered Species of
25   Wild Fauna and Flora, or CITES, was signed-
26   severely restricting trade in the products of
27   whaling, or other activities that threatened
28   endangered species.  While it is still legal to
29   trade in the products of whales which were
30   harvested before the treaty, no whale teeth
31   harvested since the signing of the treaty may
32   legally be traded in most parts of the world.
33   Today, as a result, great care must be taken to
34   acquire only legal whale teeth, and the practice
35   of scrimshaw is much less widespread- but the
36   value of antique scrimshaw has increased
37   considerably.

*Go on to the next page* ➡

13. The main purpose of this passage is to

    (A) explain why Scrimshaw is now a rare art form.

    (B) criticize the CITES treaty for restricting trade.

    (C) describe the history of Scrimshaw.

    (D) explain how Scrimshaw is produced.

14. The purpose of the second paragraph (lines 5-17) is to

    (A) show why whale teeth provided the best material for scrimshanders.

    (B) describe the wealth and leisure enjoyed by whalers.

    (C) foreshadow the end of the art of scrimshaw.

    (D) inform the reader about the origins of scrimshaw.

15. We can infer from the passage that by 1976

    (A) the market for whale teeth had already disappeared.

    (B) the whales traditionally hunted by whalers had become endangered species.

    (C) whalers had generally found other ways to entertain themselves than scrimshaw.

    (D) scrimshanders were primarily using walrus tusks rather than whale teeth.

16. Care must be taken when trading in scrimshaw because

    (A) the pigments used by early scrimshanders are not as durable as the more modern pigments.

    (B) walrus tusks are significantly more brittle than whale teeth.

    (C) the market for scrimshaw is constantly growing, even though the supply of whale teeth has been restricted.

    (D) it is illegal in many places to trade whale teeth harvested after 1976.

17. According to the passage, whalers originally chose the teeth and bones of whales for their carvings because

    (A) the growing market for whale teeth made them a valuable commodity.

    (B) they had easy access to large quantities of those materials.

    (C) whalers had too much free time.

    (D) teeth and bones could be easily dyed with tobacco and soot.

18. Which best describes the effect that the CITES treaty on the trade in scrimshaw?

    (A) The CITES treaty banned the sale of scrimshaw, but still allowed scrimshanders to make new scrimshaw.

    (B) When CITES was passed, the scrimshaw market finally reached its peak, and then declined as the whaling industry shrank.

    (C) CITES imposed new restrictions on the trade of new whale teeth, but did not prohibit the sale of antique scrimshaw.

    (D) Scrimshaw was banned under CITES, although raw whale teeth could still be harvested and traded.

*Go on to the next page* ➡

Questions 19–24

1     National Forests are largely forest and
2 woodland areas owned by the federal
3 government and managed by the United States
4 Forest Service, part of the United States
5 Department of Agriculture. Land management
6 of these areas focuses on conservation, timber
7 harvesting, livestock grazing, watershed
8 protection, wildlife, and recreation. Unlike
9 national parks and other federal lands
10 managed by the National Park Service,
11 extraction of natural resources from national
12 forests is sanctioned, and in many cases
13 encouraged.
14     The National Forest system was created
15 by the Land Revision Act of 1891. It was the
16 result of concerted action by Los Angeles-area
17 businessmen and property owners who were
18 concerned about the harm being done to the
19 watershed of the San Gabriel Mountains by
20 ranchers and miners. Before the passage of the
21 act, it was common practice in the area to burn
22 down large swathes of forest, to make room for
23 grazing land or for other purposes. Such
24 "burned over" lands are vulnerable to dramatic
25 soil erosion, and the fire-damaged and

26 diminished soil was able to absorb and hold
27 less water.
28     Under the Land Revision Act, the
29 president was granted the authority to set
30 aside lands which could otherwise have been
31 cheaply purchased from the federal
32 government under the Homestead Act and
33 other laws. Because extraction of resources and
34 other activity in US Forest Lands could be
35 managed by the Forest Service, the damage
36 from land use could be limited.
37     There are, however, still conflicts
38 between timber and mining companies,
39 environmentalists, and recreational users of
40 National Forest land- such as hunters, campers,
41 and hikers- over the use of National Forest
42 land. These conflicts center on land use, logging
43 practices, mining laws, and road-building in
44 National Forests.
45     The task of the Forest Service is to
46 balance the interests of all the users of National
47 Forest lands, and to create sustainable
48 management plans for forests which will allow
49 the public to continue to enjoy all that the
50 forests have to offer for generations to come.

*Go on to the next page* ➡

19. We can infer from the passage that before the Land Revision Act

    (A) the majority of privately owned forests had already been burned down.

    (B) miners and ranchers were able to steal federal lands for their own use.

    (C) other laws required the government to sell some of its lands to private buyers.

    (D) land use practices were much more responsible, and safeguarded the soil and water.

20. According to the passage, the creation of the National Forest system was motivated mainly by

    (A) the potential for revenues from sustainable logging and hunting.

    (B) the needs of recreational hikers, hunters, and campers.

    (C) the need to offer affordable lands for sale under the Homestead Act.

    (D) damage being done to the environment by harmful land use.

21. The purpose of lines 20-27 is to

    (A) persuade the reader that miners and ranchers cannot be good stewards of the environment.

    (B) exaggerate the harms that were caused by some uses of natural resources.

    (C) describe the mission and importance of the US Forest Service.

    (D) describe the harmful practices that prompted the passage of the Land Revision Act.

22. With regard to the conflicts that still exist over the appropriate use of National Forest lands (lines 37-44), the author appears to

    (A) side exclusively with the environmentalists, hikers, and campers.

    (B) strongly favor the position of the timber and mining companies.

    (C) support the Forest Service's mission of balancing competing interests.

    (D) support a change in the Forest Service's current policies.

23. As it is used in line 12, the word "sanctioned" most nearly means

    (A) excluded.

    (B) purchased.

    (C) permitted.

    (D) required.

24. With which of the following sentences would the author of the passage most likely agree?

    (A) With good land management, natural resources can be exploited without causing excessive harm to the environment.

    (B) National Forest lands are an underutilized resource, and the Forest Service should allow more exploitation of natural resources on federal lands.

    (C) The Forest Service is a much more important government agency than the National Park Service.

    (D) Logging and mining should not be allowed in national forest lands, which should be mainly reserved for recreational use.

*Go on to the next page* ➡

Questions 25–30

1      Jean Piaget was a psychologist and
2 philosopher best known for his work with
3 children. Piaget was interested in how people
4 develop as they get older, and more specifically
5 with how they perceive the world, and learn in
6 different ways, as they grow up.
7      Early in his career, Piaget helped to score
8 intelligence tests administered in a school
9 where he was employed, and while scoring
10 them he noticed that there were differences
11 between the results that younger children
12 achieved and the results attained by adults. At
13 the time, the prevailing belief in psychology
14 was that children thought in basically the same
15 way as adults, but that they were simply less
16 competent- so you would expect for a child not
17 to do as well as an adult on a test of
18 intelligence. But there were particular types of
19 mistakes which adults did not make, and which
20 children would consistently make. To Piaget,
21 that suggested more than just different levels
22 of intelligence: that suggested that children
23 were thinking in fundamentally different ways
24 from adults.
25      Piaget would go on to conduct a number

26 of revealing experiments with children of
27 various ages that showed the ways in which
28 their perception of the world changed as they
29 grew. Based on his observations, Piaget defined
30 a series of stages of development in children,
31 during which their perceptions of the world
32 change in significant ways. For this work, he is
33 regarded by some as the father of
34 Developmental Psychology, the field of
35 psychology concerned with the growth and
36 development of human minds.
37      Piaget's work hasn't survived without
38 criticism: many of the distinctions between the
39 stages may not be as clear as Piaget proposed,
40 and some researchers have contended that his
41 experimental results are the product of
42 phenomena other than his proposed stages of
43 development. But Piaget's work has
44 nonetheless been profoundly influential.
45 Generations of psychologists and educators
46 have studied Piaget, and his thinking has
47 helped to shape the way that school curricula
48 are designed, the ways in which psychologists
49 work with children, and the advice that some
50 parenting experts give on raising children.

*Go on to the next page* ➡

25. This passage is mainly concerned with

    (A) discussing the career and legacy of Jean Piaget.

    (B) exploring the implications of Piaget's theories for teachers and psychologists.

    (C) describing the theories of Jean Piaget.

    (D) providing a critical view of Piaget's work.

26. As it is used in line 13, the word "prevailing" most nearly means

    (A) victorious.

    (B) dominant.

    (C) singular.

    (D) improbable.

27. Which of the following statements is supported by information in the passage?

    (A) Piaget's ideas about psychology are no longer relevant, but he is still notable as a philosopher.

    (B) Psychologists and teachers continue to resist Piaget's ideas, but have been unable to disprove them.

    (C) The children that Piaget worked with developed very well, and continue to serve as a model for students and educators today.

    (D) Ideas about development have changed somewhat since Piaget's time, but his work remains important.

28. Which of the following questions would probably have been LEAST relevant to Piaget's studies?

    (A) Why do some adults do better than other adults on IQ tests?

    (B) Are there some problems that young children solve faster than older ones?

    (C) Do adults learn new activities more quickly than children?

    (D) At what age can children solve simple problems with algebra?

29. Which of the following words could replace "competent" in line 16 without changing the meaning of the sentence?

    (A) appropriate

    (B) adequate

    (C) credentialed

    (D) capable

30. Piaget first began to notice fundamental differences in the way that children and adults think when

    (A) he helped to create the first intelligence tests for children and adults.

    (B) he realized that the prevailing beliefs in psychology may be wrong.

    (C) he was helping to score intelligence tests administered to adults and children.

    (D) he conducted experiments with children of various ages.

*Go on to the next page* ➡

Questions 31–36

1    Salt is often used as a de-icing agent on
2  roads and sidewalks because a solution of salt
3  and water has a lower freezing point than pure
4  water. The ice exchanges molecules with the
5  salt, creating a solution, and because this
6  solution has a lower freezing point than pure
7  water, the ice often melts. If the temperature is
8  very cold, however, the ice may remain solid. In
9  such cases, sand is spread over the surface of
10  the ice in order to maintain traction, rather
11  than trying to melt the ice.
12    Salt is also added to ice to make cold
13  brine. The chemical reaction that occurs as the
14  salt melts the ice actually reduces the
15  temperature of the solution, resulting in liquid
16  water which is colder than the normal freezing
17  point of water. This effect is used when making
18  ice cream: a container of flavored cream is
19  frozen by submerging it in cold brine while
20  stirring, although care is taken to avoid letting
21  the brine mix with the cream.
22    It is widely believed that salt also lowers
23  the boiling point of water, which would cause
24  water to come to a boil more quickly when
25  heated. However, salt actually has the opposite
26  effect: adding salt to water increases its boiling
27  point, meaning that salted water must reach a
28  higher temperature than unsalted water before
29  it begins to boil. This is a very small effect,

30  however. Almost twelve teaspoons of salt
31  would be required to increase the boiling point
32  of an ounce of water by one degree Fahrenheit.
33  Thus, the amount of salt that is typically used in
34  cooking probably has no real impact on the
35  speed at which water boils.
36    It does, however, affect the flavor of the
37  food.  Salt has been used in food preparation
38  for as long as humans have been keeping
39  record, both because it can enhance the flavors
40  of otherwise bland or bitter foods, and because
41  it is a natural preservative.  This is because salt
42  draws in moisture, dehydrating foods treated
43  with generous applications of salt.  Such dried
44  foods are less hospitable to the bacteria that
45  cause the decomposition of fresh, moist foods,
46  and can thus be stored for long periods of time
47  without decay.
48    This process of using salt to preserve
49  foods is called curing, and requires a
50  concentration of salt of nearly 20% to be
51  effective. Curing is used especially often to
52  preserve meat or fish, but certain vegetables
53  such as cabbage can also be stored this way.
54  The primary ingredient used in curing foods is
55  simple table salt, along with other compounds
56  such as nitrates, nitrites, and sugar. Salt is
57  sometimes also used in smaller doses in other
58  forms of food preservation, such as pickling.

*Go on to the next page* ➜

31. People often spread salt on icy streets and sidewalks in order to

    (A) generate heat that will melt the ice.

    (B) increase traction.

    (C) melt the ice by lowering its freezing point.

    (D) warn drivers of icy conditions.

32. Adding a pinch of salt to a large pot of water would most likely

    (A) cause the water to boil more quickly.

    (B) cause the water to boil more slowly.

    (C) have little impact on the water's boiling point.

    (D) be enough to cure any meat in the water.

33. In line 13 the word "brine" most nearly means

    (A) a solution of salt and water.

    (B) frozen saltwater.

    (C) boiling saltwater.

    (D) a solution of sand and ice.

34. The author's style in this passage could best be described as

    (A) argumentative.

    (B) expository.

    (C) narrative.

    (D) condescending.

35. This passage is primarily about

    (A) the properties and uses of salt.

    (B) how salt is used to melt ice.

    (C) how salt interacts with water.

    (D) salt's use in food preparation.

36. The function of the third paragraph (lines 22–35) is to

    (A) argue that salt lowers the boiling point of water.

    (B) discuss salt's use as a natural preservative.

    (C) describe salt's impact on the boiling point of water.

    (D) explain the chemical composition of salt.

STOP. Do not go on until told to do so.

**STOP**

## SECTION 4

## Mathematics Achievement

**47 Questions**

**Time: 40 minutes**

Each question is followed by four suggested answers. Read each question and then decide which one of the four suggested answers is best.

Find the row of spaces on your answer document that has the same number as the question. In this row, mark the space having the same letter as the answer you have chosen. You may write in your test booklet.

---

SAMPLE QUESTION:

Sample Answer

If $a = 3$, what is the value $a^2 + (3 \times 4) \div 6$?

(A) 3.5

(B) 11

(C) 14.5

(D) 20

The correct answer is 11, so circle B is darkened.

---

STOP. Do not go on
until told to do so.

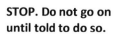

1. Which number has the most unique prime factors?

   (A) 15

   (B) 17

   (C) 27

   (D) 43

2. If $y = 2$ and $\frac{xy}{x-y^2} = 0$, then which of the following could be a value of $x$?

   (A) $y^2$

   (B) $2y$

   (C) $2 - y$

   (D) $y^2 - 2$

3. How many millimeters are in 0.345km?

   (A) 345 mm

   (B) $3.45 \times 10^3$ mm

   (C) $3.45 \times 10^5$ mm

   (D) $3.45 \times 10^6$ mm

4. $\sqrt{-36} =$

   (A) $6i$

   (B) $-6i$

   (C) 6

   (D) $-6$

5. There are 3 blue marbles, 5 red marbles, and 7 yellow marbles. Shania is randomly removing marbles from the bag and giving them to her brother. What is the probability that she gives her brother first a blue marble and then a red marble?

   (A) $\frac{1}{15}$

   (B) $\frac{1}{14}$

   (C) $\frac{1}{7}$

   (D) $\frac{8}{15}$

6. At Frank's bakery, a batch of cupcakes requires 12 eggs and 32 cups of flour. If Frank wants to scale down this recipe and make cupcakes at home with 3 eggs, how many cups of flour should he use?

   (A) 4

   (B) 8

   (C) $\frac{32}{3}$

   (D) 20

7. One-fifth of 1.6 plus one-tenth of 3.2 equals

   (A) 0.32.

   (B) 0.64.

   (C) 1.28.

   (D) 4.8.

8. The formula for the volume of a sphere is $V = \frac{4}{3}\pi r^3$. Sphere $A$ has a radius of 2cm and Sphere $B$ has a radius of 4cm. How many times greater is the volume of Sphere $B$ than the volume of Sphere $A$?

   (A) 2

   (B) $\frac{16}{3}$

   (C) 8

   (D) $\frac{32}{3}$

9. Jen's office is 30km away from her house. On the way to the office, she drove at an average speed of 90km/hour. On the way home, she drove at an average speed of 60km/hour. How long was her entire roundtrip, in minutes?

   (A) 150

   (B) 90

   (C) 75

   (D) 50

*Go on to the next page* ➡

10. The students at Sandbanks Elementary School were asked about their favorite sports.

**Students' Favorite Sports**

- ■ Hockey
- ▨ Soccer
- ▨ Basketball
- ▨ Volleyball

If 91 students picked hockey, approximately how many students are there at the school?

(A) 182

(B) 320

(C) 360

(D) 400

---

11. Julio recorded the heights of several plants in his garden in inches: 2, 3, 5, 7, and 8. What is the product of the average and the range of this list of numbers?

(A) 30

(B) 40

(C) 50

(D) 60

12. A diner offers a lunch combo: customers can choose one of 4 different sandwiches, one of 3 different soups, and either coffee or tea. How many different lunch combinations are possible?

(A) 9

(B) 12

(C) 14

(D) 24

13. David has taken four tests so far in his math class. His scores were 80, 85, 78, and 90. What does David need to get on his fifth test in order to bring his average up to an 86?

(A) 86

(B) 94

(C) 95

(D) 97

14. Which expression is equivalent to the expression $x(x-1) - x + 1$?

(A) 0

(B) $(x-1)^2$

(C) $x^2 - x + 1$

(D) $x^2 + 1$

*Go on to the next page* ➡

15. The figure below shows a square with side lengths of $\sqrt{2}$ cm that has been inscribed in a circle. What is the area of the shaded region?

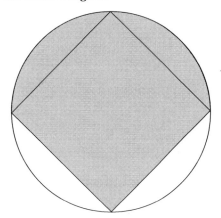

(A) $\frac{\pi}{2} - 2$ cm²

(B) $\pi - 1$ cm²

(C) $\frac{\pi}{2}$ cm²

(D) $\frac{\pi}{2} + 1$ cm²

16. A sequence is shown below. What is the 7th term in this sequence?

$$-\frac{1}{4}, \frac{1}{2}, -1, 2, -4, \ldots$$

(A) $-16$

(B) $6$

(C) $8$

(D) $16$

17. Use these two functions to answer this question.

$$j(x) = 10x - 3$$
$$k(x) = 3$$

At which point do these two functions intersect?

(A) $(3, 3)$

(B) $(3, \frac{6}{10})$

(C) $(\frac{3}{5}, 3)$

(D) $(10, 3)$

18. The solution set of which inequality is graphed below?

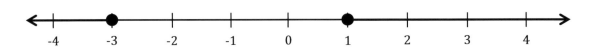

(A) $|x + 1| \geq 2$

(B) $|x - 1| \geq 2$

(C) $|x + 1| > 2$

(D) $|x + 1| \leq 2$

*Go on to the next page* ➡

19. The stem-and-leaf plot below represents the ages of people at an office.

| Stem | Leaf |
|------|------|
| 2 | 7 8 |
| 3 | 0 2 3 6 |
| 4 | 1 1 5 6 7 8 |
| 5 | 2 3 4 7 9 9 |
| 6 | 1 2 6 9 |
| 7 | 3 |

5 | 2 represents a 52 year old

What is the median age?

(A) 41
(B) 47
(C) 48
(D) 52

20. The points $(-5, 4)$ and $(7, 12)$ are the endpoints of the diameter of a circle. What are the coordinates of the center of this circle?

(A) $(2, 16)$
(B) $(6, 16)$
(C) $(1, 8)$
(D) $(6, 8)$

21. What is the $y$-intercept of $y = 3x - 5$?

(A) $\frac{5}{3}$
(B) 3
(C) 5
(D) $-5$

22. Angles A and B are complementary. If the measure of angle A is $30°$, what is the measure of angle B?

(A) $30°$
(B) $60°$
(C) $90°$
(D) $150°$

23. If $\frac{1600}{x} = 32$, what is the value of $x$?

(A) 5
(B) 20
(C) 50
(D) 500

24. Which expression is equivalent to $\sqrt[5]{x^{20}}$?

(A) $x^4$
(B) $x^{10}$
(C) $x^{15}$
(D) $x^{25}$

25. What is the sum of angles A, B, and C in the diagram below?

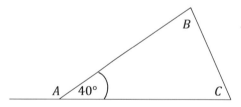

(A) $180°$
(B) $280°$
(C) $300°$
(D) $320°$

*Go on to the next page* ➡

26. If $f(x) = 4x - 3$, what is the value of $f(7)$?

    (A) 4

    (B) 25

    (C) 27

    (D) 28

27. What is the product of 243 and 9?

    (A) 2185

    (B) 2186

    (C) 2187

    (D) 2188

28. The probability that Meghan scores a goal in soccer is 75%. If she tries 48 times to score a goal, how many times is she expected to miss?

    (A) 4

    (B) 12

    (C) 20

    (D) 36

29. Two runners who run at exactly the same speed run laps around a track, shown below.

    If the radius of the outer circle is twice the radius of the inner circle, how many laps will the runner on the outside run in the time that it takes the runner on the inside to run 10 laps?

    (A) 2.5

    (B) 5

    (C) 15

    (D) 20

30. The table below comes from an equation for a graph.

    | $x$ | $y$ |
    |-----|-----|
    | -1  | 0   |
    | 0   | 1   |
    | 1   | 2   |
    | 2   | 9   |

    What is a possible equation for the graph?

    (A) $y = x + 1$

    (B) $y = x^3$

    (C) $y = x^3 + 1$

    (D) $y = 3x + 1$

31. The country of Westerovia has an alternate system for money. In this system, 1 coin is equal to 12 papers, 1 paper is equal to 4 beads, and 17 beads are equal to 1 jewel. Which expression represents the number of coins that equals the value of 5 jewels?

    (A) $\frac{5}{12 \times 4 \times 17}$

    (B) $\frac{17}{4 \times 12}$

    (C) $\frac{5 \times 17}{4 \times 12}$

    (D) $\frac{5 \times 4 \times 12}{17}$

32. At 10:00AM, a ship is 50km away from the mainland. If it continues sailing in the same direction away from the mainland at 30km/hour, which expression represents its distance from the mainland ($D$) in terms of the number of hours past 10:00AM ($t$)?

    (A) $D = 50t + 30$

    (B) $D = 10t + 50$

    (C) $D = 10t + 30$

    (D) $D = 30t + 50$

*Go on to the next page* ➡

33. What is the solution set for this inequality?

$$-7 < -4x + 1 < 13$$

(A) $-3 < x < -2$

(B) $-3 < x < \frac{3}{2}$

(C) $-3 < x < 2$

(D) $2 < x < 6$

34. Joe and Tyson work on an assembly line at a factory doing quality control. Joe samples $\frac{7}{9}$ of the pens and Tyson samples $\frac{7}{8}$ of the pens. Out of a batch of 72 pens, what is the least number of pens that will be checked by *both* workers?

(A) 16

(B) 47

(C) 56

(D) 63

35. Which is the most reasonable unit to measure the weight of an eraser?

(A) liters

(B) milligrams

(C) grams

(D) kilograms

36. Which numerical expression does NOT represent an integer?

(A) $\frac{\sqrt{12}}{\sqrt{3}}$

(B) $\sqrt{5 + \sqrt{16}}$

(C) $(\sqrt{9})^2 + (\sqrt{2})^2$

(D) $(\sqrt{9} + \sqrt{2})^2$

37. The figure below represents a cake that Luke wants to bake. The formula used to find the volume of a cylinder is $V = r^2 h \pi$, where $r$ is the radius of the cylinder and $h$ is the height of the cylinder.

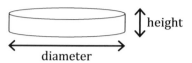

If Luke wants the cake to have a diameter of 10 inches and a height of 3 inches, what will the volume of his cake be?

(A) $45\pi$ inches³

(B) $60\pi$ inches³

(C) $75\pi$ inches³

(D) $90\pi$ inches³

38. Tyler washes the dishes at a rate of fifteen dishes every ten minutes. Harry can only dry the dishes at a rate of fifteen dishes every half hour. If Tyler spends fifty minutes washing the dishes, how long does it take Harry to dry them?

(A) 5 hours and 45 minutes

(B) 3 hours and 20 minutes

(C) 2 hours and 30 minutes

(D) 1 hour and 30 minutes

*Go on to the next page* ➡

39. Three vertices of a kite are plotted on the graph below.

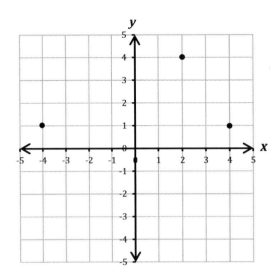

At which point should the fourth vertex be plotted to complete the kite?

(A) $(-2, -2)$

(B) $(-2, 4)$

(C) $(-2, 2)$

(D) $(2, -2)$

---

40. Corwin used 5 cups of pecans to bake a pie. Each cup of pecans holds about 20 individual nuts. If he is going to split his pie evenly among 8 of his friends, approximately how many pecans will each person get to eat?

(A) 12.5

(B) 10

(C) 2.5

(D) $\frac{5}{8}$

41. The formula for the volume of a cone is $V = \frac{1}{3}\pi r^2 h$, where $r$ is the cone's radius and $h$ is the cone's height.

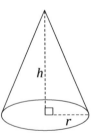

The cone shown above has a height of 5 in. and a radius of $\sqrt{3}$ in. What is the cone's volume?

(A) $\sqrt{3}\pi$ in²

(B) $3\pi$ in²

(C) $5\pi$ in²

(D) $15\pi$ in²

*Go on to the next page* ➡

42. If $3(y - 9^m) = 3y - 9$, what is the value of $m$?

(A) 3

(B) $\sqrt{3}$

(C) $\frac{1}{2}$

(D) 0

43. In the figure below, two congruent regular pentagons have been joined at their bases.

If the perimeter of the entire figure is 40, what is the length of one of the pentagons' sides?

(A) 2

(B) 5

(C) 8

(D) 16

44. The graph below shows the population size and land area of three different towns.

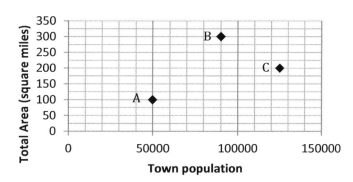

The population density of a town is measured by dividing the town population by the total land size. What is the ratio of the population density of Town A to the population density of Town C?

(A) 3 to 8

(B) 1 to 2

(C) 3 to 4

(D) 4 to 5

*Go on to the next page* ➡

45. If $w$ is a positive integer, which expression is equivalent to the expression $\sqrt{81x^{4w} - 16y^2}$?

(A) $(3x^w - 4y)(3x^w + 4y)$

(B) $(9x^w - 8y)(9x^w + 8y)$

(C) $(3x^{2w} - 4y^2)(3x^{2w} + 4y^2)$

(D) $(81x^{4w} - 4y^2)(81x^{4w} + 4y^2)$

46. If $A = \begin{bmatrix} 2 & 8 \\ -3 & 7 \end{bmatrix}$ and $B = \begin{bmatrix} 5 & -10 \\ 13 & -11 \end{bmatrix}$, what is $A + B$?

(A) $\begin{bmatrix} 10 & -80 \\ -39 & 77 \end{bmatrix}$

(B) $\begin{bmatrix} 7 & -2 \\ 10 & 4 \end{bmatrix}$

(C) $\begin{bmatrix} -3 & 18 \\ -16 & 4 \end{bmatrix}$

(D) $\begin{bmatrix} 7 & -2 \\ 10 & -4 \end{bmatrix}$

47. Use the triangle below to answer this question.

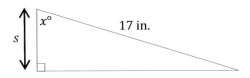

The value of which expression is equal to the length of side $s$?

(A) $\frac{17\tan(x)}{5}$

(B) $17\sin(x)$

(C) $17\cos(x)$

(D) $\frac{17}{2}\sin(x)$

STOP. Do not go on until told to do so.

**STOP**

# Essay Topic Sheet

The directions for the Essay portion of the ISEE are printed in the box below. Use the pre-lined pages on pages 218-219 for this part of the Practice Test.

You will have 30 minutes to plan and write an essay on the topic printed on the other side of this page. **Do not write on another topic. An essay on another topic is not acceptable.**

The essay is designed to give you an opportunity to show how well you can write. You should try to express your thoughts clearly. How well you write is much more important than how much you write, but you need to say enough for a reader to understand what you mean.

You will probably want to write more than a short paragraph. You should also be aware that a copy of your essay will be sent to each school that will be receiving your test results. You are to write only in the appropriate section of the answer sheet. Please write or print so that your writing may be read by someone who is not familiar with your handwriting.

You may make notes and plan your essay on the reverse side of the page. Allow enough time to copy the final form onto your answer sheet. You must copy the essay topic onto your answer sheet, on page 218, in the box provided.

Please remember to write only the final draft of the essay on pages 218-219 of your answer sheet and to write it in blue or black pen. Again, you may use cursive writing or you may print. Only pages 218-219 will be sent to the schools.

*Directions continue on the next page.*

**REMINDER:** Please write this essay topic on the first few lines of the first page of your essay sheet.

### Essay Topic

Your local government has a surprising budget surplus, leaving it with extra funds to spend. How do you think the extra funds should be used to improve your community?

- Only write on this essay question
- Only pages 218 and 219 will be sent to the schools
- Only write in blue or black pen

# NOTES

_____

_____

_____

_____

_____

_____

_____

_____

_____

_____

_____

_____

_____

_____

_____

_____

_____

_____

_____

# PRACTICE TEST 6

## UPPER LEVEL

# HOW TO TAKE THIS PRACTICE TEST

To simulate an accurate testing environment, sit at a desk in a quiet location free of distractions—no TV, computers, phones, music, or noise—and clear your desk of all materials except pencils and erasers. Remember that no calculators, rulers, protractors, dictionaries, or other aids are allowed on the ISEE.

Give yourself the following amounts of time for each section:

| SECTION | SUBJECT | TIME LIMIT |
|---------|---------|------------|
| 1 | Verbal Reasoning | 20 minutes |
| 2 | Quantitative Reasoning | 35 minutes |
| *5 minute break* | | |
| 3 | Reading Comprehension | 35 minutes |
| 4 | Mathematics Achievement | 40 minutes |
| *5 minute break* | | |
| 5 | Essay | 30 minutes |

Have an adult help you monitor your time, or use a watch and time yourself. Only give yourself the allotted time for each section; put your pencil down when your time is up.

Follow the instructions carefully. As you take your test, bubble your answers into the answer sheets provided. Use the test booklet as scratch paper for notes and calculations. Remember that you are not granted time at the end of a section to transfer your answers to the answer sheet, so you must do this as you go along.

When you are finished, check your answers against the answer keys provided. Then, score your exam using the directions at the end of the book.

**Ivy Global**

Note: students with diagnosed learning disabilities who apply for testing with accommodations may receive extra time, or may be allowed to use certain assistive devices during the ISEE. For more information, visit http://erblearn.org/parents/admission/isee/accommodations.

# Ivy Global

# ISEE
## UPPER LEVEL TEST 2

### MARKING INSTRUCTIONS

- Use a #2 or HB pencil only on pages 266 and 267.
- Use a ballpoint pen for your essay on pages 268 and 269.
- Make dark marks that completely fill the circle.
- Erase clearly any mark you wish to change.
- Make no stray marks on this form.
- Do not fold or crease this form.

Correct Mark          Incorrect Marks

### 1 VERBAL REASONING

| | | | |
|---|---|---|---|
| 1 Ⓐ Ⓑ Ⓒ Ⓓ | 15 Ⓐ Ⓑ Ⓒ Ⓓ | 29 Ⓐ Ⓑ Ⓒ Ⓓ | |
| 2 Ⓐ Ⓑ Ⓒ Ⓓ | 16 Ⓐ Ⓑ Ⓒ Ⓓ | 30 Ⓐ Ⓑ Ⓒ Ⓓ | |
| 3 Ⓐ Ⓑ Ⓒ Ⓓ | 17 Ⓐ Ⓑ Ⓒ Ⓓ | 31 Ⓐ Ⓑ Ⓒ Ⓓ | |
| 4 Ⓐ Ⓑ Ⓒ Ⓓ | 18 Ⓐ Ⓑ Ⓒ Ⓓ | 32 Ⓐ Ⓑ Ⓒ Ⓓ | |
| 5 Ⓐ Ⓑ Ⓒ Ⓓ | 19 Ⓐ Ⓑ Ⓒ Ⓓ | 33 Ⓐ Ⓑ Ⓒ Ⓓ | |
| 6 Ⓐ Ⓑ Ⓒ Ⓓ | 20 Ⓐ Ⓑ Ⓒ Ⓓ | 34 Ⓐ Ⓑ Ⓒ Ⓓ **Lower Level Ends** | |
| 7 Ⓐ Ⓑ Ⓒ Ⓓ | 21 Ⓐ Ⓑ Ⓒ Ⓓ | 35 Ⓐ Ⓑ Ⓒ Ⓓ | |
| 8 Ⓐ Ⓑ Ⓒ Ⓓ | 22 Ⓐ Ⓑ Ⓒ Ⓓ | 36 Ⓐ Ⓑ Ⓒ Ⓓ | |
| 9 Ⓐ Ⓑ Ⓒ Ⓓ | 23 Ⓐ Ⓑ Ⓒ Ⓓ | 37 Ⓐ Ⓑ Ⓒ Ⓓ | |
| 10 Ⓐ Ⓑ Ⓒ Ⓓ | 24 Ⓐ Ⓑ Ⓒ Ⓓ | 38 Ⓐ Ⓑ Ⓒ Ⓓ | |
| 11 Ⓐ Ⓑ Ⓒ Ⓓ | 25 Ⓐ Ⓑ Ⓒ Ⓓ | 39 Ⓐ Ⓑ Ⓒ Ⓓ | |
| 12 Ⓐ Ⓑ Ⓒ Ⓓ | 26 Ⓐ Ⓑ Ⓒ Ⓓ | 40 Ⓐ Ⓑ Ⓒ Ⓓ **Middle/Upper Level Ends** | |
| 13 Ⓐ Ⓑ Ⓒ Ⓓ | 27 Ⓐ Ⓑ Ⓒ Ⓓ | | |
| 14 Ⓐ Ⓑ Ⓒ Ⓓ | 28 Ⓐ Ⓑ Ⓒ Ⓓ | | |

## 2 QUANTITATIVE REASONING

| | | | | | |
|---|---|---|---|---|---|
| 1 Ⓐ Ⓑ Ⓒ Ⓓ | 15 Ⓐ Ⓑ Ⓒ Ⓓ | 29 Ⓐ Ⓑ Ⓒ Ⓓ |
| 2 Ⓐ Ⓑ Ⓒ Ⓓ | 16 Ⓐ Ⓑ Ⓒ Ⓓ | 30 Ⓐ Ⓑ Ⓒ Ⓓ |
| 3 Ⓐ Ⓑ Ⓒ Ⓓ | 17 Ⓐ Ⓑ Ⓒ Ⓓ | 31 Ⓐ Ⓑ Ⓒ Ⓓ |
| 4 Ⓐ Ⓑ Ⓒ Ⓓ | 18 Ⓐ Ⓑ Ⓒ Ⓓ | 32 Ⓐ Ⓑ Ⓒ Ⓓ |
| 5 Ⓐ Ⓑ Ⓒ Ⓓ | 19 Ⓐ Ⓑ Ⓒ Ⓓ | 33 Ⓐ Ⓑ Ⓒ Ⓓ |
| 6 Ⓐ Ⓑ Ⓒ Ⓓ | 20 Ⓐ Ⓑ Ⓒ Ⓓ | 34 Ⓐ Ⓑ Ⓒ Ⓓ |
| 7 Ⓐ Ⓑ Ⓒ Ⓓ | 21 Ⓐ Ⓑ Ⓒ Ⓓ | 35 Ⓐ Ⓑ Ⓒ Ⓓ |
| 8 Ⓐ Ⓑ Ⓒ Ⓓ | 22 Ⓐ Ⓑ Ⓒ Ⓓ | 36 Ⓐ Ⓑ Ⓒ Ⓓ |
| 9 Ⓐ Ⓑ Ⓒ Ⓓ | 23 Ⓐ Ⓑ Ⓒ Ⓓ | 37 Ⓐ Ⓑ Ⓒ Ⓓ **Middle/Upper Level Ends** |
| 10 Ⓐ Ⓑ Ⓒ Ⓓ | 24 Ⓐ Ⓑ Ⓒ Ⓓ | 38 Ⓐ Ⓑ Ⓒ Ⓓ **Lower Level Ends** |
| 11 Ⓐ Ⓑ Ⓒ Ⓓ | 25 Ⓐ Ⓑ Ⓒ Ⓓ | |
| 12 Ⓐ Ⓑ Ⓒ Ⓓ | 26 Ⓐ Ⓑ Ⓒ Ⓓ | |
| 13 Ⓐ Ⓑ Ⓒ Ⓓ | 27 Ⓐ Ⓑ Ⓒ Ⓓ | |
| 14 Ⓐ Ⓑ Ⓒ Ⓓ | 28 Ⓐ Ⓑ Ⓒ Ⓓ | |

## 4 MATHEMATICS ACHIEVEMENT

| | | |
|---|---|---|
| 1 Ⓐ Ⓑ Ⓒ Ⓓ | 18 Ⓐ Ⓑ Ⓒ Ⓓ | 35 Ⓐ Ⓑ Ⓒ Ⓓ |
| 2 Ⓐ Ⓑ Ⓒ Ⓓ | 19 Ⓐ Ⓑ Ⓒ Ⓓ | 36 Ⓐ Ⓑ Ⓒ Ⓓ |
| 3 Ⓐ Ⓑ Ⓒ Ⓓ | 20 Ⓐ Ⓑ Ⓒ Ⓓ | 37 Ⓐ Ⓑ Ⓒ Ⓓ |
| 4 Ⓐ Ⓑ Ⓒ Ⓓ | 21 Ⓐ Ⓑ Ⓒ Ⓓ | 38 Ⓐ Ⓑ Ⓒ Ⓓ |
| 5 Ⓐ Ⓑ Ⓒ Ⓓ | 22 Ⓐ Ⓑ Ⓒ Ⓓ | 39 Ⓐ Ⓑ Ⓒ Ⓓ |
| 6 Ⓐ Ⓑ Ⓒ Ⓓ | 23 Ⓐ Ⓑ Ⓒ Ⓓ | 40 Ⓐ Ⓑ Ⓒ Ⓓ |
| 7 Ⓐ Ⓑ Ⓒ Ⓓ | 24 Ⓐ Ⓑ Ⓒ Ⓓ | 41 Ⓐ Ⓑ Ⓒ Ⓓ |
| 8 Ⓐ Ⓑ Ⓒ Ⓓ | 25 Ⓐ Ⓑ Ⓒ Ⓓ | 42 Ⓐ Ⓑ Ⓒ Ⓓ |
| 9 Ⓐ Ⓑ Ⓒ Ⓓ | 26 Ⓐ Ⓑ Ⓒ Ⓓ | 43 Ⓐ Ⓑ Ⓒ Ⓓ |
| 10 Ⓐ Ⓑ Ⓒ Ⓓ | 27 Ⓐ Ⓑ Ⓒ Ⓓ | 44 Ⓐ Ⓑ Ⓒ Ⓓ |
| 11 Ⓐ Ⓑ Ⓒ Ⓓ | 28 Ⓐ Ⓑ Ⓒ Ⓓ | 45 Ⓐ Ⓑ Ⓒ Ⓓ |
| 12 Ⓐ Ⓑ Ⓒ Ⓓ | 29 Ⓐ Ⓑ Ⓒ Ⓓ | 46 Ⓐ Ⓑ Ⓒ Ⓓ |
| 13 Ⓐ Ⓑ Ⓒ Ⓓ | 30 Ⓐ Ⓑ Ⓒ Ⓓ **Lower Level Ends** | 47 Ⓐ Ⓑ Ⓒ Ⓓ **Middle/Upper Level Ends** |
| 14 Ⓐ Ⓑ Ⓒ Ⓓ | 31 Ⓐ Ⓑ Ⓒ Ⓓ | |
| 15 Ⓐ Ⓑ Ⓒ Ⓓ | 32 Ⓐ Ⓑ Ⓒ Ⓓ | |
| 16 Ⓐ Ⓑ Ⓒ Ⓓ | 33 Ⓐ Ⓑ Ⓒ Ⓓ | |
| 17 Ⓐ Ⓑ Ⓒ Ⓓ | 34 Ⓐ Ⓑ Ⓒ Ⓓ | |

## 3 READING COMPREHENSION

| | | |
|---|---|---|
| 1 Ⓐ Ⓑ Ⓒ Ⓓ | 15 Ⓐ Ⓑ Ⓒ Ⓓ | 29 Ⓐ Ⓑ Ⓒ Ⓓ |
| 2 Ⓐ Ⓑ Ⓒ Ⓓ | 16 Ⓐ Ⓑ Ⓒ Ⓓ | 30 Ⓐ Ⓑ Ⓒ Ⓓ |
| 3 Ⓐ Ⓑ Ⓒ Ⓓ | 17 Ⓐ Ⓑ Ⓒ Ⓓ | 31 Ⓐ Ⓑ Ⓒ Ⓓ |
| 4 Ⓐ Ⓑ Ⓒ Ⓓ | 18 Ⓐ Ⓑ Ⓒ Ⓓ | 32 Ⓐ Ⓑ Ⓒ Ⓓ |
| 5 Ⓐ Ⓑ Ⓒ Ⓓ | 19 Ⓐ Ⓑ Ⓒ Ⓓ | 33 Ⓐ Ⓑ Ⓒ Ⓓ |
| 6 Ⓐ Ⓑ Ⓒ Ⓓ | 20 Ⓐ Ⓑ Ⓒ Ⓓ | 34 Ⓐ Ⓑ Ⓒ Ⓓ |
| 7 Ⓐ Ⓑ Ⓒ Ⓓ | 21 Ⓐ Ⓑ Ⓒ Ⓓ | 35 Ⓐ Ⓑ Ⓒ Ⓓ |
| 8 Ⓐ Ⓑ Ⓒ Ⓓ | 22 Ⓐ Ⓑ Ⓒ Ⓓ | 36 Ⓐ Ⓑ Ⓒ Ⓓ **Middle/Upper Level Ends** |
| 9 Ⓐ Ⓑ Ⓒ Ⓓ | 23 Ⓐ Ⓑ Ⓒ Ⓓ | |
| 10 Ⓐ Ⓑ Ⓒ Ⓓ | 24 Ⓐ Ⓑ Ⓒ Ⓓ | |
| 11 Ⓐ Ⓑ Ⓒ Ⓓ | 25 Ⓐ Ⓑ Ⓒ Ⓓ **Lower Level Ends** | |
| 12 Ⓐ Ⓑ Ⓒ Ⓓ | 26 Ⓐ Ⓑ Ⓒ Ⓓ | |
| 13 Ⓐ Ⓑ Ⓒ Ⓓ | 27 Ⓐ Ⓑ Ⓒ Ⓓ | |
| 14 Ⓐ Ⓑ Ⓒ Ⓓ | 28 Ⓐ Ⓑ Ⓒ Ⓓ | |

**Ivy Global**

STUDENT NAME _____  GRADE APPLYING FOR _____

Use a blue or black ballpoint pen to write the final draft of your essay on this sheet.

You must write your essay topic in this space.

_____

_____

_____

Use specific details and examples in your response.

_____

_____

_____

_____

_____

_____

_____

_____

_____

_____

_____

_____

_____

_____

_____

_____

_____

_____

_____

_____

_____

_____

_____

_____

Ivy Global

# Section 1
# Verbal Reasoning

40 Questions   Time: 20 minutes

This section is divided into two parts that contain two different types of questions. As soon as you have completed Part One, answer the questions in Part Two. You may write in your test booklet. For each answer you select, fill in the corresponding circle on your answer document.

## PART ONE — SYNONYMS

Each question in Part One consists of a word in capital letters followed by four answer choices. Select the one word that is most nearly the same in meaning as the word in capital letters.

---

SAMPLE QUESTION:                                         Sample Answer

CHARGE:                                                  Ⓐ Ⓑ ● Ⓓ

(A) release

(B) belittle

(C) accuse

(D) conspire

The correct answer is "accuse," so circle C is darkened.

---

*Go on to the next page* ➡

# VR

## PART TWO — SENTENCE COMPLETION

Each question in Part Two is made up of a sentence with one blank. Each blank indicates that a word or phrase is missing. The sentence is followed by four answer choices. Select the word or phrase that will best complete the meaning of the sentence as a whole.

---

SAMPLE QUESTIONS:                                                                          <u>Sample Answer</u>

    It rained so much that the streets were -------.                ● Ⓑ Ⓒ Ⓓ

(A) flooded

(B) arid

(C) paved

(D) crowded

The correct answer is "flooded," so circle A is darkened.


    The house was so dirty that it took -------.                    Ⓐ Ⓑ Ⓒ ●

(A) less than ten minutes to wash it.

(B) four months to demolish it.

(C) over a week to walk across it.

(D) two days to clean it.

The correct answer is "two days to clean it," so circle D is darkened.

---

STOP. Do not go on
until told to do so.

**Directions:** Select the word that is most nearly the same in meaning as the word in capital letters.

1.  FROLIC

    (A) prance

    (B) jimmy

    (C) laugh

    (D) stride

2.  CRUDE

    (A) naked

    (B) insolent

    (C) colorful

    (D) unrefined

3.  APPREHEND

    (A) charge

    (B) sentence

    (C) seek

    (D) capture

4.  WIRED

    (A) crackling

    (B) captured

    (C) remote

    (D) excited

5.  HEEDLESS

    (A) hungry

    (B) inconsiderate

    (C) open

    (D) remorseless

6.  ASSIMILATE

    (A) anticipate

    (B) raise

    (C) reject

    (D) incorporate

7.  REGIMEN

    (A) army

    (B) king

    (C) plan

    (D) dynasty

8.  ASSENT

    (A) justify

    (B) prove

    (C) cultivate

    (D) approve

9.  SKULK

    (A) cry

    (B) blossom

    (C) run

    (D) sneak

10. CANTANKEROUS

    (A) grumpy

    (B) uncouth

    (C) immoral

    (D) undeterred

11. TROUNCE

    (A) rout

    (B) denounce

    (C) fish

    (D) captivate

12. MOLTEN

    (A) shed

    (B) pursued

    (C) burnt

    (D) liquefied

*Go on to the next page* ➡

13. RIGOROUS

    (A) envious

    (B) tactful

    (C) thorough

    (D) cruel

14. CURTAIL

    (A) circle

    (B) rejoice

    (C) limit

    (D) frown

15. AMBITIOUS

    (A) perfect

    (B) bold

    (C) lazy

    (D) careful

16. OVERWHELM

    (A) overpower

    (B) overcook

    (C) overlook

    (D) overthink

17. ADJUST

    (A) judge

    (B) try

    (C) tweak

    (D) carry

18. SQUALL

    (A) snow

    (B) gust

    (C) storm

    (D) thunder

19. BURLY

    (A) belligerent

    (B) muscular

    (C) dour

    (D) angry

*Go on to the next page* ➡

## PART TWO – SENTENCE COMPLETION

**Directions:** Select the word that best completes the sentence.

20. Amish communities tend to be rather
------, choosing to live in isolated rural
areas where they can practice their
religion in peace.

   (A) insular
   (B) outgoing
   (C) grave
   (D) fortunate

21. President Abraham Lincoln was known
for possessing the virtue of ------; that
was how he got the nickname "Honest
Abe."

   (A) truthfulness
   (B) malevolence
   (C) caution
   (D) fervor

22. While professional psychics are ------ in
their abilities, in experimental settings
their predictions are rarely better than
random guesses.

   (A) shallow
   (B) confident
   (C) redundant
   (D) noticeable

23. When Watson and Crick discovered the
double-helix shape of DNA, it completely
changed the ------ of genetic science and
opened the door for new genetic research.

   (A) trademarks
   (B) decorations
   (C) fundamentals
   (D) pages

24. While frostbite causes ------ during its
onset, affected areas become very painful
as they thaw.

   (A) tartness
   (B) dexterity
   (C) numbness
   (D) folly

25. Though I tried to be ------ with my prose,
I still went over the word limit for the
essay.

   (A) unorthodox
   (B) excessive
   (C) concise
   (D) proper

26. Months of snowstorms and frigid
temperatures left many people quite
------ of the weather and ready for spring.

   (A) ignorant
   (B) enamored
   (C) expectant
   (D) weary

27. Canyons are created by the action of
rivers ----- their riverbeds over the course
of centuries, slowly channeling deep rifts
through the earth.

   (A) foraging
   (B) eroding
   (C) regrouping
   (D) replacing

*Go on to the next page* ➜

28. Journalists prefer to interview ------- people whose answers don't sound forced or rehearsed.

    (A) disheveled

    (B) reluctant

    (C) candid

    (D) meticulous

29. Almost all pastry recipes include a small amount of salt in order to ------- the sweetness of the sugar.

    (A) overwhelm

    (B) counteract

    (C) compound

    (D) taste

30. The ------- of our newly built table proved to be unsound; it collapsed after we put a tablecloth on it.

    (A) intuition

    (B) organization

    (C) abstraction

    (D) construction

31. Garden variety ants are actually capable of ------- feats of strength; worker ants can lift objects many times their own body weight.

    (A) impressive

    (B) nonchalant

    (C) requisite

    (D) complex

32. While bunny slopes are ------ enough for beginning skiers to master, double diamond slopes are ------- for even the most experienced of skiers.

    (A) simple...effortless

    (B) convoluted...unforgiving

    (C) intricate...average

    (D) easy...demanding

33. Working long hours can be financially -------, but ultimately ------ to one's health and social life.

    (A) risky...harmful

    (B) prudent...detrimental

    (C) wise...advantageous

    (D) fortunate...supportive

34. While defense lawyers ------- for their client's interests, the job of the prosecutors is to ------ the state's case against them.

    (A) obfuscate...prove

    (B) support...predict

    (C) advocate...argue

    (D) provoke...restrict

35. In fairy tales, knights are often models of ------- who exhibit all virtues and never commit ------- deeds.

    (A) excellence...altruistic

    (B) chivalry...malicious

    (C) opulence...sinister

    (D) rebellion...arrogant

36. While children are often ------- by the tricks of magicians, adults usually find them too ------- to be entertaining.

    (A) enraged...simplistic

    (B) overjoyed...perplexing

    (C) fascinated...transparent

    (D) amused...realistic

37. Large cities produce such ------- amounts of garbage that finding landfills ------- enough to hold all the refuse can be difficult.

    (A) copious...sizeable

    (B) colossal...fallacious

    (C) frequent...adequate

    (D) fearful...comical

*Go on to the next page* ➡

38. Cooking good risotto requires much ------- on the part of the chef; cook the risotto too quickly, and it will clump together and become -------.

    (A) patience...inedible

    (B) aptitude...appetizing

    (C) frustration...unsalvageable

    (D) preparation...mysterious

39. The Soviet Union invested ------- in the Kola Superdeep Borehole, yet still ultimately failed to ------- their target depth of 15,000 meter.

    (A) endlessly...relieve

    (B) tremendously...achieve

    (C) intermittently...possess

    (D) retroactively...accomplish

40. Though eating junk food is often ------- in the moment, it can make you feel ------- and bloated afterward.

    (A) sickening...refreshed

    (B) gratifying...disorganized

    (C) fattening...fabulous

    (D) satisfying...uncomfortable

**STOP. Do not go on until told to do so.** STOP

## Section 2
## Quantitative Reasoning

| 38 Questions | Time: 35 minutes |

Each question is followed by four suggested answers. Read each question and then decide which one of the four suggested answers is best.

Find the row of spaces on your answer document that has the same number as the question. In this row, mark the space having the same letter as the answer you have chosen. You may write in your test booklet.

---

SAMPLE QUESTIONS:                                         Sample Answer

What is the value of the expression $(4 + 6) \div 2$?     Ⓐ Ⓑ ● Ⓓ

(A) 2

(B) 4

(C) 5

(D) 7

The correct answer is 5, so circle C is darkened.

A square has an area of 25cm². What is the length of one of its     Ⓐ ● Ⓒ Ⓓ
sides?

(A) 1 cm

(B) 5 cm

(C) 10 cm

(D) 25 cm

The correct answer is 5, so circle B is darkened.

---

*Go on to the next page* ➔

## PART TWO — QUANTITATIVE COMPARISONS

All questions in Part Two are quantitative comparisons between the quantities shown in Column A and Column B. Using the information given in each question, compare the quantity in Column A to the quantity in Column B, and choose one of these four answer choices:

- (A) The quantity in Column A is greater.
- (B) The quantity in Column B is greater.
- (C) The two quantities are equal.
- (D) The relationship cannot be determined from the information given.

---

SAMPLE QUESTIONS:

| <u>Column A</u> | <u>Column B</u> | <u>Sample Answer</u> |
|:---:|:---:|:---:|
| 5 | $\sqrt{25}$ | Ⓐ Ⓑ ● Ⓓ |

The quantity in <u>Column A</u> (5) is the same as the quantity in <u>Column B</u> (5), so circle C is darkened.

---

$$x = 6^2 - 3 \times 4$$

| <u>Column A</u> | <u>Column B</u> | <u>Sample Answer</u> |
|:---:|:---:|:---:|
| $x$ | 22 | ● Ⓑ Ⓒ Ⓓ |

The quantity in <u>Column A</u> (24) is greater than the quantity in <u>Column B</u> (22), so circle A is darkened.

---

**STOP. Do not go on until told to do so.**  **STOP**

## PART ONE – WORD PROBLEMS

**Directions:** Choose the best answer from the four choices given.

1. If $5 \geq x > -3$, what is the minimum value for $y$ if $y = x^2 - 9$?

   (A) -9

   (B) -3

   (C) 0

   (D) 3

2. Jerry has $b$ car brand names available. Once a brand name is selected, it cannot be selected again. If Jerry selects two cars at random, what is the probability that one of his choices will be a Cool Look brand name car?

   (A) $\frac{2}{b}$

   (B) $\frac{b-2}{b}$

   (C) $\frac{1}{b^2}$

   (D) $2b$

3. A train is moving at 55 miles per hour. A car is moving in the exact opposite direction at $s$ miles per hour. After 2 hours what will be the distance between the train and the car?

   (A) $55 + 2s$ miles

   (B) $2(55 + s)$ miles

   (C) $2s$ miles

   (D) $2(55 - s)$ miles

4. $g^{\nearrow} = \left(\frac{5}{g}\right)^2 - 4^g$. What is the value of $\frac{1}{x}^{\nearrow}$ ?

   (A) $\frac{1}{\left(\frac{5}{x}\right)^2 - 4^x}$

   (B) $(5x)^2 - 2$

   (C) $(5x)^2 - \sqrt[x]{4}$

   (D) $(5x)^2 - \frac{1}{4^x}$

5. A company wants to use sixty-four trucks to bring goods from its warehouses to its headquarters. All the warehouses are located along one highway. Each warehouse loads three quarters of the trucks that arrive or loads one truck, whichever is greater. A truck that has been loaded returns to headquarters, while the remaining empty trucks drive to the next warehouse. How many warehouses will the fleet of sixty-four trucks visit before every truck has returned to headquarters?

   (A) 1

   (B) 2

   (C) 3

   (D) 4

6. What is the value of the expression $\frac{8^{(2/3)} + 4^{(3/2)}}{2^3}$ ?

   (A) $\frac{17}{16}$

   (B) $\frac{3}{2}$

   (C) $\frac{\sqrt[3]{4}}{2\sqrt{2}}$

   (D) $\frac{1280}{3}$

7. The product of all integers from $-1$ to $-100$, inclusive is $z$. What is the product of all integers from $-2$ to $-102$ inclusive?

   (A) $-z$

   (B) $\frac{-z \times 10302}{2}$

   (C) $-z \times 10302$

   (D) $z \times 10302$

*Go on to the next page* ➡

8. If $2y - x = 6$, then which expression is equal to $x$?

   (A) $-2(3 + y)$

   (B) $-2(3 - y)$

   (C) $2(3 - y)$

   (D) $2(3 + y)$

9. Helen ran an average of 15 miles per day for 5 days. After six days of running, her mean distance was 12.5 miles. How many miles did Helen run on the sixth day?

   (A) 0

   (B) 2.5

   (C) 12.5

   (D) 15

10. A trapezoid has two bases. One of the bases measures 5 inches and the other measures 7 inches. If its total area is 36 inches², what is the measure of its height?

    (A) 6 inches

    (B) 12 inches

    (C) 35 inches

    (D) 36 inches

11. A general manager is trying to figure out the cost of making a fruit drink. She knows that the cost of berries and bananas together are equal to the cost of the drink and that a fruit drink with only bananas is $1 less expensive than one with both bananas and berries. What other information does she need in order to complete her calculation of the cost of the fruit drink?

    (A) the cost of electricity used to make the fruit drink

    (B) the comparable cost of pomegranates

    (C) that berries are selling for one half the cost of a banana

    (D) that berries are the most desired fruit for customers

12. A right angle triangle's hypotenuse increases 25 percent from 20cm. If the triangle's new base is 20cm, what is the new triangle's area?

    (A) 96cm²

    (B) 150cm²

    (C) 300cm²

    (D) 500cm²

13. An equilateral triangle is inscribed within a circle.

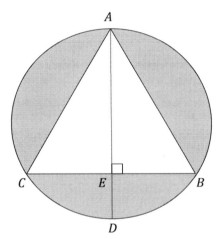

If $\overline{AD} = 2$, $\overline{AE} = \frac{3}{2}$, and $\overline{CB} = \sqrt{3}$, what is area of the entire shaded region?

   (A) $\frac{3\sqrt{3}}{4}$

   (B) $\pi - \frac{3\sqrt{3}}{4}$

   (C) $4\pi - 3\sqrt{3}$

   (D) $2\pi$

*Go on to the next page* ➡

14. The number of days of sunshine per month in Toronto are represented on a histogram.

**Days of Sunshine**

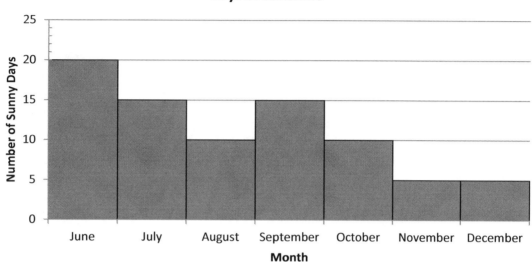

Which of the following statements is correct?

(A) On average from June to December, Toronto is sunny more often than not.

(B) The graph has a single mode of 5 sunny days.

(C) The median number of sunny days is equal to the number of sunny days in August.

(D) The average number of sunny days per month is greater than the range of sunny days per month.

---

15. $A$ is the least common multiple of 12 and 18. $B$ is the smallest prime factor of 12 and 18. What is $A/B$?

(A) $\frac{1}{6}$

(B) 6

(C) 12

(D) 18

16. What is the value of the expression $\frac{\sqrt[3]{3^4}}{\sqrt[6]{3^{-2}}}$ ?

(A) 1

(B) $\sqrt[3]{3}$

(C) 3

(D) $3\sqrt[3]{3^2}$

*Go on to the next page* ➜

17. If $x$ is a negative integer and $x^2 - 9 = 0$, what is the value of $x$?

    (A) -9

    (B) -6

    (C) -3

    (D) -1

18. A sphere is placed inside a pyramid as shown below. The pyramid's base is 12 and its height is $\sqrt{6}$. The formula used to find the volume of a pyramid is $V = \frac{base \times height}{3}$.

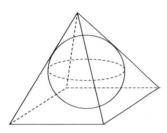

    If the volume of the sphere is $\frac{4\pi}{3}$, what is the volume of the empty space left inside the pyramid?

    (A) $2\sqrt{3} - \frac{4}{3}\pi$

    (B) $4\sqrt{6} - \frac{4}{3}\pi$

    (C) $8\sqrt{3} - \frac{4}{3}\pi$

    (D) $8\sqrt{6} - \frac{4}{3}\pi$

19. An isosceles triangle is shown.

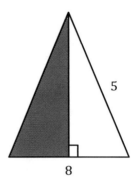

    *Note: Figure not drawn to scale.*

    The triangle has a base of 8, a side of 5, and is bisected through the middle. What is the perimeter of the shaded region?

    (A) 12

    (B) 14

    (C) 18

    (D) 24

*Go on to the next page* ➡

20. The time for 10 competitors at an eating competition is shown on a graph. The competitors each eat one at a time and their times are recorded.

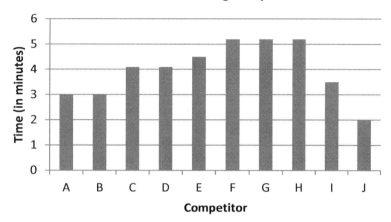

**Time Trials for an Eating Competition**

Which of the following statements is true?

(A) The range for the competitors' times is greater than the competitors' mean time.

(B) The competition lasted approximately 35 minutes.

(C) The mode time for the competitors is less than the competitors' mean time.

(D) The range of the competitors' times is less than the competitors' mean time.

*Go on to the next page* ➡

# PART TWO – QUANTITATIVE COMPARISONS

**Directions:** Using the information given in each question, compare the quantity in column A to the quantity in Column B. All questions in Part Two have these answer choices:

(A) The quantity in Column A is greater.

(B) The quantity in Column B is greater.

(C) The two quantities are equal.

(D) The relationship cannot be determined from the information given.

---

$$\&j = 2(2^j - 6)$$

| | Column A | Column B |
|---|---|---|
| 21. | &3 | 6 |

| | Column A | Column B |
|---|---|---|
| 22. | $\sqrt[3]{3^{-3}}$ | $\dfrac{1}{2}$ |

| | Column A | Column B |
|---|---|---|
| 23. | $3 \times -2 + \left(\dfrac{3}{2} - 4\right) \times 2$ | -12 |

| | Column A | Column B |
|---|---|---|
| 24. | $-\dfrac{1}{3}$ | The slope of the line perpendicular to the expression $2x + 5 - y = 0$ |

*Note: Figure not drawn to scale.*

| | Column A | Column B |
|---|---|---|
| 25. | $2y^2$ | The area of the rectangle |

An 8 sided number octahedron, labelled 1-8, is rolled twice.

| | Column A | Column B |
|---|---|---|
| 26. | The probability that the sum of the rolls will equal eight | $\dfrac{1}{8}$ |

There are two types of house, Modern and Classic, and each house may be painted red, yellow, green, blue, grey, or white.

| | Column A | Column B |
|---|---|---|
| 27. | The probability that James will pick a Modern type of house with a blue color | The probability that James will pick a Classic house with a color other than yellow |

| | Column A | Column B |
|---|---|---|
| 28. | The area of a circle with a radius of $b$. | The area of a square with a side of $2b$. |

*Go on to the next page* ➡

## ANSWER CHOICES FOR ALL QUESTIONS ON THIS PAGE:

(A) The quantity in Column A is greater.

(B) The quantity in Column B is greater.

(C) The two quantities are equal.

(D) The relationship cannot be determined from the information given.

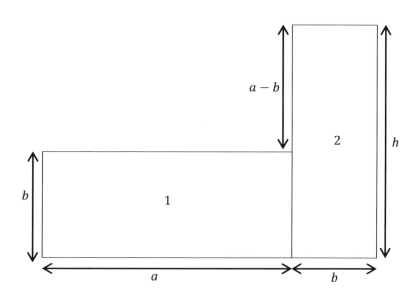

*Note: Figures not drawn to scale.*

|  | Column A | Column B |
|---|---|---|
| 29. | The area of rectangle *2* if $h = 2b$ | The area of rectangle *1* if $h = 2b$ |

A box-and-whisker graph represents the difference of high to low tide in 19 locations by the sea.

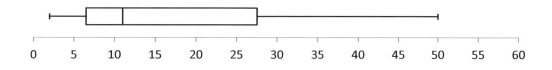

|  | Column A | Column B |
|---|---|---|
| 30. | The median difference in high to low tide | 10 |

*Go on to the next page* ➜

**ANSWER CHOICES FOR ALL QUESTIONS ON THIS PAGE:**

(A) The quantity in Column A is greater.

(B) The quantity in Column B is greater.

(C) The two quantities are equal.

(D) The relationship cannot be determined from the information given.

|  | Column A | Column B |
|---|---|---|
| 31. | $2 + \dfrac{2p + 4}{3}$ | $\dfrac{2p}{3} + 4$ |

Gum costs \$2.80 and is paid for by Eduardo using nickels and dimes. Eduardo paid with 3 times as many dimes as nickels.

*One nickel=\$0.05, one dime=\$0.10*

|  | Column A | Column B |
|---|---|---|
| 32. | The number of nickels that Eduardo uses | 8 |

In January, 2014 the cost of crude oil was approximately \$108 dollar per barrel. By the end of February, 2014 the price increased by 20%. By the end of March, 2014 the price decreased by 20%.

|  | Column A | Column B |
|---|---|---|
| 33. | The price of a barrel of oil at the end of March, 2014 | \$108 |

$$a = 2 \times \left(3 - 5\left(\dfrac{8}{2^2} - 1\right) + \dfrac{3^2}{2}\right) - 2$$

|  | Column A | Column B |
|---|---|---|
| 34. | 25% of $a$ | $3/b$ |

The area of rectangle $C$ is three times the area of rectangle $B$.

Rectangle $B$        Rectangle $C$

$3d$          $3e$

$d$          $e$

*Note: Figures not drawn to scale.*

|  | Column A | Column B |
|---|---|---|
| 35. | The perimeter of rectangle $B$ | $\dfrac{8e}{\sqrt{3}}$ |

Jill rolls a 2 on a 6 sided cube, numbered 1-6. She then rolls the 6 cube two more times.

|  | Column A | Column B |
|---|---|---|
| 36. | The probability that she rolls two more 2s | $\dfrac{1}{36}$ |

A jar is filled with nickels and dimes and the sum of the money in the jar = $s$. There are three times more dimes than nickels in the jar. (One nickel = \$0.05 and one dime = \$0.10.)

|  | Column A | Column B |
|---|---|---|
| 37. | The number of nickels in the jar | $\dfrac{s}{0.30}$ |

STOP. Do not go on until told to do so.

STOP

## Section 3
## Reading Comprehension

This section contains six short reading passages. Each passage is followed by six questions based on its content. Answer the questions following each passage on the basis of what is <u>stated</u> or <u>implied</u> in that passage. You may write in your test booklet.

STOP. Do not go on until told to do so.

Questions 1–6

1  According to a press release from the
2  University of Buffalo, university researchers
3  are developing an underwater wireless
4  network that they are dubbing a "deep-sea"
5  Internet. If this network proves successful, it
6  could lead to improvements in tsunami
7  detection, offshore oil and natural gas
8  exploration, surveillance, pollution monitoring
9  and other marine activities.
10  "A submerged wireless network will give
11  us an unprecedented ability to collect and
12  analyze data from our oceans in real time," said
13  Tommaso Melodia, an associate professor of
14  electrical engineering and the project's lead
15  researcher. "Making this information available
16  to anyone with a smartphone or computer,
17  especially when a tsunami or other type of
18  disaster occurs, could help save lives."
19  The need for a submerged wireless
20  network arises from the limitations of land-
21  based wireless networks. These networks rely
22  on radio waves that transmit data via satellites
23  and antennae. While very effective at
24  transmitting information over land, radio
25  waves work poorly underwater. In order to
26  communicate underwater, organizations like
27  the Navy and National Oceanic and
28  Atmospheric Administration must use sound
29  wave-based techniques instead. For example,
30  NOAA relies on acoustic waves to send data
31  from tsunami sensors on the seafloor to surface
32  buoys. The buoys then convert the acoustic
33  waves into radio waves to send the data to a
34  satellite, which then redirects the radio waves
35  back to land-based computers. This can be a
36  cumbersome process because each system has
37  a different infrastructure specific to the type of
38  waves it can receive, and data must be
39  converted from one system to the next.
40  Melodia's new framework builds upon
41  existing sound-wave based technology to
42  eliminate many of these tedious steps. Instead
43  of shuttling data back and forth among
44  different sensors, it would transmit data from
45  existing underwater sensor networks to
46  laptops, smartphones and other wireless
47  devices in real time.
48  The system was recently tested in Lake
49  Erie. Melodia and his fellow researchers
50  lowered two 40-pound sensors into the water,
51  typed a command into a laptop, and seconds
52  later a series of high-pitched chirps ricocheted
53  off a nearby concrete wall. These chirps acted
54  as an aural confirmation of the network's
55  success.
56  Melodia believes that the implications of
57  such technology are many. "We could even use
58  it to monitor fish and marine mammals, and
59  find out how to best protect them from
60  shipping traffic and other dangers," Melodia
61  explained. "An Internet underwater has so
62  many possibilities."

*Go on to the next page* ➜

1. The primary purpose of the passage is to

   (A) explain the structure of the Internet and contrast it with its marine counterpart.

   (B) discredit Tommaso Melodia's ideas.

   (C) discuss the potential impact of a developing marine technology.

   (D) promote doing electronic activities underwater.

2. In line 36, the word "cumbersome" most nearly means

   (A) inefficient

   (B) heavy

   (C) streamlined

   (D) erratic

3. According to the third paragraph (lines 19-39), one reason that the current system of underwater sound wave technology works poorly is that

   (A) data must be converted numerous times between different systems.

   (B) buoys can only absorb acoustic waves.

   (C) the Navy and NOAA don't understand it very well.

   (D) we have no underwater satellites.

4. The first quote from Tommaso Melodia (lines 10-12) implies that

   (A) a submerged wireless network would replace the Internet over time.

   (B) we have previously been unable to process underwater data in real time.

   (C) there are not enough data analysts to process all of the underwater data.

   (D) this submerged wireless network is replacing an older one.

5. The experiment conducted in Lake Erie (lines 49-55) demonstrated that

   (A) the new framework could be disruptive to fish, marine mammals, and shipping traffic.

   (B) this new technology only works in bodies of freshwater.

   (C) commands from land-based wireless devices could be successfully converted into acoustic waves.

   (D) the submerged wireless network is not yet operational.

6. The final quote from Tommaso Melodia (lines 57-60) implies that

   (A) "underwater Internet" has only a limited range of possible effects.

   (B) protecting marine mammals is the entire goal of the submerged wireless network.

   (C) saving marine life is one possible benefit of the submerged wireless network.

   (D) a submerged wireless network would be bad for the shipping industry.

*Go on to the next page* ➡

Questions 7–12

1     People have always been attracted to
2 water. Many of the great civilizations of the
3 past originated near seas, lakes, and rivers.
4 There are many good reasons to live near
5 bodies of water. Rivers flowing to the sea
6 provide fresh water for people, livestock, and
7 crops. Floodplains and sediments enrich the
8 soil, making farming easier and crops more
9 abundant. Even the salty seas provide access to
10 plentiful fisheries, supplying ample food for the
11 human population, as well as access to
12 navigable waterways that make large scale
13 commerce possible by allowing people to load
14 goods onto boats for transportation over long
15 distances.
16     By some estimates, more than half of the
17 planet's current population lives in coastal
18 regions, and the population of coastal regions is
19 growing more rapidly than the non-coastal
20 population. Living near the coast is a mixed
21 blessing, however. The sea still offers access to
22 shipping lanes, fisheries, and other natural
23 resources, but coastal waters are becoming
24 increasingly polluted. Sewage discharge in
25 densely populated areas is a major contributor
26 to marine pollution and is responsible for the
27 spread of infection and disease. Pesticides from
28 farms, and industrial pollutants from factories,
29 power plants, and other sources also find their

30 way into the sea from inland farms and
31 factories and can taint fish stocks, shellfish, and
32 even seaweed, making food harvested from the
33 sea potentially unsafe for human consumption.
34 Additionally, as the planet warms and sea
35 levels rise, coastal areas are under increasing
36 threat from storm surges, or, in some cases, in
37 danger of being entirely submerged by rising
38 waters. Millions of people could be displaced
39 by rising seas in the century to come and
40 billions of dollars' worth of real estate washed
41 away by the mounting waters.
42     But disaster is not inevitable:
43 governments, non-profit organizations, and
44 major corporations are all exploring ways of
45 confronting the challenges faced by coastal
46 regions. Plans are being drawn and projects are
47 underway to help clean up polluted coastal
48 regions and prepare for the dangers of a
49 climatically changing world. Some of the
50 measures being considered, such as high
51 seawalls designed to protect cities from rising
52 waters, are massive and incredibly expensive
53 projects. But even with increasing
54 environmental threats, the human population
55 is unlikely to abandon the coasts any time soon,
56 and such investments may be necessary to
57 secure our future by the sea.

*Go on to the next page* ➡

7.  The tone of the second paragraph could best be described as

    (A) indecisive.

    (B) ambitious.

    (C) bleak.

    (D) pithy.

8.  What is the main purpose of the first paragraph?

    (A) to persuade readers to move to the coast

    (B) to describe the ancient civilizations that arose along coasts

    (C) to discuss the benefits of living near water

    (D) to foreshadow changes that would later happen in coastal areas

9.  In line 31, the word "taint" most nearly means

    (A) improve

    (B) massacre

    (C) corrupt

    (D) contaminate

10. In the second paragraph (lines 16-41), the author cites all of the following coastal pollution sources EXCEPT

    (A) fuel runoff from shipping boats.

    (B) sewage discharge from highly populated areas.

    (C) pesticides from agricultural activities.

    (D) pollutants from power plants.

11. The final paragraph (lines 42-57) implies that

    (A) the measures necessary to combat coastal pollution are too expensive to enact.

    (B) human beings will do whatever is necessary to continue living in coastal areas.

    (C) it is too late to effect serious change in coastal regions.

    (D) only sea-based industries are interested in stemming coastal pollution.

12. The primary message of this passage is that

    (A) without expensive sea walls, coastal cities may be more vulnerable to flooding in the future.

    (B) pollution and climate change pose growing threats to coastal populations.

    (C) coastal regions will inevitably disappear.

    (D) the sea was more useful to ancient human populations than current ones.

*Go on to the next page* ➡

Questions 13–18

1      Henri Marie Raymond de Toulouse-
2 Lautrec-Monfa—or more simply, Henri de
3 Toulouse-Lautrec—was a French painter and
4 illustrator whose immersion in the colorful life
5 of Paris in the last decades of the 19th century
6 yielded a collection of exciting, elegant, and
7 provocative images. Henri owed his long name
8 to his aristocratic heritage, to which he also
9 owed his serious life-long health problems.
10 Henri's parents, the Count and Countess of
11 Toulouse and Lautrec, were first cousins, and
12 Henri suffered from health conditions often
13 found in the offspring of close relatives. At the
14 age of 13, Henri fractured his right thigh bone,
15 and at 14, his left. The breaks did not heal
16 properly, and his legs ceased to grow, so that as
17 an adult he was just over five feet tall, having
18 developed an adult-sized torso while retaining
19 his child-sized legs. Physically unable to
20 participate in many activities typically enjoyed
21 by men of his age, Henri immersed himself in
22 art.
23      Under the tutelage of Bonnat and later

24 Fernand Cormon, Henri developed his
25 characteristically vivid painting style and his
26 taste for the Paris social scene as his main
27 artistic subject. He was masterful at capturing
28 crowd scenes in which all of the figures are
29 highly individualized; the evocative images
30 buzz with life, bringing the observer into the
31 humming and colorful social events of Paris.
32 Along with Cézanne, Van Gogh, and Gauguin,
33 Henri Toulouse-Lautrec would come to be
34 known as one of the greatest painters of the
35 period.
36      Sadly, as with many great artists, Henri's
37 life was cut short by tragedy. Constantly
38 mocked for his short stature and physical
39 appearance, Henri drowned his sorrows in
40 alcohol. His alcoholism eventually became so
41 debilitating that his mother briefly had him
42 institutionalized. Despite her and the rest of his
43 family's best efforts, Henri died from
44 complications due to alcoholism at the young
45 age of 36. One wonders what Henri's art career
46 would have been like if he had lived to old age.

*Go on to the next page* ➡

13. Based on the description in the passage, the paintings of Henri de Toulouse-Lautrec are most likely

    (A) drab.

    (B) abstract.

    (C) satirical.

    (D) vibrant.

14. The author states that Henri's long name and physical ailments were both a result of

    (A) malnutrition as a child.

    (B) his talent as a painter.

    (C) his lack of athletic ability.

    (D) his aristocratic origins.

15. According to the author's description in the second paragraph (lines 23-35), Henri's masterpieces

    (A) were inspired by his engagement in the social life of his city.

    (B) were successful due to his family's influence.

    (C) cured him of his disabilities.

    (D) allowed him to keep living the life of an aristocrat.

16. According to the passage, Henri's stunted growth

    (A) raised his social status.

    (B) prevented him from enjoying certain experiences with his peers.

    (C) directly caused his death.

    (D) was common among artists in Paris during this period.

17. Which of the following does the author consider one of Henri's greatest strengths as a painter?

    (A) His inspiring biography.

    (B) His ability to spark controversy with his illustrations.

    (C) His memorable appearance.

    (D) His ability to portray individual people within a large crowd.

18. Based on the information in the passage, Fernand Cormon was most likely

    (A) one of Henri's childhood friends.

    (B) one of Henri's relatives.

    (C) one of Henri's art teachers.

    (D) Henri's patron in London.

*Go on to the next page* ➡

Questions 19–24

1　　　In a settlement called Pormpuraaw, on
2　the northern tip of the Cape York Peninsula in
3　Queensland, Australia, live a people called the
4　Thaayorre. The Thaayorre speak a language
5　called Kuuk Thaayorre, which shares several
6　important features with other aboriginal
7　languages: it is spoken by only a few hundred
8　people (two hundred and fifty, at the last
9　count); most of the dialects have been lost as
10　the number of speakers has dwindled; and, in
11　Kuuk Thaayorre, there is no word for "left" or
12　"right." In fact, in Kuuk Thaayorre there is no
13　subjective direction at all. All sixteen words for
14　direction relate to the cardinal directions:
15　North, East, South and West.
16　　　Kuuk Thaayorre uses cardinal directions
17　instead of subjective direction at all scales,
18　large and small. If you were speaking Kuuk
19　Thaayorre, not only might you have to say
20　something familiar like "you must walk north
21　to reach the store," but you might also have to
22　say something like "your southeastern shoe is
23　untied." If you lost track of your position
24　relative to the cardinal directions, then you
25　wouldn't be able to communicate effectively at
26　all.
27　　　Owing to this peculiarity of their
28　language, the Thaayorre people must always

29　know which direction they are facing, even
30　when they are inside or in unfamiliar
31　surroundings. Fortunately, as recent research
32　demonstrates, the Thaayorre and other people
33　who speak similar languages have a special
34　talent for this. They're even better at tracking
35　their orientation than scientists had previously
36　thought was possible among human beings.
37　　　This absolute dependence on cardinal
38　directions may affect other areas of the
39　Thaayorre people's lives as well. For example,
40　when asked to arrange a sequence of pictures
41　in temporal order, Kuuk Thaayorre speakers
42　consistently arrange them so that time runs
43　east to west, regardless of their own bodily
44　orientation. Speakers of English, however,
45　generally arrange them so that time runs from
46　left to right from the perspective of the person
47　arranging the pictures. Researchers are
48　intrigued by this difference in the visualization
49　of time, and have speculated about the
50　possibility of broader differences.
51　　　The Thaayorre's abilities and
52　peculiarities raise questions about the power of
53　the human mind to achieve what was once
54　thought impossible, and about the relationship
55　between language and thought processes.

*Go on to the next page* ➡

19. What does the author mean by "subjective direction" (line 17)?

    (A) Directions which are always the opposite of objective directions.

    (B) Directions unique to aboriginal languages.

    (C) Directions that rely on descriptions of landmarks.

    (D) Directions that are unrelated to the cardinal directions.

20. The author would most likely agree with which of the following statements about the Thaayorre people?

    (A) They cannot communicate effectively.

    (B) They think more clearly about things than most other people.

    (C) Their culture will soon be extinct.

    (D) Their language and abilities raise questions about human potential.

21. The author implies that English speakers, unlike the Kuuk Thayyorre, normally use cardinal directions only

    (A) on large scales, for things that are big or far away.

    (B) when they are inside.

    (C) on small scales, for things that are small or nearby.

    (D) when they cannot tell which way they are facing.

22. We can infer from the passage that

    (A) other aboriginal languages also rely heavily on cardinal directions.

    (B) scientists don't understand how we track subjective directions.

    (C) cardinal directions are better than subjective directions.

    (D) English has no words for cardinal directions.

23. What is the structure of this passage?

    (A) Two differing opinions are given about a popular issue, but evidence is provided for only one side.

    (B) A specific phenomenon is discussed, along with speculation about its implications.

    (C) One author discredits the ideas of another author.

    (D) A complicated but important concept is explained in detail.

24. In line 37, the word "absolute" most nearly means

    (A) sole.

    (B) radical.

    (C) ineffective.

    (D) ludicrous.

*Go on to the next page* ➡

Questions 25–30

1     Charlotte, Emily, and Anne Bronte were
2 born in the early 19th century to Patrick, a
3 priest, and Maria Bronte. The sisters had two
4 elder sisters who died in childhood, and a
5 brother, Patrick Branwell, with whom they
6 were very close. The Bronte family lived a very
7 modest life and did not have the funds to send
8 the sisters to private schools, so they were
9 largely educated at home. Even at a young age,
10 the girls demonstrated a talent for narrative,
11 using their brother's twelve wooden toy
12 soldiers to create endless stories. They soon
13 began writing these stories down, creating epic
14 sagas about the fictional kingdoms of Glass
15 Town and the Empire of Agria.
16     The first work the sisters ever published,
17 appearing in 1846, was a joint collection of
18 poems entitled *Poems* by Currer, Ellis, and
19 Acton Bell. The sisters were forced to employ
20 these quasi-masculine pseudonyms because
21 the publishing company was worried that
22 poetry written by female authors simply
23 wouldn't sell. The sisters selected names that
24 would match their own initials so they could
25 reserve at least some ownership of the text.
26     In 1847, all three sisters published what
27 would come to be their most famous novels:
28 Charlotte's *Jane Eyre*, Emily's *Wuthering*
29 *Heights*, and Anne's *Agnes Grey*. Though
30 originally published under the same
31 pseudonyms, Charlotte and Emily Bronte
32 ended their anonymity when they travelled to
33 London to prove to their publisher that they
34 were indeed independent authors (a rumor
35 had started that "Ellis Bell" was in fact the
36 author of all three novels) and also female.
37 Though their gender had originally been feared
38 as a potential detriment to their novels'
39 success, this never came to pass; *Jane Eyre* and
40 *Wuthering Heights* were wildly successful and
41 remain popular literature today.

*Go on to the next page* ➡

25. The primary purpose of the passage is to

    (A) discuss the development of female authorship.

    (B) explain the origins of pseudonyms.

    (C) compare the careers of Charlotte, Emily, and Anne Bronte.

    (D) provide the history of three famous literary sisters.

26. In line 38, the word "detriment" most nearly means

    (A) boost.

    (B) hindrance.

    (C) fluke.

    (D) foreshadowing.

27. You would most likely expect to find this passage in

    (A) a piece in a literary history magazine.

    (B) an article in a scientific journal.

    (C) a blog post about different ways to use pseudonyms.

    (D) an advertisement for creative writing classes.

28. In the second paragraph (lines 16-25), the author implies that

    (A) the Bronte sisters stylistically preferred their pseudonyms to their given names.

    (B) publishing under a pseudonym was very fashionable in the 19th century.

    (C) Currer, Acton, and Ellis Bell helped the Bronte sisters write the poems.

    (D) the Bronte sisters were reluctant to publish anonymously.

29. The tone of the final paragraph could best be described as

    (A) triumphant.

    (B) critical.

    (C) timid.

    (D) perplexed.

30. Based on information given in the first paragraph, it can be inferred that

    (A) the Bronte sisters possessed enough talent to overcome their lack of formal education.

    (B) it was typical not to educate young girls during this time period.

    (C) Patrick Branwell didn't play with his toy soldiers.

    (D) the Bronte sisters' parents frowned upon their narrative exploits.

*Go on to the next page* ➜

Questions 31–36

Hard as it is to believe, it was once standard public health policy to isolate those who were sick with infectious disease in isolation hospitals until they were no longer ill. Whereas nowadays doctors realize that isolation is only necessary in the cases of extremely infectious diseases and only for short periods of time, doctors in the early twentieth century thought that isolation was the most effective way to prevent the spread of nearly all diseases. Public health officials ran into a problem, however, when they discovered that there could be apparently healthy people carrying the bacteria of deadly diseases inside their bodies. The problem is well-illustrated by the story of Typhoid Mary.

Mary Mallon, aka "Typhoid Mary," was the first known healthy carrier of typhoid fever. Mary worked as a cook in the homes of wealthy New Yorkers in the early 20th century. New York public health officials traced several outbreaks of typhoid fever to her cooking. The officials determined that Mary transferred typhoid bacteria from her unwashed hands to the food she served the families. Laboratory tests confirmed that Mary was playing host to billions of typhoid bacteria, even though she claimed to have never suffered from the disease herself.

Once public health officials had located Mary, they had to decide what to do with her. Ultimately, the officials decided that Mary was too dangerous to be allowed to roam freely, particularly since she adamantly believed that she was not a typhoid carrier and vowed to continue cooking. The officials forcibly isolated her in a one-room bungalow on North Brother Island for nearly three decades until her death in 1938. Her only companion was a small dog, and journalists who came to interview her (for by that point "Typhoid Mary" had become a minor celebrity) were not even allowed to accept a glass of water from her for fear of contagion.

Such procedures seem unreasonably draconian nowadays; it would be impossible to restrict an individual's liberty to such an extent in the present day. The case of Typhoid Mary serves to show how quickly the relationship between individual freedom and public health has evolved in the last century.

*Go on to the next page* ➡

31. The main purpose of this passage is to

    (A) advocate for Typhoid Mary's immediate release from isolation.

    (B) discuss the case of Typhoid Mary as an example of changing public health policies.

    (C) explain the biological workings of typhoid fever.

    (D) demonstrate the importance of washing one's hands, especially in the foodservice industry.

32. In line 21, the word "traced" most nearly means

    (A) outlined.

    (B) connected.

    (C) drew.

    (D) discovered.

33. According to the passage, public health officials considered Mary Mallon a threat because

    (A) she might have children who would be typhoid carriers.

    (B) she refused to believe she was a typhoid carrier.

    (C) she routinely used disease-causing ingredients in her cooking.

    (D) she interacted primarily with wealthy people.

34. In the last paragraph (lines 45-51), it is implied that

    (A) public health standards have deteriorated since the time of Mary Mallon.

    (B) modern isolation facilities are much more pleasant than those which existed in the early 20th century.

    (C) Mary Mallon would have received different treatment if she had been discovered in the present day.

    (D) America will always value public health over individual freedom.

35. In line 46, the word "draconian" most nearly means

    (A) severe.

    (B) relaxed.

    (C) rational.

    (D) dangerous.

36. Which of the following sentences best describes the structure of the passage?

    (A) A debate between two ideas is presented, with evidence for each side.

    (B) A weak argument is followed by criticism, and rejection.

    (C) A specific historical example is discussed in relation to a broader problem.

    (D) A chronology of important events is presented, leaving the reader to draw conclusions.

**STOP. Do not go on until told to do so.**

**STOP**

# SECTION 4

# Mathematics Achievement

Each question is followed by four suggested answers. Read each question and then decide which one of the four suggested answers is best.

Find the row of spaces on your answer document that has the same number as the question. In this row, mark the space having the same letter as the answer you have chosen. You may write in your test booklet.

---

SAMPLE QUESTION:                            <u>Sample Answer</u>

If $a = 3$, what is the value $a^2 + (3 \times 4) \div 6$?        Ⓐ ● Ⓒ Ⓓ

(A) 3.5

(B) 11

(C) 14.5

(D) 20

The correct answer is 11, so circle B is darkened.

---

STOP. Do not go on
until told to do so.

**STOP**

**Ivy Global**

1. If $3 \geq Q + 1 > -2$, what could be a value of Q?

   (A) -3

   (B) -1

   (C) 3

   (D) 5

2. Which expression describes the values of $x$ for which $|2x + 2| \leq 3$?

   (A) $x \leq \frac{1}{2}$

   (B) $-\frac{5}{2} \leq x$

   (C) $-\frac{5}{2} \leq x \leq \frac{1}{2}$

   (D) $x \leq -\frac{5}{2}$ or $x \geq \frac{1}{2}$

3. Mr. Jones has 8 white shirts, 4 black shirts, 5 blue shirts, and 3 yellow shirts. He chooses one shirt at random from his drawer, then puts it back and chooses another shirt at random. What is the probability that one shirt will be blue and that the other shirt will be white?

   (A) $\frac{1}{5} \times \frac{1}{8}$

   (B) $\frac{1}{4} \times \frac{2}{5}$

   (C) $\frac{7}{20}$

   (D) $\frac{13}{20}$

4. Which of the following expressions is equal to $5.214 \times 10^8$?

   (A) $5.21 \times 10^5 + 4 \times 10^3$

   (B) $(5.21 \times 10^5) \times (4 \times 10^3)$

   (C) $5.21 \times 10^8 + 4 \times 10^5$

   (D) $(5.21 \times 10^8) \times (4 \times 10^5)$

5. What is the value of the numerical expression $\sqrt{169 - 144}$?

   (A) 1

   (B) 2

   (C) 5

   (D) 10

6. Which of the following is equivalent to the expression $\frac{2^6 \times 4^2}{2^3 \times 2^2}$?

   (A) $2^3$

   (B) $2^4$

   (C) $2^5$

   (D) $2^6$

7. Mr. Gomez's 10 students take a quiz. The mean score is 8. If 2 more kids join the class and each receives a score of 9 on the quiz, what is the new mean score for the class?

   (A) $\frac{13}{6}$

   (B) $\frac{47}{6}$

   (C) 8

   (D) $\frac{49}{6}$

8. Sally and Jim both worked 8 hours yesterday and Jim makes half as much money per hour as Sally. If their total income was $120.00, what is Sally's hourly wage?

   (A) $5.00

   (B) $10.00

   (C) $15.00

   (D) $20.00

*Go on to the next page* ➜

9. Nathan needs to jump four long jumps that have an average length of 4.5 meters in order to qualify for the Olympics. His first three jumps had lengths of 3 meters, 4.5 meters, and 5 meters. What is the minimum length that he must jump on his fourth jump in order to qualify?

(A) 4 meters

(B) 4.5 meters

(C) 5 meters

(D) 5.5 meters

10. The number of frogs in various ponds is calculated and shown in the table below.

| FROGS IN POND | |
|---|---|
| Number of Frogs | Number of Ponds Containing that Number of Frogs |
| 0 | 2 |
| 20 | 4 |
| 40 | 3 |
| 60 | 6 |
| 80 | 9 |

Based on this data, what is the median number of frogs per pond?

(A) 20

(B) 40

(C) 60

(D) 80

11. Which expression is equivalent to the expression $\frac{z^3 2y^3 - 2z^3 y^4}{z^2 y^2}$?

(A) $z^2$

(B) $2zy - 2zy^2$

(C) $2z^2 y - 2zy^2$

(D) $z^3 y - 2z^2 y^2$

*Questions 12-13 refer to the stem-and-leaf plot below.*

12. The stem-and-leaf plot shown represents exam scores for an algebra test.

| Stem | Leaf |
|---|---|
| 5 | 2 4 8 |
| 6 | 0 0 0 2 |
| 7 | 1 2 8 |
| 8 | 3 4 4 5 |
| 9 | 1 1 2 3 3 |

What is the mode exam score?

(A) 52

(B) 60

(C) 84

(D) 93

13. What is the median exam score?

(A) 60

(B) 72

(C) 78

(D) 83

14. A lock keypad requires the correct three digit code to activate it. You can use the numbers 0-9 for the code. The first and last numbers may be the same, but the middle number must be different than both the first and the last numbers. How many unique codes are possible for the keypad?

(A) 120

(B) 720

(C) 810

(D) 3,628,800

*Go on to the next page* ➜

15. Triangle $ABC$ is shown. The length $\overline{BC}$ is 3 inches. The measure of $ACB$ is 30º.

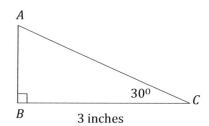

The value of which expression is equal to the length of side $\overline{AB}$?

(A) $\tan 30° \times 3$

(B) $\dfrac{\tan 30°}{3}$

(C) $\sin 30° \times 3$

(D) $\dfrac{\sin 30°}{3}$

16. The center of a circle is located at (0,-1). Point (2,2) is found on the circle's perimeter. What is the circle's radius?

(A) 2

(B) $\sqrt{5}$

(C) 3

(D) $\sqrt{13}$

17. What is the solution set for the expression $2y^2 + 162 = 0$?

(A) -9

(B) 9

(C) $9i$

(D) $\pm 9i$

18. Which expression is equivalent to the expression $\dfrac{1}{\sqrt{64x^{64}}}$?

(A) $\dfrac{x^{-32}}{8}$

(B) $x^{-32}$

(C) $2x^{32}$

(D) $(8x^8)^{-1}$

19. For what value(s) does $\dfrac{(y+2)(y-5)}{y(y^2-4)} = 0$?

(A) 5

(B) -2 and 2

(C) -2 and 5

(D) -2, 2 and 5

20. The surface area for the cone shown measures $24\pi$. The formula for the surface area of a cone is $SA = \pi r^2 + r\pi s$, where $r$ is the radius of the base of the cone and $s$ is the cone's slant height.

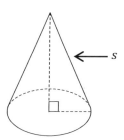

If the radius, $r$, is equal to 3, what is the slant height, $s$, of the cone?

(A) 2.5

(B) 5

(C) 25

(D) 12

*Go on to the next page* ➡

21. The following graph represents the solution set for which of following inequalities?

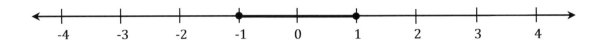

(A) $-1 \geq x + 3 \geq 1$

(B) $4 \geq 2x + 6 \geq 2$

(C) $8 \geq 2x + 6 \geq 4$

(D) $16 \geq 2x + 6 \geq 4$

*Questions 22 to 23 are based on the box-and-whisker plot below.*

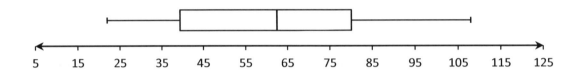

22. Which inequality best represents the median of the data found in the box-and-whisker plot above?

(A) $35 < median < 45$

(B) $55 < median < 65$

(C) $75 < median < 85$

(D) $95 < median < 115$

23. Which number falls within the third quartile of the box-and-whisker plot above?

(A) 35

(B) 45

(C) 55

(D) 75

*Go on to the next page* ➡

24. When measuring the volume of a cup of coffee, what is the best unit to use?

    (A) milligram

    (B) centimeter

    (C) milliliter

    (D) millisecond

25. Two similar triangles are shown below.

    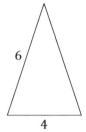

    *Note: Figures not drawn to scale.*

    What is the value of $b$?

    (A) $\frac{2}{3}$

    (B) 1

    (C) $\frac{4}{3}$

    (D) 4

26. George wants to determine the average number of children per family in his city. Which sample will provide him with the most reliable information about the average number of children per family in his city?

    (A) the families that he knows on his city block

    (B) the families that show up at a picnic in his city's park

    (C) a random sample of the families that sign up for recreational sports in his city

    (D) a random sample of all the families in his city

27. Which expression is equivalent to the expression $(3x + 3)(3x + 3)$?

    (A) $9x^2 - 9$

    (B) $9x^3 - 9$

    (C) $9x^2 + 18x + 9$

    (D) $9x^3 + 18x + 9$

28. Which expression is equivalent to the expression $(x - 2)(x^2 + 2x + 4)$?

    (A) $x^2 - 4$

    (B) $2x^2 - 4$

    (C) $x^3 - 8$

    (D) $x^3 + 8$

29. The graph of a line is shown.

    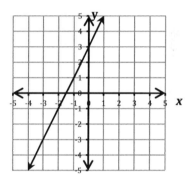

    What is the slope of the line?

    (A) -2

    (B) -1

    (C) 1

    (D) 2

*Go on to the next page* ➡

30. The results of 10 Olympic scores are shown in a bar graph.

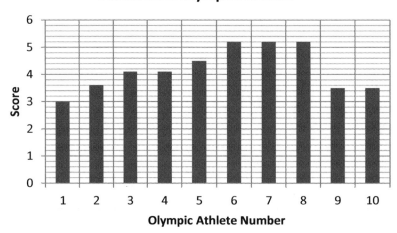

**Scores from Olympic Athletes**

What is the mode of the scores?

(A) 1

(B) 3.5

(C) 4.1

(D) 5.2

---

31. A rectangle bisects two identical circles as shown.

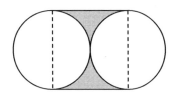

If the radius of the circles is 3, what is the area of the shaded space within the rectangle?

(A) $36 - \pi$

(B) $36 - 9\pi$

(C) $36 - \frac{9\pi}{2}$

(D) $36$

32. A backpack contains 3 conch shells, 4 oyster shells, 6 snail shells, and 2 nassa shells. Joon randomly removes one shell from the backpack and leaves it by the sea. Joon's sister then randomly removes a shell from the backpack. If the shell Joon removed from the backpack is a conch shell, what is the probability that the shell his sister removed is a snail shell?

(A) $\frac{1}{7}$

(B) $\frac{1}{6}$

(C) $\frac{6}{15}$

(D) $\frac{3}{7}$

*Go on to the next page* ➡

33. Which value is equal to $3\frac{2}{9}$?

    (A) $\frac{19}{6}$

    (B) 3.3333333

    (C) $3.\overline{2}$

    (D) 3.2222

34. If $za + 2z = 4a + 8$ and $a \neq -2$, what is a possible value for z?

    (A) -3

    (B) 0

    (C) 2

    (D) 4

35. Abena has 8 kinds of ingredients and cooking a meal requires 4 different ingredients. If the order of the ingredients makes no difference to the meal, and Abena uses no more than the 4 ingredients required for each meal, how many different meals can Abena make?

    (A) 8

    (B) 32

    (C) 70

    (D) 1680

36. If $a$ and $d$ are prime numbers, what is the greatest common factor of $a\sqrt{81d}$, $27da$, and $18a$?

    (A) $3a\sqrt{d}$

    (B) $3ad$

    (C) $9a\sqrt{d}$

    (D) $9ad$

37. Factory A makes four times the waste of factory B. If the total waste from the two factories weighs 40 tons, how much waste was made by factory B?

    (A) 4 tons

    (B) 8 tons

    (C) 16 tons

    (D) 32 tons

38. Which expression represents an integer?

    (A) $2\pi$

    (B) $\sqrt{16-4}$

    (C) $\frac{3^{0.5} \times 3}{3^{-0.5}}$

    (D) $\sqrt{-1}$

39. The area of each grid unit is 3 cm$^2$.

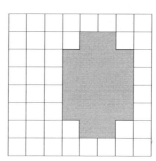

    What is the area of the unshaded region?

    (A) 20 cm$^2$

    (B) 60 cm$^2$

    (C) 64 cm$^2$

    (D) 132 cm$^2$

*Go on to the next page* ➡

*Questions 40 to 41 refer to the histogram below.*

40. A histogram shows the height of the population in Greenville.

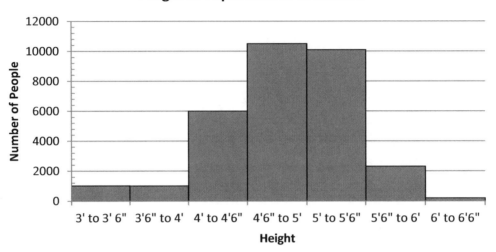

What is the range of the height of the population in Greenville?

(A) 3'

(B) 3'6"

(C) 4'6"

(D) 6'6"

41. What is the median height category of the population in Greenville?

(A) 4'to 4'6"

(B) 4'6" to 5'

(C) 5' to 5'6"

(D) 5'6" to 6'

*Go on to the next page* ➡

42. The graph of a line is shown.

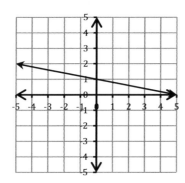

Which of the following could be the equation of a line that is perpendicular to this line?

(A) $y = -\frac{1}{5}x$

(B) $y = -\frac{1}{5}x + 1$

(C) $y = \frac{1}{5}x + 1$

(D) $y = 5x + 1$

43. Two lines bisect each other, forming two isosceles triangles.

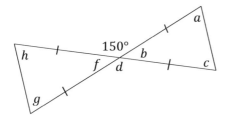

What is the value for angle $h$?

(A) 30°

(B) 75°

(C) 90°

(D) 150°

44. A cylinder is shown below. The formula for the volume of a cylinder is $V = r^2 h\pi$, where $r$ is the cylinder's radius and $h$ is the cylinder's height.

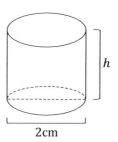

2cm

If the cylinder has a diameter of 2 cm and a volume of $4\pi$ cm³, what is its height?

(A) 1 cm

(B) 2 cm

(C) 4 cm

(D) 8 cm

45. Points $(-3, -2)$, $(-1, 1)$, and $(2, -2)$ form three points of a parallelogram. What are the coordinates of the remaining point?

(A) $(-4, 1)$

(B) $(-2, 2)$

(C) $(2, 1)$

(D) $(4, 1)$

*Go on to the next page* ➡

46. A sphere is placed in a cube. The formula used to find the volume of a sphere is $V = \frac{4}{3}\pi r^3$, where $r$ is the radius of the sphere. The cube has a volume of 8 cm³ and the length of one side of the cube is equal to the diameter of the sphere.

What is the volume of the empty space remaining in the cube after the sphere is placed in the cube?

(A) $8 - \frac{32}{3}\pi$

(B) $8 - \frac{4}{3}\pi$

(C) $\frac{4}{3}\pi$

(D) $\frac{32}{3}\pi$

47. What is the result of the expression $\begin{bmatrix} -1 & 3 \\ 5 & 1 \end{bmatrix} - \begin{bmatrix} 2 & 3 \\ 2 & 4 \end{bmatrix}$?

(A) $\begin{bmatrix} -3 & 0 \\ 3 & -3 \end{bmatrix}$

(B) $\begin{bmatrix} 2 & 3 \\ 2 & 4 \end{bmatrix}$

(C) $\begin{bmatrix} -1 & 3 \\ 5 & 1 \end{bmatrix}$

(D) $\begin{bmatrix} 4 & 9 \\ 12 & 19 \end{bmatrix}$

**STOP. Do not go on until told to do so.** STOP

# Essay Topic Sheet

The directions for the Essay portion of the ISEE are printed in the box below. Use the pre-lined pages on pages 268-269 for this part of the Practice Test.

---

You will have 30 minutes to plan and write an essay on the topic printed on the other side of this page. **Do not write on another topic. An essay on another topic is not acceptable.**

The essay is designed to give you an opportunity to show how well you can write. You should try to express your thoughts clearly. How well you write is much more important than how much you write, but you need to say enough for a reader to understand what you mean.

You will probably want to write more than a short paragraph. You should also be aware that a copy of your essay will be sent to each school that will be receiving your test results. You are to write only in the appropriate section of the answer sheet. Please write or print so that your writing may be read by someone who is not familiar with your handwriting.

You may make notes and plan your essay on the reverse side of the page. Allow enough time to copy the final form onto your answer sheet. You must copy the essay topic onto your answer sheet, on page 268, in the box provided.

Please remember to write only the final draft of the essay on pages 268-269 of your answer sheet and to write it in blue or black pen. Again, you may use cursive writing or you may print. Only pages 268-269 will be sent to the schools.

---

*Directions continue on the next page.*

**REMINDER:** Please write this essay topic on the first few lines of the first page of your essay sheet.

**Essay Topic**

What piece of modern technology do you think has most improved your own life? Explain why it has been important to you.

- Only write on this essay question
- Only pages 268 and 269 will be sent to the schools
- Only write in blue or black pen

# NOTES

_____

_____

_____

_____

_____

_____

_____

_____

_____

_____

_____

_____

_____

_____

_____

_____

_____

_____

_____

_____

**Ivy Global**

# ANSWER KEYS

CHAPTER 4

# PRACTICE TEST 1

## SECTION 1 – VERBAL REASONING (PAGES 40-43)

| | | | | | | |
|---|---|---|---|---|---|---|
| 1. C | 6. D | 11. A | 16. B | 21. D | 26. B | 31. B |
| 2. C | 7. B | 12. D | 17. C | 22. B | 27. B | 32. B |
| 3. D | 8. D | 13. D | 18. C | 23. A | 28. D | 33. C |
| 4. C | 9. A | 14. A | 19. A | 24. C | 29. C | 34. A |
| 5. A | 10. D | 15. A | 20. D | 25. A | 30. A | |

## SECTION 2 – QUANTITATIVE REASONING (PAGES 45-52)

| | | | | | | | |
|---|---|---|---|---|---|---|---|
| 1. D | 6. B | 11. D | 16. B | 21. A | 26. B | 31. B | 36. C |
| 2. D | 7. D | 12. A | 17. A | 22. C | 27. C | 32. D | 37. B |
| 3. B | 8. D | 13. C | 18. B | 23. D | 28. B | 33. A | 38. C |
| 4. A | 9. A | 14. C | 19. D | 24. C | 29. C | 34. C | |
| 5. C | 10. C | 15. B | 20. B | 25. B | 30. B | 35. A | |

## SECTION 3 – READING COMPREHENSION (PAGES 54-63)

| | | | | | | |
|---|---|---|---|---|---|---|
| 1. D | 5. A | 9. D | 13. D | 17. B | 21. B | 25. D |
| 2. B | 6. C | 10. A | 14. D | 18. C | 22. A | |
| 3. D | 7. C | 11. C | 15. A | 19. B | 23. B | |
| 4. D | 8. A | 12. C | 16. D | 20. D | 24. C | |

## SECTION 4 – MATHEMATICS ACHIEVEMENT (PAGES 65-70)

| | | | | | | | |
|---|---|---|---|---|---|---|---|
| 1. D | 5. C | 9. C | 13. D | 17. D | 21. C | 25. C | 29. D |
| 2. C | 6. C | 10. B | 14. C | 18. B | 22. C | 26. D | 30. C |
| 3. B | 7. D | 11. C | 15. D | 19. C | 23. A | 27. B | |
| 4. B | 8. C | 12. C | 16. D | 20. D | 24. C | 28. D | |

# SCORING YOUR TEST

On the ISEE, you receive one point for every question you answered correctly, and you receive no points for questions you answered incorrectly or skipped. In each section, the ISEE also includes 5 or 6 experimental questions that do not count towards your score. You won't be told which questions are unscored, and for this reason, these practice tests do not have specific questions marked as experimental. This also means that it isn't possible to determine an exact score for each section of these practice tests, but you can estimate your score using the procedures below.

To estimate your **raw score** for your practice test, first count up the number of questions you answered correctly in each section. Then, follow the table below to subtract 3, 4, or 5 points for each section, accounting for the experimental questions that would not be scored on your actual ISEE exam.

| MY RAW SCORE | | | |
|---|---|---|---|
| **Section** | **# of Questions Correct** | | **Raw Score** |
| Verbal Reasoning | | – 4 = | |
| Quantitative Reasoning | | – 3 = | |
| Reading Comprehension | | – 5 = | |
| Mathematics Achievement | | – 5 = | |

## SCALED SCORE

Once you have found your raw score, convert it into an approximate **scaled score** using the scoring charts that follow. These charts provide an estimated range for your ISEE scaled score based on your performance on this practice test. Keep in mind that this estimate may differ slightly from your scaled score when you take your actual ISEE exam, depending on the ISEE's specific scaling for that exam and any differences in your own test-taking process.

| Raw Score | Verbal Reasoning | Quantitative Reasoning | Reading Comprehension | Mathematics Achievement |
|:---:|:---:|:---:|:---:|:---:|
| | **LOWER LEVEL SCALED SCORE RANGES** | | | |
| 35 | | 875 – 905 | | |
| 34 | | 875 – 905 | | |
| 33 | | 870 – 900 | | |
| 32 | | 865 – 895 | | |
| 31 | | 865 – 895 | | |
| 30 | 875 – 905 | 860 – 890 | | |
| 29 | 870 – 900 | 860 – 890 | | |
| 28 | 865 – 895 | 855 – 885 | | |
| 27 | 865 – 895 | 850 – 880 | | |
| 26 | 860 – 890 | 850 – 880 | | |
| 25 | 855 – 885 | 845 – 875 | | 875 – 905 |
| 24 | 850 – 880 | 840 – 870 | | 875 – 905 |
| 23 | 845 – 875 | 840 – 870 | | 870 – 900 |
| 22 | 845 – 875 | 835 – 865 | | 860 – 890 |
| 21 | 840 – 870 | 830 – 860 | | 860 – 890 |
| 20 | 835 – 865 | 830 – 860 | 885 – 905 | 855 – 885 |
| 19 | 830 – 860 | 825 – 855 | 875 – 905 | 850 – 880 |
| 18 | 830 – 860 | 820 – 850 | 870 – 900 | 845 – 875 |
| 17 | 825 – 855 | 820 – 850 | 865 – 895 | 845 – 875 |
| 16 | 820 – 850 | 815 – 845 | 860 – 890 | 840 – 870 |
| 15 | 820 – 850 | 815 – 845 | 855 – 885 | 835 – 865 |
| 14 | 815 – 845 | 810 – 840 | 845 – 875 | 830 – 860 |
| 13 | 810 – 840 | 805 – 835 | 840 – 870 | 830 – 860 |

| | | | | |
|---|---|---|---|---|
| 12 | 805 – 835 | 805 – 835 | 835 – 865 | 825 – 855 |
| 11 | 800 – 830 | 800 – 830 | 830 – 860 | 820 – 850 |
| 10 | 800 – 830 | 800 – 830 | 825 – 855 | 820 – 850 |
| 9 | 795 – 825 | 795 – 825 | 815 – 845 | 815 – 845 |
| 8 | 790 – 820 | 790 – 820 | 810 – 840 | 810 – 840 |
| 7 | 785 – 815 | 790 – 820 | 805 – 835 | 805 – 835 |
| 6 | 780 – 810 | 785 – 815 | 800 – 830 | 805 – 835 |
| 5 | 780 – 810 | 780 – 810 | 790 – 820 | 800 – 830 |
| 4 | 775 – 805 | 780 – 810 | 785 – 815 | 795 – 825 |
| 3 | 770 – 800 | 775 – 805 | 780 – 810 | 790 – 820 |
| 2 | 765 – 795 | 770 – 800 | 775 – 805 | 790 – 820 |
| 1 | 765 – 795 | 770 – 800 | 770 – 800 | 785 – 815 |
| 0 | 760 – 790 | 765 – 795 | 765 – 795 | 780 – 810 |

## PERCENTILE

When you take your actual ISEE exam, you will receive a **percentile** ranking comparing your performance against the performance of other students in the same grade who have taken the ISEE that year. For example, a percentile of 62 means that you scored higher than 62% of other ISEE test-takers applying to the same grade. Because your percentile ranking shows how well you performed according to your own grade level, these rankings are frequently given high consideration by admissions offices.

The following charts provide an estimate of your ISEE percentile rankings for this practice test, compared against other students applying to the same grade. For example, if you are scoring at or above the 75th percentile, you are scoring higher than 75% of other ISEE test-takers applying to the same grade. Keep in mind that these percentiles are estimates only, and your actual ISEE percentile will depend on the specific group of students taking the exam in your year.

Ivy Global

| LOWER LEVEL VERBAL REASONING PERCENTILES | | | |
|---|---|---|---|
| Grade Applying To | 75th percentile | 50th percentile | 25th percentile |
| Grade 5 | 857 | 840 | 821 |
| Grade 6 | 871 | 856 | 837 |

| LOWER LEVEL QUANTITATIVE REASONING PERCENTILES | | | |
|---|---|---|---|
| Grade Applying To | 75th percentile | 50th percentile | 25th percentile |
| Grade 5 | 859 | 843 | 828 |
| Grade 6 | 870 | 856 | 840 |

| LOWER LEVEL READING COMPREHENSION PERCENTILES | | | |
|---|---|---|---|
| Grade Applying To | 75th percentile | 50th percentile | 25th percentile |
| Grade 5 | 854 | 834 | 815 |
| Grade 6 | 868 | 848 | 828 |

| LOWER LEVEL MATHEMATICS ACHIEVEMENT PERCENTILES | | | |
|---|---|---|---|
| Grade Applying To | 75th percentile | 50th percentile | 25th percentile |
| Grade 5 | 863 | 848 | 833 |
| Grade 6 | 876 | 863 | 848 |

## STANINE

When you receive the score report for your actual ISEE exam, your percentile score will also be broken down into a **stanine**. A stanine is a number from 1-9 obtained by dividing the entire range of students' scores into 9 segments, as shown in the table below:

| PERCENTILE RANK | STANINE |
|:---:|:---:|
| 1 – 3 | 1 |
| 4 – 10 | 2 |
| 11 – 22 | 3 |
| 23 – 39 | 4 |
| 40 – 59 | 5 |
| 60 – 76 | 6 |
| 77 – 88 | 7 |
| 89 – 95 | 8 |
| 96 – 99 | 9 |

Although it isn't possible to calculate your exact stanine from this practice test, you can estimate a stanine score range by looking at your estimated percentile score on each section. For example, if you scored between the 50th and 75th percentile in one of your test sections, your stanine score would be between 5 and 6.

# PRACTICE TEST 2

## LOWER LEVEL

## SECTION 1 – VERBAL REASONING (PAGES 82-85)

| | | | | | | |
|---|---|---|---|---|---|---|
| 1. B | 6. B | 11. A | 16. B | 21. A | 26. D | 31. B |
| 2. C | 7. D | 12. C | 17. C | 22. A | 27. A | 32. B |
| 3. B | 8. B | 13. B | 18. B | 23. C | 28. D | 33. D |
| 4. C | 9. C | 14. C | 19. C | 24. D | 29. B | 34. C |
| 5. A | 10. D | 15. C | 20. D | 25. A | 30. A | |

## SECTION 2 – QUANTITATIVE REASONING (PAGES 87-95)

| | | | | | | | |
|---|---|---|---|---|---|---|---|
| 1. B | 6. B | 11. B | 16. C | 21. A | 26. C | 31. C | 36. D |
| 2. C | 7. B | 12. A | 17. A | 22. D | 27. A | 32. B | 37. C |
| 3. A | 8. D | 13. C | 18. B | 23. C | 28. B | 33. B | 38. A |
| 4. D | 9. A | 14. B | 19. B | 24. B | 29. C | 34. A | |
| 5. D | 10. A | 15. D | 20. D | 25. C | 30. C | 35. B | |

## SECTION 3 – READING COMPREHENSION (PAGES 97-106)

| | | | | | | |
|---|---|---|---|---|---|---|
| 1. A | 5. B | 9. C | 13. C | 17. B | 21. A | 25. D |
| 2. C | 6. D | 10. D | 14. D | 18. A | 22. C | |
| 3. D | 7. A | 11. A | 15. B | 19. B | 23. B | |
| 4. A | 8. C | 12. C | 16. B | 20. D | 24. D | |

## SECTION 4 – MATHEMATICS ACHIEVEMENT (PAGES 108-113)

| | | | | | | | |
|---|---|---|---|---|---|---|---|
| 1. D | 5. B | 9. B | 13. C | 17. C | 21. B | 25. D | 29. C |
| 2. C | 6. C | 10. B | 14. C | 18. A | 22. C | 26. B | 30. A |
| 3. B | 7. C | 11. B | 15. A | 19. C | 23. A | 27. C | |
| 4. D | 8. C | 12. A | 16. C | 20. B | 24. B | 28. D | |

# SCORING YOUR TEST

On the ISEE, you receive one point for every question you answered correctly, and you receive no points for questions you answered incorrectly or skipped. In each section, the ISEE also includes 5 or 6 experimental questions that do not count towards your score. You won't be told which questions are unscored, and for this reason, these practice tests do not have specific questions marked as experimental. This also means that it isn't possible to determine an exact score for each section of these practice tests, but you can estimate your score using the procedures below.

To estimate your **raw score** for your practice test, first count up the number of questions you answered correctly in each section. Then, follow the table below to subtract 3, 4, or 5 points for each section, accounting for the experimental questions that would not be scored on your actual ISEE exam.

| MY RAW SCORE | | | |
|---|---|---|---|
| **Section** | **# of Questions Correct** | | **Raw Score** |
| Verbal Reasoning | | – 4 = | |
| Quantitative Reasoning | | – 3 = | |
| Reading Comprehension | | – 5 = | |
| Mathematics Achievement | | – 5 = | |

## SCALED SCORE

Once you have found your raw score, convert it into an approximate **scaled score** using the scoring charts that follow. These charts provide an estimated range for your ISEE scaled score based on your performance on this practice test. Keep in mind that this estimate may differ slightly from your scaled score when you take your actual ISEE exam, depending on the ISEE's specific scaling for that exam and any differences in your own test-taking process.

| Raw Score | Verbal Reasoning | Quantitative Reasoning | Reading Comprehension | Mathematics Achievement |
|---|---|---|---|---|
| 35 | | 875 – 905 | | |
| 34 | | 875 – 905 | | |
| 33 | | 870 – 900 | | |
| 32 | | 865 – 895 | | |
| 31 | | 865 – 895 | | |
| 30 | 875 – 905 | 860 – 890 | | |
| 29 | 870 – 900 | 860 – 890 | | |
| 28 | 865 – 895 | 855 – 885 | | |
| 27 | 865 – 895 | 850 – 880 | | |
| 26 | 860 – 890 | 850 – 880 | | |
| 25 | 855 – 885 | 845 – 875 | | 875 – 905 |
| 24 | 850 – 880 | 840 – 870 | | 875 – 905 |
| 23 | 845 – 875 | 840 – 870 | | 870 – 900 |
| 22 | 845 – 875 | 835 – 865 | | 860 – 890 |
| 21 | 840 – 870 | 830 – 860 | | 860 – 890 |
| 20 | 835 – 865 | 830 – 860 | 885 – 905 | 855 – 885 |
| 19 | 830 – 860 | 825 – 855 | 875 – 905 | 850 – 880 |
| 18 | 830 – 860 | 820 – 850 | 870 – 900 | 845 – 875 |
| 17 | 825 – 855 | 820 – 850 | 865 – 895 | 845 – 875 |
| 16 | 820 – 850 | 815 – 845 | 860 – 890 | 840 – 870 |
| 15 | 820 – 850 | 815 – 845 | 855 – 885 | 835 – 865 |
| 14 | 815 – 845 | 810 – 840 | 845 – 875 | 830 – 860 |
| 13 | 810 – 840 | 805 – 835 | 840 – 870 | 830 – 860 |

**Ivy Global**

| 12 | 805 – 835 | 805 – 835 | 835 – 865 | 825 – 855 |
|----|-----------|-----------|-----------|-----------|
| 11 | 800 – 830 | 800 – 830 | 830 – 860 | 820 – 850 |
| 10 | 800 – 830 | 800 – 830 | 825 – 855 | 820 – 850 |
| 9 | 795 – 825 | 795 – 825 | 815 – 845 | 815 – 845 |
| 8 | 790 – 820 | 790 – 820 | 810 – 840 | 810 – 840 |
| 7 | 785 – 815 | 790 – 820 | 805 – 835 | 805 – 835 |
| 6 | 780 – 810 | 785 – 815 | 800 – 830 | 805 – 835 |
| 5 | 780 – 810 | 780 – 810 | 790 – 820 | 800 – 830 |
| 4 | 775 – 805 | 780 – 810 | 785 – 815 | 795 – 825 |
| 3 | 770 – 800 | 775 – 805 | 780 – 810 | 790 – 820 |
| 2 | 765 – 795 | 770 – 800 | 775 – 805 | 790 – 820 |
| 1 | 765 – 795 | 770 – 800 | 770 – 800 | 785 – 815 |
| 0 | 760 – 790 | 765 – 795 | 765 – 795 | 780 – 810 |

## PERCENTILE

When you take your actual ISEE exam, you will receive a **percentile** ranking comparing your performance against the performance of other students in the same grade who have taken the ISEE that year. For example, a percentile of 62 means that you scored higher than 62% of other ISEE test-takers applying to the same grade. Because your percentile ranking shows how well you performed according to your own grade level, these rankings are frequently given high consideration by admissions offices.

The following charts provide an estimate of your ISEE percentile rankings for this practice test, compared against other students applying to the same grade. For example, if you are scoring at or above the 75th percentile, you are scoring higher than 75% of other ISEE test-takers applying to the same grade. Keep in mind that these percentiles are estimates only, and your actual ISEE percentile will depend on the specific group of students taking the exam in your year.

Ivy Global

## LOWER LEVEL VERBAL REASONING PERCENTILES

| Grade Applying To | 75th percentile | 50th percentile | 25th percentile |
|---|---|---|---|
| Grade 5 | 857 | 840 | 821 |
| Grade 6 | 871 | 856 | 837 |

## LOWER LEVEL QUANTITATIVE REASONING PERCENTILES

| Grade Applying To | 75th percentile | 50th percentile | 25th percentile |
|---|---|---|---|
| Grade 5 | 859 | 843 | 828 |
| Grade 6 | 870 | 856 | 840 |

## LOWER LEVEL READING COMPREHENSION PERCENTILES

| Grade Applying To | 75th percentile | 50th percentile | 25th percentile |
|---|---|---|---|
| Grade 5 | 854 | 834 | 815 |
| Grade 6 | 868 | 848 | 828 |

## LOWER LEVEL MATHEMATICS ACHIEVEMENT PERCENTILES

| Grade Applying To | 75th percentile | 50th percentile | 25th percentile |
|---|---|---|---|
| Grade 5 | 863 | 848 | 833 |
| Grade 6 | 876 | 863 | 848 |

## STANINE

When you receive the score report for your actual ISEE exam, your percentile score will also be broken down into a **stanine**. A stanine is a number from 1-9 obtained by dividing the entire range of students' scores into 9 segments, as shown in the table below:

| PERCENTILE RANK | STANINE |
|:---:|:---:|
| 1 – 3 | 1 |
| 4 – 10 | 2 |
| 11 – 22 | 3 |
| 23 – 39 | 4 |
| 40 – 59 | 5 |
| 60 – 76 | 6 |
| 77 – 88 | 7 |
| 89 – 95 | 8 |
| 96 – 99 | 9 |

Although it isn't possible to calculate your exact stanine from this practice test, you can estimate a stanine score range by looking at your estimated percentile score on each section. For example, if you scored between the 50th and 75th percentile in one of your test sections, your stanine score would be between 5 and 6.

# PRACTICE TEST 3

MIDDLE LEVEL

## SECTION 1 – VERBAL REASONING (PAGES 125-129)

| | | | | | | | | | | | | | | |
|---|---|---|---|---|---|---|---|---|---|---|---|---|---|---|
| 1. | C | 6. | B | 11. | C | 16. | B | 21. | D | 26. | D | 31. | C | 36. | D |
| 2. | B | 7. | D | 12. | A | 17. | C | 22. | B | 27. | D | 32. | A | 37. | D |
| 3. | A | 8. | A | 13. | C | 18. | C | 23. | A | 28. | C | 33. | B | 38. | A |
| 4. | C | 9. | B | 14. | A | 19. | B | 24. | C | 29. | C | 34. | B | 39. | A |
| 5. | B | 10. | A | 15. | B | 20. | B | 25. | A | 30. | B | 35. | C | 40. | B |

## SECTION 2 – QUANTITATIVE REASONING (PAGES 132-139)

| | | | | | | | | | | | | | | |
|---|---|---|---|---|---|---|---|---|---|---|---|---|---|---|
| 1. | D | 6. | D | 11. | B | 16. | D | 21. | C | 26. | A | 31. | B | 36. | D |
| 2. | C | 7. | D | 12. | B | 17. | B | 22. | A | 27. | D | 32. | C | 37. | C |
| 3. | A | 8. | C | 13. | B | 18. | C | 23. | B | 28. | C | 33. | C | | |
| 4. | A | 9. | C | 14. | B | 19. | B | 24. | B | 29. | B | 34. | B | | |
| 5. | D | 10. | A | 15. | D | 20. | B | 25. | C | 30. | B | 35. | A | | |

## SECTION 3 – READING COMPREHENSION (PAGES 141-152)

| | | | | | | | | | | | | | | |
|---|---|---|---|---|---|---|---|---|---|---|---|---|---|---|
| 1. | C | 6. | A | 11. | D | 16. | D | 21. | D | 26. | D | 31. | B | 36. | B |
| 2. | A | 7. | C | 12. | D | 17. | A | 22. | C | 27. | B | 32. | A | | |
| 3. | B | 8. | B | 13. | C | 18. | A | 23. | A | 28. | B | 33. | D | | |
| 4. | B | 9. | A | 14. | D | 19. | B | 24. | A | 29. | A | 34. | C | | |
| 5. | C | 10. | A | 15. | A | 20. | B | 25. | A | 30. | D | 35. | D | | |

## SECTION 4 – MATHEMATICS ACHIEVEMENT (PAGES 154-162)

| | | | | | | | | | | | | | | | | |
|---|---|---|---|---|---|---|---|---|---|---|---|---|---|---|---|---|
| 1. | B | 7. | D | 13. | B | 19. | A | 25. | C | 31. | A | 37. | D | 43. | B |
| 2. | D | 8. | D | 14. | C | 20. | D | 26. | B | 32. | B | 38. | B | 44. | D |
| 3. | A | 9. | D | 15. | A | 21. | B | 27. | B | 33. | C | 39. | D | 45. | B |
| 4. | C | 10. | C | 16. | B | 22. | A | 28. | B | 34. | B | 40. | C | 46. | A |
| 5. | D | 11. | B | 17. | B | 23. | A | 29. | C | 35. | B | 41. | B | 47. | C |
| 6. | B | 12. | D | 18. | C | 24. | C | 30. | D | 36. | B | 42. | D | | |

# SCORING YOUR TEST

On the ISEE, you receive one point for every question you answered correctly, and you receive no points for questions you answered incorrectly or skipped. In each section, the ISEE also includes 5 or 6 experimental questions that do not count towards your score. You won't be told which questions are unscored, and for this reason, these practice tests do not have specific questions marked as experimental. This also means that it isn't possible to determine an exact score for each section of these practice tests, but you can estimate your score using the procedures below.

To estimate your **raw score** for your practice test, first count up the number of questions you answered correctly in each section. Then, follow the table below to subtract 5 or 6 points for each section, accounting for the experimental questions that would not be scored on your actual ISEE exam.

| | MY RAW SCORE | | |
|---|---|---|---|
| **Section** | **# of Questions Correct** | | **Raw Score** |
| Verbal Reasoning | | – 5 = | |
| Quantitative Reasoning | | – 5 = | |
| Reading Comprehension | | – 6 = | |
| Mathematics Achievement | | – 5 = | |

## SCALED SCORE

Once you have found your raw score, convert it into an approximate **scaled score** using the scoring charts that follow. These charts provide an estimated range for your ISEE scaled score based on your performance on this practice test. Keep in mind that this estimate may differ slightly from your scaled score when you take your actual ISEE exam, depending on the ISEE's specific scaling for that exam and any differences in your own test-taking process.

| | MIDDLE LEVEL SCALED SCORE RANGES | | | |
|---|---|---|---|---|
| Raw Score | Verbal Reasoning | Quantitative Reasoning | Reading Comprehension | Mathematics Achievement |
| 42 | | | | 875 – 905 |
| 41 | | | | 875 – 905 |
| 40 | | | | 870 – 900 |
| 39 | | | | 870 – 900 |
| 38 | | | | 865 – 895 |
| 37 | | | | 865 – 895 |
| 36 | | | | 860 – 890 |
| 35 | 895 – 925 | | | 860 – 890 |
| 34 | 890 – 920 | | | 855 – 885 |
| 33 | 890 – 920 | | | 855 – 885 |
| 32 | 885 – 915 | 895 – 925 | | 850 – 880 |
| 31 | 885 – 915 | 895 – 925 | | 850 – 880 |
| 30 | 880 – 910 | 890 – 920 | 915 – 940 | 845 – 875 |
| 29 | 875 – 905 | 885 – 915 | 910 – 940 | 845 – 875 |
| 28 | 875 – 905 | 885 – 915 | 905 – 935 | 845 – 875 |
| 27 | 870 – 900 | 880 – 910 | 905 – 935 | 840 – 870 |
| 26 | 865 – 895 | 875 – 905 | 900 – 930 | 840 – 870 |
| 25 | 865 – 895 | 875 – 905 | 895 – 925 | 835 – 865 |
| 24 | 860 – 890 | 870 – 900 | 890 – 920 | 835 – 865 |
| 23 | 855 – 885 | 865 – 895 | 885 – 915 | 830 – 860 |
| 22 | 855 – 885 | 865 – 895 | 885 – 915 | 830 – 860 |
| 21 | 850 – 880 | 860 – 890 | 880 – 910 | 825 – 855 |
| 20 | 845 – 875 | 855 – 885 | 875 – 905 | 825 – 855 |

**Ivy Global**

| 19 | 845 – 875 | 855 – 885 | 870 – 900 | 820 – 850 |
|----|-----------|-----------|-----------|-----------|
| 18 | 840 – 870 | 850 – 880 | 870 – 900 | 820 – 850 |
| 17 | 835 – 865 | 845 – 875 | 865 – 895 | 815 – 845 |
| 16 | 835 – 865 | 845 – 875 | 860 – 890 | 815 – 845 |
| 15 | 830 – 860 | 840 – 870 | 855 – 885 | 810 – 840 |
| 14 | 825 – 855 | 835 – 865 | 855 – 885 | 810 – 840 |
| 13 | 825 – 855 | 835 – 865 | 850 – 880 | 805 – 835 |
| 12 | 820 – 850 | 830 – 860 | 845 – 875 | 805 – 835 |
| 11 | 815 – 845 | 830 – 860 | 840 – 870 | 800 – 830 |
| 10 | 815 – 845 | 825 – 855 | 835 – 865 | 800 – 830 |
| 9  | 810 – 840 | 820 – 850 | 835 – 865 | 795 – 825 |
| 8  | 810 – 840 | 820 – 850 | 830 – 860 | 795 – 825 |
| 7  | 805 – 835 | 815 – 845 | 825 – 855 | 790 – 820 |
| 6  | 800 – 830 | 810 – 840 | 820 – 850 | 790 – 820 |
| 5  | 800 – 830 | 810 – 840 | 820 – 850 | 785 – 815 |
| 4  | 795 – 825 | 805 – 835 | 815 – 845 | 785 – 815 |
| 3  | 790 – 820 | 800 – 830 | 810 – 840 | 780 – 810 |
| 2  | 790 – 820 | 800 – 830 | 805 – 835 | 780 – 810 |
| 1  | 785 – 815 | 795 – 825 | 805 – 835 | 775 – 805 |
| 0  | 780 – 810 | 790 – 820 | 800 – 830 | 775 – 805 |

Ivy Global

# PERCENTILE

When you take your actual ISEE exam, you will receive a **percentile** ranking comparing your performance against the performance of other students in the same grade who have taken the ISEE that year. For example, a percentile of 62 means that you scored higher than 62% of other ISEE test-takers applying to the same grade. Because your percentile ranking shows how well you performed according to your own grade level, these rankings are frequently given high consideration by admissions offices.

The following charts provide an estimate of your ISEE percentile rankings for this practice test, compared against other students applying to the same grade. For example, if you are scoring at or above the 75th percentile, you are scoring higher than 75% of other ISEE test-takers applying to the same grade. Keep in mind that these percentiles are estimates only, and your actual ISEE percentile will depend on the specific group of students taking the exam in your year.

| MIDDLE LEVEL VERBAL REASONING PERCENTILES | | | |
|---|---|---|---|
| **Grade Applying To** | **75th percentile** | **50th percentile** | **25th percentile** |
| Grade 7 | 880 | 868 | 853 |
| Grade 8 | 890 | 878 | 867 |

| MIDDLE LEVEL QUANTITATIVE REASONING PERCENTILES | | | |
|---|---|---|---|
| **Grade Applying To** | **75th percentile** | **50th percentile** | **25th percentile** |
| Grade 7 | 877 | 865 | 853 |
| Grade 8 | 884 | 873 | 864 |

| MIDDLE LEVEL READING COMPREHENSION PERCENTILES | | | |
|---|---|---|---|
| **Grade Applying To** | **75th percentile** | **50th percentile** | **25th percentile** |
| Grade 7 | 885 | 869 | 850 |
| Grade 8 | 897 | 883 | 868 |

| MIDDLE LEVEL MATHEMATICS ACHIEVEMENT PERCENTILES | | | |
|---|---|---|---|
| Grade Applying To | 75th percentile | 50th percentile | 25th percentile |
| Grade 7 | 882 | 871 | 861 |
| Grade 8 | 886 | 876 | 867 |

## STANINE

When you receive the score report for your actual ISEE exam, your percentile score will also be broken down into a **stanine**. A stanine is a number from 1-9 obtained by dividing the entire range of students' scores into 9 segments, as shown in the table below:

| PERCENTILE RANK | STANINE |
|---|---|
| 1 – 3 | 1 |
| 4 – 10 | 2 |
| 11 – 22 | 3 |
| 23 – 39 | 4 |
| 40 – 59 | 5 |
| 60 – 76 | 6 |
| 77 – 88 | 7 |
| 89 – 95 | 8 |
| 96 – 99 | 9 |

Although it isn't possible to calculate your exact stanine from this practice test, you can estimate a stanine score range by looking at your estimated percentile score on each section. For example, if you scored between the 50th and 75th percentile in one of your test sections, your stanine score would be between 5 and 6.

**Ivy Global**

# PRACTICE TEST 4

MIDDLE LEVEL

## SECTION 1 – VERBAL REASONING (PAGES 173-177)

| | | | | | | | |
|---|---|---|---|---|---|---|---|
| 1. C | 6. C | 11. C | 16. D | 21. B | 26. B | 31. A | 36. B |
| 2. C | 7. A | 12. A | 17. D | 22. D | 27. C | 32. C | 37. A |
| 3. B | 8. B | 13. A | 18. C | 23. A | 28. C | 33. C | 38. D |
| 4. D | 9. D | 14. C | 19. B | 24. A | 29. D | 34. A | 39. B |
| 5. C | 10. D | 15. C | 20. C | 25. D | 30. C | 35. D | 40. A |

## SECTION 2 – QUANTITATIVE REASONING (PAGES 180-187)

| | | | | | | | |
|---|---|---|---|---|---|---|---|
| 1. B | 6. B | 11. D | 16. C | 21. B | 26. B | 31. C | 36. D |
| 2. C | 7. C | 12. D | 17. C | 22. B | 27. B | 32. B | 37. C |
| 3. B | 8. B | 13. C | 18. B | 23. C | 28. D | 33. B | |
| 4. B | 9. B | 14. A | 19. B | 24. B | 29. B | 34. B | |
| 5. B | 10. B | 15. B | 20. B | 25. A | 30. B | 35. A | |

## SECTION 3 – READING COMPREHENSION (PAGES 189-200)

| | | | | | | | |
|---|---|---|---|---|---|---|---|
| 1. C | 6. C | 11. C | 16. D | 21. C | 26. C | 31. B | 36. A |
| 2. C | 7. C | 12. B | 17. C | 22. C | 27. C | 32. A | |
| 3. B | 8. B | 13. C | 18. C | 23. A | 28. A | 33. C | |
| 4. A | 9. B | 14. B | 19. A | 24. C | 29. D | 34. D | |
| 5. C | 10. C | 15. A | 20. D | 25. B | 30. B | 35. B | |

## SECTION 4 – MATHEMATICS ACHIEVEMENT (PAGES 202-210)

| | | | | | | | |
|---|---|---|---|---|---|---|---|
| 1. B | 7. A | 13. B | 19. A | 25. C | 31. C | 37. D | 43. B |
| 2. B | 8. C | 14. B | 20. A | 26. B | 32. B | 38. B | 44. D |
| 3. A | 9. D | 15. B | 21. B | 27. C | 33. D | 39. C | 45. B |
| 4. B | 10. C | 16. D | 22. D | 28. B | 34. D | 40. C | 46. C |
| 5. D | 11. C | 17. A | 23. C | 29. A | 35. C | 41. D | 47. A |
| 6. C | 12. C | 18. D | 24. C | 30. D | 36. B | 42. A | |

# SCORING YOUR TEST

On the ISEE, you receive one point for every question you answered correctly, and you receive no points for questions you answered incorrectly or skipped. In each section, the ISEE also includes 5 or 6 experimental questions that do not count towards your score. You won't be told which questions are unscored, and for this reason, these practice tests do not have specific questions marked as experimental. This also means that it isn't possible to determine an exact score for each section of these practice tests, but you can estimate your score using the procedures below.

To estimate your **raw score** for your practice test, first count up the number of questions you answered correctly in each section. Then, follow the table below to subtract 5 or 6 points for each section, accounting for the experimental questions that would not be scored on your actual ISEE exam.

| MY RAW SCORE | | | |
|---|---|---|---|
| **Section** | **# of Questions Correct** | | **Raw Score** |
| Verbal Reasoning | | – 5 = | |
| Quantitative Reasoning | | – 5 = | |
| Reading Comprehension | | – 6 = | |
| Mathematics Achievement | | – 5 = | |

## SCALED SCORE

Once you have found your raw score, convert it into an approximate **scaled score** using the scoring charts that follow. These charts provide an estimated range for your ISEE scaled score based on your performance on this practice test. Keep in mind that this estimate may differ slightly from your scaled score when you take your actual ISEE exam, depending on the ISEE's specific scaling for that exam and any differences in your own test-taking process.

| | MIDDLE LEVEL SCALED SCORE RANGES | | | |
|---|---|---|---|---|
| Raw Score | Verbal Reasoning | Quantitative Reasoning | Reading Comprehension | Mathematics Achievement |
| 42 | | | | 875 – 905 |
| 41 | | | | 875 – 905 |
| 40 | | | | 870 – 900 |
| 39 | | | | 870 – 900 |
| 38 | | | | 865 – 895 |
| 37 | | | | 865 – 895 |
| 36 | | | | 860 – 890 |
| 35 | 895 – 925 | | | 860 – 890 |
| 34 | 890 – 920 | | | 855 – 885 |
| 33 | 890 – 920 | | | 855 – 885 |
| 32 | 885 – 915 | 895 – 925 | | 850 – 880 |
| 31 | 885 – 915 | 895 – 925 | | 850 – 880 |
| 30 | 880 – 910 | 890 – 920 | 915 – 940 | 845 – 875 |
| 29 | 875 – 905 | 885 – 915 | 910 – 940 | 845 – 875 |
| 28 | 875 – 905 | 885 – 915 | 905 – 935 | 845 – 875 |
| 27 | 870 – 900 | 880 – 910 | 905 – 935 | 840 – 870 |
| 26 | 865 – 895 | 875 – 905 | 900 – 930 | 840 – 870 |
| 25 | 865 – 895 | 875 – 905 | 895 – 925 | 835 – 865 |
| 24 | 860 – 890 | 870 – 900 | 890 – 920 | 835 – 865 |
| 23 | 855 – 885 | 865 – 895 | 885 – 915 | 830 – 860 |
| 22 | 855 – 885 | 865 – 895 | 885 – 915 | 830 – 860 |
| 21 | 850 – 880 | 860 – 890 | 880 – 910 | 825 – 855 |
| 20 | 845 – 875 | 855 – 885 | 875 – 905 | 825 – 855 |

| | | | | |
|---|---|---|---|---|
| 19 | 845 – 875 | 855 – 885 | 870 – 900 | 820 – 850 |
| 18 | 840 – 870 | 850 – 880 | 870 – 900 | 820 – 850 |
| 17 | 835 – 865 | 845 – 875 | 865 – 895 | 815 – 845 |
| 16 | 835 – 865 | 845 – 875 | 860 – 890 | 815 – 845 |
| 15 | 830 – 860 | 840 – 870 | 855 – 885 | 810 – 840 |
| 14 | 825 – 855 | 835 – 865 | 855 – 885 | 810 – 840 |
| 13 | 825 – 855 | 835 – 865 | 850 – 880 | 805 – 835 |
| 12 | 820 – 850 | 830 – 860 | 845 – 875 | 805 – 835 |
| 11 | 815 – 845 | 830 – 860 | 840 – 870 | 800 – 830 |
| 10 | 815 – 845 | 825 – 855 | 835 – 865 | 800 – 830 |
| 9 | 810 – 840 | 820 – 850 | 835 – 865 | 795 – 825 |
| 8 | 810 – 840 | 820 – 850 | 830 – 860 | 795 – 825 |
| 7 | 805 – 835 | 815 – 845 | 825 – 855 | 790 – 820 |
| 6 | 800 – 830 | 810 – 840 | 820 – 850 | 790 – 820 |
| 5 | 800 – 830 | 810 – 840 | 820 – 850 | 785 – 815 |
| 4 | 795 – 825 | 805 – 835 | 815 – 845 | 785 – 815 |
| 3 | 790 – 820 | 800 – 830 | 810 – 840 | 780 – 810 |
| 2 | 790 – 820 | 800 – 830 | 805 – 835 | 780 – 810 |
| 1 | 785 – 815 | 795 – 825 | 805 – 835 | 775 – 805 |
| 0 | 780 – 810 | 790 – 820 | 800 – 830 | 775 – 805 |

**Ivy Global**

# PERCENTILE

When you take your actual ISEE exam, you will receive a **percentile** ranking comparing your performance against the performance of other students in the same grade who have taken the ISEE that year. For example, a percentile of 62 means that you scored higher than 62% of other ISEE test-takers applying to the same grade. Because your percentile ranking shows how well you performed according to your own grade level, these rankings are frequently given high consideration by admissions offices.

The following charts provide an estimate of your ISEE percentile rankings for this practice test, compared against other students applying to the same grade. For example, if you are scoring at or above the 75th percentile, you are scoring higher than 75% of other ISEE test-takers applying to the same grade. Keep in mind that these percentiles are estimates only, and your actual ISEE percentile will depend on the specific group of students taking the exam in your year.

| MIDDLE LEVEL VERBAL REASONING PERCENTILES | | | |
|---|---|---|---|
| Grade Applying To | 75th percentile | 50th percentile | 25th percentile |
| Grade 7 | 880 | 868 | 853 |
| Grade 8 | 890 | 878 | 867 |

| MIDDLE LEVEL QUANTITATIVE REASONING PERCENTILES | | | |
|---|---|---|---|
| Grade Applying To | 75th percentile | 50th percentile | 25th percentile |
| Grade 7 | 877 | 865 | 853 |
| Grade 8 | 884 | 873 | 864 |

| MIDDLE LEVEL READING COMPREHENSION PERCENTILES | | | |
|---|---|---|---|
| Grade Applying To | 75th percentile | 50th percentile | 25th percentile |
| Grade 7 | 885 | 869 | 850 |
| Grade 8 | 897 | 883 | 868 |

| MIDDLE LEVEL MATHEMATICS ACHIEVEMENT PERCENTILES | | | |
|---|---|---|---|
| Grade Applying To | 75th percentile | 50th percentile | 25th percentile |
| Grade 7 | 882 | 871 | 861 |
| Grade 8 | 886 | 876 | 867 |

## STANINE

When you receive the score report for your actual ISEE exam, your percentile score will also be broken down into a **stanine**. A stanine is a number from 1-9 obtained by dividing the entire range of students' scores into 9 segments, as shown in the table below:

| PERCENTILE RANK | STANINE |
|---|---|
| $1 - 3$ | 1 |
| $4 - 10$ | 2 |
| $11 - 22$ | 3 |
| $23 - 39$ | 4 |
| $40 - 59$ | 5 |
| $60 - 76$ | 6 |
| $77 - 88$ | 7 |
| $89 - 95$ | 8 |
| $96 - 99$ | 9 |

Although it isn't possible to calculate your exact stanine from this practice test, you can estimate a stanine score range by looking at your estimated percentile score on each section. For example, if you scored between the 50th and 75th percentile in one of your test sections, your stanine score would be between 5 and 6.

# PRACTICE TEST 5

## SECTION 1 – VERBAL REASONING (PAGES 222-226)

| | | | | | | | |
|---|---|---|---|---|---|---|---|
| 1. A | 6. D | 11. C | 16. A | 21. D | 26. B | 31. A | 36. A |
| 2. D | 7. C | 12. D | 17. B | 22. C | 27. D | 32. C | 37. D |
| 3. A | 8. B | 13. C | 18. D | 23. D | 28. C | 33. C | 38. A |
| 4. C | 9. A | 14. D | 19. B | 24. B | 29. B | 34. B | 39. B |
| 5. B | 10. B | 15. B | 20. C | 25. D | 30. D | 35. B | 40. C |

## SECTION 2 – QUANTITATIVE REASONING (PAGES 229-237)

| | | | | | | | |
|---|---|---|---|---|---|---|---|
| 1. B | 6. A | 11. D | 16. D | 21. A | 26. B | 31. A | 36. A |
| 2. C | 7. C | 12. C | 17. A | 22. D | 27. C | 32. A | 37. C |
| 3. A | 8. D | 13. B | 18. B | 23. B | 28. B | 33. A | |
| 4. D | 9. A | 14. A | 19. B | 24. A | 29. C | 34. B | |
| 5. B | 10. C | 15. C | 20. B | 25. A | 30. C | 35. B | |

## SECTION 3 – READING COMPREHENSION (PAGES 238-250)

| | | | | | | | |
|---|---|---|---|---|---|---|---|
| 1. C | 6. D | 11. A | 16. D | 21. D | 26. B | 31. C | 36. C |
| 2. A | 7. A | 12. B | 17. B | 22. C | 27. D | 32. C | |
| 3. B | 8. C | 13. C | 18. C | 23. C | 28. A | 33. A | |
| 4. C | 9. C | 14. D | 19. C | 24. A | 29. D | 34. B | |
| 5. D | 10. B | 15. B | 20. D | 25. A | 30. C | 35. A | |

## SECTION 4 – MATHEMATICS ACHIEVEMENT (PAGES 252-260)

| | | | | | | | |
|---|---|---|---|---|---|---|---|
| 1. A | 7. B | 13. D | 19. C | 25. B | 31. C | 37. C | 43. B |
| 2. C | 8. C | 14. B | 20. C | 26. B | 32. D | 38. C | 44. D |
| 3. C | 9. D | 15. D | 21. D | 27. C | 33. C | 39. D | 45. A |
| 4. A | 10. C | 16. A | 22. B | 28. B | 34. B | 40. A | 46. D |
| 5. B | 11. A | 17. C | 23. C | 29. B | 35. C | 41. C | 47. C |
| 6. B | 12. D | 18. A | 24. A | 30. C | 36. D | 42. C | |

# SCORING YOUR TEST

On the ISEE, you receive one point for every question you answered correctly, and you receive no points for questions you answered incorrectly or skipped. In each section, the ISEE also includes 5 or 6 experimental questions that do not count towards your score. You won't be told which questions are unscored, and for this reason, these practice tests do not have specific questions marked as experimental. This also means that it isn't possible to determine an exact score for each section of these practice tests, but you can estimate your score using the procedures below.

To estimate your **raw score** for your practice test, first count up the number of questions you answered correctly in each section. Then, follow the table below to subtract 5 or 6 points for each section, accounting for the experimental questions that would not be scored on your actual ISEE exam.

| MY RAW SCORE | | | |
|---|---|---|---|
| Section | # of Questions Correct | | Raw Score |
| Verbal Reasoning | | − 5 = | |
| Quantitative Reasoning | | − 5 = | |
| Reading Comprehension | | − 6 = | |
| Mathematics Achievement | | − 5 = | |

## SCALED SCORE

Once you have found your raw score, convert it into an approximate **scaled score** using the scoring charts that follow. These charts provide an estimated range for your ISEE scaled score based on your performance on this practice test. Keep in mind that this estimate may differ slightly from your scaled score when you take your actual ISEE exam, depending on the ISEE's specific scaling for that exam and any differences in your own test-taking process.

| Raw Score | Verbal Reasoning | Quantitative Reasoning | Reading Comprehension | Mathematics Achievement |
|---|---|---|---|---|
| | UPPER LEVEL SCALED SCORE RANGES | | | |
| 42 | | | | 920 – 950 |
| 41 | | | | 920 – 950 |
| 40 | | | | 915 – 945 |
| 39 | | | | 915 – 945 |
| 38 | | | | 910 – 940 |
| 37 | | | | 910 – 935 |
| 36 | | | | 905 – 935 |
| 35 | 910 – 940 | | | 900 – 930 |
| 34 | 910 – 940 | | | 900 – 930 |
| 33 | 905 – 935 | | | 895 – 925 |
| 32 | 905 – 935 | 915 – 945 | | 895 – 925 |
| 31 | 900 – 930 | 910 – 940 | | 890 – 920 |
| 30 | 900 – 930 | 910 – 940 | 910 – 940 | 890 – 920 |
| 29 | 895 – 925 | 905 – 935 | 905 – 935 | 885 – 915 |
| 28 | 890 – 920 | 900 – 930 | 900 – 930 | 880 – 910 |
| 27 | 890 – 920 | 900 – 930 | 900 – 930 | 880 – 910 |
| 26 | 885 – 915 | 895 – 925 | 895 – 925 | 875 – 905 |
| 25 | 885 – 910 | 890 – 920 | 890 – 920 | 875 – 905 |
| 24 | 880 – 910 | 890 – 920 | 885 – 915 | 870 – 900 |
| 23 | 875 – 905 | 885 – 915 | 885 – 915 | 870 – 900 |
| 22 | 875 – 905 | 880 – 910 | 880 – 910 | 865 – 895 |
| 21 | 870 – 900 | 880 – 910 | 875 – 905 | 865 – 895 |
| 20 | 870 – 900 | 875 – 905 | 870 – 900 | 860 – 890 |

**Ivy Global**

| | | | | |
|---|---|---|---|---|
| 19 | 865 – 895 | 870 – 900 | 870 – 900 | 860 – 890 |
| 18 | 860 – 890 | 870 – 900 | 865 – 895 | 855 – 885 |
| 17 | 860 – 890 | 865 – 895 | 860 – 890 | 855 – 885 |
| 16 | 855 – 885 | 860 – 890 | 855 – 885 | 850 – 880 |
| 15 | 850 – 880 | 860 – 890 | 855 – 885 | 845 – 875 |
| 14 | 850 – 880 | 855 – 885 | 850 – 880 | 845 – 875 |
| 13 | 845 – 875 | 850 – 880 | 845 – 875 | 840 – 870 |
| 12 | 845 – 875 | 845 – 875 | 840 – 870 | 840 – 870 |
| 11 | 840 – 870 | 845 – 875 | 840 – 870 | 835 – 865 |
| 10 | 840 – 870 | 840 – 870 | 835 – 865 | 835 – 865 |
| 9 | 835 – 865 | 835 – 865 | 830 – 860 | 830 – 860 |
| 8 | 835 – 865 | 835 – 865 | 825 – 855 | 830 – 860 |
| 7 | 830 – 860 | 830 – 860 | 825 – 855 | 825 – 855 |
| 6 | 825 – 855 | 825 – 855 | 820 – 850 | 825 – 855 |
| 5 | 825 – 855 | 825 – 855 | 815 – 845 | 820 – 850 |
| 4 | 820 – 850 | 820 – 850 | 810 – 840 | 820 – 850 |
| 3 | 815 – 845 | 815 – 845 | 810 – 840 | 815 – 845 |
| 2 | 815 – 845 | 815 – 845 | 805 – 835 | 810 – 840 |
| 1 | 810 – 840 | 810 – 840 | 800 – 830 | 810 – 840 |
| 0 | 805 – 840 | 805 – 835 | 795 – 825 | 805 – 835 |

# PERCENTILE

When you take your actual ISEE exam, you will receive a **percentile** ranking comparing your performance against the performance of other students in the same grade who have taken the ISEE that year. For example, a percentile of 62 means that you scored higher than 62% of other ISEE test-takers applying to the same grade. Because your percentile ranking shows how well you performed according to your own grade level, these rankings are frequently given high consideration by admissions offices.

The following charts provide an estimate of your ISEE percentile rankings for this practice test, compared against other students applying to the same grade. For example, if you are scoring at or above the 75th percentile, you are scoring higher than 75% of other ISEE test-takers applying to the same grade. Keep in mind that these percentiles are estimates only, and your actual ISEE percentile will depend on the specific group of students taking the exam in your year.

| UPPER LEVEL VERBAL REASONING PERCENTILES | | | |
|---|---|---|---|
| Grade Applying To | 75th percentile | 50th percentile | 25th percentile |
| Grade 9 | 893 | 879 | 866 |
| Grade 10 | 899 | 883 | 867 |
| Grade 11 | 902 | 886 | 869 |
| Grade 12 | 898 | 881 | 863 |

| UPPER LEVEL QUANTITATIVE REASONING PERCENTILES | | | |
|---|---|---|---|
| Grade Applying To | 75th percentile | 50th percentile | 25th percentile |
| Grade 9 | 892 | 878 | 866 |
| Grade 10 | 897 | 882 | 868 |
| Grade 11 | 901 | 885 | 870 |
| Grade 12 | 897 | 884 | 872 |

## UPPER LEVEL READING COMPREHENSION PERCENTILES

| Grade Applying To | 75th percentile | 50th percentile | 25th percentile |
|---|---|---|---|
| Grade 9 | 897 | 880 | 865 |
| Grade 10 | 902 | 886 | 868 |
| Grade 11 | 903 | 889 | 868 |
| Grade 12 | 899 | 880 | 862 |

## UPPER LEVEL MATHEMATICS ACHIEVEMENT PERCENTILES

| Grade Applying To | 75th percentile | 50th percentile | 25th percentile |
|---|---|---|---|
| Grade 9 | 894 | 882 | 869 |
| Grade 10 | 900 | 886 | 871 |
| Grade 11 | 905 | 890 | 875 |
| Grade 12 | 903 | 889 | 875 |

## STANINE

When you receive the score report for your actual ISEE exam, your percentile score will also be broken down into a **stanine**. A stanine is a number from 1-9 obtained by dividing the entire range of students' scores into 9 segments, as shown in the table below:

| PERCENTILE RANK | STANINE |
|---|---|
| 1 – 3 | 1 |
| 4 – 10 | 2 |
| 11 – 22 | 3 |
| 23 – 39 | 4 |

| | |
|---|---|
| 40 – 59 | 5 |
| 60 – 76 | 6 |
| 77 – 88 | 7 |
| 89 – 95 | 8 |
| 96 – 99 | 9 |

Although it isn't possible to calculate your exact stanine from this practice test, you can estimate a stanine score range by looking at your estimated percentile score on each section. For example, if you scored between the 50th and 75th percentile in one of your test sections, your stanine score would be between 5 and 6.

# PRACTICE TEST 6

UPPER LEVEL

## SECTION 1 – VERBAL REASONING (PAGES 272-276)

| | | | | | | | |
|---|---|---|---|---|---|---|---|
| 1. A | 6. D | 11. A | 16. A | 21. A | 26. D | 31. A | 36. C |
| 2. D | 7. C | 12. D | 17. C | 22. B | 27. B | 32. D | 37. A |
| 3. D | 8. D | 13. C | 18. B | 23. C | 28. C | 33. B | 38. A |
| 4. D | 9. D | 14. C | 19. B | 24. C | 29. B | 34. C | 39. B |
| 5. B | 10. A | 15. B | 20. A | 25. C | 30. D | 35. B | 40. D |

## SECTION 2 – QUANTITATIVE REASONING (PAGES 279-286)

| | | | | | | | |
|---|---|---|---|---|---|---|---|
| 1. A | 6. B | 11. C | 16. D | 21. B | 26. B | 31. B | 36. C |
| 2. A | 7. C | 12. B | 17. C | 22. B | 27. D | 32. C | 37. B |
| 3. B | 8. B | 13. B | 18. B | 23. A | 28. B | 33. B | |
| 4. C | 9. A | 14. C | 19. A | 24. A | 29. C | 34. D | |
| 5. D | 10. A | 15. D | 20. D | 25. D | 30. A | 35. C | |

## SECTION 3 – READING COMPREHENSION (PAGES 288-298)

| | | | | | | | |
|---|---|---|---|---|---|---|---|
| 1. C | 6. C | 11. B | 16. B | 21. A | 26. B | 31. B | 36. C |
| 2. A | 7. C | 12. B | 17. D | 22. A | 27. A | 32. B | |
| 3. A | 8. C | 13. D | 18. C | 23. B | 28. D | 33. B | |
| 4. B | 9. D | 14. D | 19. D | 24. A | 29. A | 34. C | |
| 5. C | 10. A | 15. A | 20. D | 25. D | 30. A | 35. A | |

## SECTION 4 – MATHEMATICS ACHIEVEMENT (PAGES 301-310)

| | | | | | | | |
|---|---|---|---|---|---|---|---|
| 1. B | 7. D | 13. C | 19. C | 25. C | 31. B | 37. B | 43. B |
| 2. C | 8. B | 14. C | 20. B | 26. D | 32. D | 38. C | 44. C |
| 3. B | 9. D | 15. A | 21. C | 27. C | 33. C | 39. D | 45. D |
| 4. C | 10. C | 16. D | 22. B | 28. C | 34. D | 40. B | 46. B |
| 5. C | 11. B | 17. D | 23. D | 29. D | 35. C | 41. B | 47. A |
| 6. C | 12. B | 18. A | 24. C | 30. D | 36. C | 42. D | |

Ivy Global

# SCORING YOUR TEST

On the ISEE, you receive one point for every question you answered correctly, and you receive no points for questions you answered incorrectly or skipped. In each section, the ISEE also includes 5 or 6 experimental questions that do not count towards your score. You won't be told which questions are unscored, and for this reason, these practice tests do not have specific questions marked as experimental. This also means that it isn't possible to determine an exact score for each section of these practice tests, but you can estimate your score using the procedures below.

To estimate your **raw score** for your practice test, first count up the number of questions you answered correctly in each section. Then, follow the table below to subtract 5 or 6 points for each section, accounting for the experimental questions that would not be scored on your actual ISEE exam.

| MY RAW SCORE | | | |
|---|---|---|---|
| **Section** | **# of Questions Correct** | | **Raw Score** |
| Verbal Reasoning | | – 5 = | |
| Quantitative Reasoning | | – 5 = | |
| Reading Comprehension | | – 6 = | |
| Mathematics Achievement | | – 5 = | |

## SCALED SCORE

Once you have found your raw score, convert it into an approximate **scaled score** using the scoring charts that follow. These charts provide an estimated range for your ISEE scaled score based on your performance on this practice test. Keep in mind that this estimate may differ slightly from your scaled score when you take your actual ISEE exam, depending on the ISEE's specific scaling for that exam and any differences in your own test-taking process.

| Raw Score | Verbal Reasoning | Quantitative Reasoning | Reading Comprehension | Mathematics Achievement |
|---|---|---|---|---|
| | | UPPER LEVEL SCALED SCORE RANGES | | |
| 42 | | | | 920 – 950 |
| 41 | | | | 920 – 950 |
| 40 | | | | 915 – 945 |
| 39 | | | | 915 – 945 |
| 38 | | | | 910 – 940 |
| 37 | | | | 910 – 935 |
| 36 | | | | 905 – 935 |
| 35 | 910 – 940 | | | 900 – 930 |
| 34 | 910 – 940 | | | 900 – 930 |
| 33 | 905 – 935 | | | 895 – 925 |
| 32 | 905 – 935 | 915 – 945 | | 895 – 925 |
| 31 | 900 – 930 | 910 – 940 | | 890 – 920 |
| 30 | 900 – 930 | 910 – 940 | 910 – 940 | 890 – 920 |
| 29 | 895 – 925 | 905 – 935 | 905 – 935 | 885 – 915 |
| 28 | 890 – 920 | 900 – 930 | 900 – 930 | 880 – 910 |
| 27 | 890 – 920 | 900 – 930 | 900 – 930 | 880 – 910 |
| 26 | 885 – 915 | 895 – 925 | 895 – 925 | 875 – 905 |
| 25 | 885 – 910 | 890 – 920 | 890 – 920 | 875 – 905 |
| 24 | 880 – 910 | 890 – 920 | 885 – 915 | 870 – 900 |
| 23 | 875 – 905 | 885 – 915 | 885 – 915 | 870 – 900 |
| 22 | 875 – 905 | 880 – 910 | 880 – 910 | 865 – 895 |
| 21 | 870 – 900 | 880 – 910 | 875 – 905 | 865 – 895 |
| 20 | 870 – 900 | 875 – 905 | 870 – 900 | 860 – 890 |

**Ivy Global**

| | | | | |
|---|---|---|---|---|
| 19 | 865 – 895 | 870 – 900 | 870 – 900 | 860 – 890 |
| 18 | 860 – 890 | 870 – 900 | 865 – 895 | 855 – 885 |
| 17 | 860 – 890 | 865 – 895 | 860 – 890 | 855 – 885 |
| 16 | 855 – 885 | 860 – 890 | 855 – 885 | 850 – 880 |
| 15 | 850 – 880 | 860 – 890 | 855 – 885 | 845 – 875 |
| 14 | 850 – 880 | 855 – 885 | 850 – 880 | 845 – 875 |
| 13 | 845 – 875 | 850 – 880 | 845 – 875 | 840 – 870 |
| 12 | 845 – 875 | 845 – 875 | 840 – 870 | 840 – 870 |
| 11 | 840 – 870 | 845 – 875 | 840 – 870 | 835 – 865 |
| 10 | 840 – 870 | 840 – 870 | 835 – 865 | 835 – 865 |
| 9 | 835 – 865 | 835 – 865 | 830 – 860 | 830 – 860 |
| 8 | 835 – 865 | 835 – 865 | 825 – 855 | 830 – 860 |
| 7 | 830 – 860 | 830 – 860 | 825 – 855 | 825 – 855 |
| 6 | 825 – 855 | 825 – 855 | 820 – 850 | 825 – 855 |
| 5 | 825 – 855 | 825 – 855 | 815 – 845 | 820 – 850 |
| 4 | 820 – 850 | 820 – 850 | 810 – 840 | 820 – 850 |
| 3 | 815 – 845 | 815 – 845 | 810 – 840 | 815 – 845 |
| 2 | 815 – 845 | 815 – 845 | 805 – 835 | 810 – 840 |
| 1 | 810 – 840 | 810 – 840 | 800 – 830 | 810 – 840 |
| 0 | 805 – 840 | 805 – 835 | 795 – 825 | 805 – 835 |

# PERCENTILE

When you take your actual ISEE exam, you will receive a **percentile** ranking comparing your performance against the performance of other students in the same grade who have taken the ISEE that year. For example, a percentile of 62 means that you scored higher than 62% of other ISEE test-takers applying to the same grade. Because your percentile ranking shows how well you performed according to your own grade level, these rankings are frequently given high consideration by admissions offices.

The following charts provide an estimate of your ISEE percentile rankings for this practice test, compared against other students applying to the same grade. For example, if you are scoring at or above the 75th percentile, you are scoring higher than 75% of other ISEE test-takers applying to the same grade. Keep in mind that these percentiles are estimates only, and your actual ISEE percentile will depend on the specific group of students taking the exam in your year.

| UPPER LEVEL VERBAL REASONING PERCENTILES | | | |
|---|---|---|---|
| **Grade Applying To** | **75th percentile** | **50th percentile** | **25th percentile** |
| Grade 9 | 893 | 879 | 866 |
| Grade 10 | 899 | 883 | 867 |
| Grade 11 | 902 | 886 | 869 |
| Grade 12 | 898 | 881 | 863 |

| UPPER LEVEL QUANTITATIVE REASONING PERCENTILES | | | |
|---|---|---|---|
| **Grade Applying To** | **75th percentile** | **50th percentile** | **25th percentile** |
| Grade 9 | 892 | 878 | 866 |
| Grade 10 | 897 | 882 | 868 |
| Grade 11 | 901 | 885 | 870 |
| Grade 12 | 897 | 884 | 872 |

**Ivy Global**

| UPPER LEVEL READING COMPREHENSION PERCENTILES | | | |
|---|---|---|---|
| Grade Applying To | 75th percentile | 50th percentile | 25th percentile |
| Grade 9 | 897 | 880 | 865 |
| Grade 10 | 902 | 886 | 868 |
| Grade 11 | 903 | 889 | 868 |
| Grade 12 | 899 | 880 | 862 |

| UPPER LEVEL MATHEMATICS ACHIEVEMENT PERCENTILES | | | |
|---|---|---|---|
| Grade Applying To | 75th percentile | 50th percentile | 25th percentile |
| Grade 9 | 894 | 882 | 869 |
| Grade 10 | 900 | 886 | 871 |
| Grade 11 | 905 | 890 | 875 |
| Grade 12 | 903 | 889 | 875 |

## STANINE

When you receive the score report for your actual ISEE exam, your percentile score will also be broken down into a **stanine**. A stanine is a number from 1-9 obtained by dividing the entire range of students' scores into 9 segments, as shown in the table below:

| PERCENTILE RANK | STANINE |
|---|---|
| 1 – 3 | 1 |
| 4 – 10 | 2 |
| 11 – 22 | 3 |
| 23 – 39 | 4 |

| 40 – 59 | 5 |
|---------|---|
| 60 – 76 | 6 |
| 77 – 88 | 7 |
| 89 – 95 | 8 |
| 96 – 99 | 9 |

Although it isn't possible to calculate your exact stanine from this practice test, you can estimate a stanine score range by looking at your estimated percentile score on each section. For example, if you scored between the 50th and 75th percentile in one of your test sections, your stanine score would be between 5 and 6.

**Ivy Global**